1986

Other Books by John C. Lilly, M.D.

Simulations of God: the Science of Belief
Man and Dolphin
The Mind of the Dolphin
Programming and Metaprogramming in the Human Biocomputer
The Center of the Cyclone
Lilly on Dolphins: Humans of the Sea

John Lilly

Antonietta Lilly

The
Dyadic
Cyclone

The Autobiography of a Couple

SIMON AND SCHUSTER : NEW YORK

John Lilly and Antonietta Lilly

The author gratefully acknowledges permission from the following sources to reprint material:

Encyclopaedia Britannica, 14th edition, for material from "Gnosticism," copyright © 1960, Encyclopaedia Britannica.

Farrar, Straus & Giroux, Inc., for material from *This Timeless Moment* by Laura Huxley, copyright © 1968 by Laura Archera Huxley.

The Julian Press, Inc., for material from *The Center of the Cyclone: An Autobiography of Inner Space* by John C. Lilly, copyright © 1972 by John C. Lilly, M.D.; from *Programming and Metaprogramming in the Human Biocomputer* by John C. Lilly, copyright © 1967, 1968 by John C. Lilly, M.D.; from *The Laws of Form* by G. Spencer-Brown, copyright © 1972 by G. Spencer-Brown; all titles also published in paperback editions by Bantam Books; and for material from *The Philosophy of Consciousness Without an Object: Reflections on the Nature of Transcendental Consciousness* by Franklin Merrell-Wolff, copyright © 1973 by Franklin F. Wolff; from *Pathways Through to Space* by Franklin Merrell-Wolff, copyright © 1973 by Franklin F. Wolff.

Penguin Books, Inc., for material from Stewart Brand's review of *The Laws of Form* in *The Updated Last Whole Earth Catalog*, edited by Stewart Brand, © 1971, 1974 by Point.

Erma Sims for the use of her poetry.

Designed by Irving Perkins
Manufactured in the United States of America

1   2   3   4   5   6   7   8   9   10

Library of Congress Cataloging in Publication Data
Lilly, John Cunningham, 1915–
    The dyadic cyclone.
    Bibliography: p.
    1. Marriage. 2. Consciousness. 3. Interpersonal
relations. I. Lilly, Antonietta, joint author.
II. Title.
HQ734.L565   158'24   75–45307
ISBN 0–671–22218–X

Dedication

To the author, director and actor Burgess Meredith, who has given unstintingly of his time, energy and wise counsel at critical times in our dyad. His professional advice has furnished us with a realistic context for our rather unconventional forays into experiments into transforms of the conventional media of communication of mood, of ideas, and of the "inexpressible" content of mystical experience. His own inner experiences of these domains and his representations of them have aided us in expressing our domains to others. Sharing his performances with us (Ulysses in Night Town, both the original off-Broadway and the recent Broadway productions, as director; The Little Foxes, as actor; his autobiography, as author), he has exemplified a model of talent and professional competence that has given us new insights into the how of communicating deep human experience through the theater, the motion picture and the written word.

Contents

I tell you, as long as I can conceive something better than myself I cannot be easy unless I am striving to bring it into existence or clearing the way for it. This is the law of my life. That is the working within me of Life's incessant aspiration to higher organization, wider, deeper, intenser self-consciousness and clearer self-understanding.

Man and Superman
GEORGE BERNARD SHAW

Prologue

"The center of the cyclone is that rising quiet central low-pressure place in which one can learn to live eternally. Just outside of this Center is the rotating storm of one's own ego, competing with other egos in a furious high-velocity circular dance. As one leaves center, the roar of the rotating wind deafens one more and more as one joins this dance. One's centered thinking-feeling-being, one's own Satoris, are in the center only, not outside. One's pushed-pulled driven states, one's anti-Satori modes of functioning, one's self-created hells, are outside the center. In the center of the cyclone one is off the wheel of Karma, of life, rising to join the Creators of the Universe, the Creators of us.

"Here we find that we have created Them who are Us."*

The Dyadic Cyclone is the combination of two personal centers. In this book it is a male and female combination—two rotating cyclones with their enclosed centers, one rotating to the right and the other rotating to the left. In *The Dyadic Cyclone*, Toni and John ask the question "Is it possible to merge two centers, two cyclones, one male, one female, in such a way that

* John C. Lilly, *The Center of the Cyclone*, epigraph, Julian Press.

15

there can be a rising, quiet center shared by both?" In our five years together, we have sought means to achieve this between us. This book is the story of that five years insofar as we can tell it at this time.

Preface

I would like to begin this book with a love letter. One written to our friend Laura Archera Huxley by her husband Aldous, published in *This Timeless Moment*, by Laura.*

". . . the only piece of paper I found in my pocket. So I scratch this out and write you a letter, my darling, while I drink my coffee in Córso Vittorio Emanuele.

A letter to tell you that you really must be a *stréga* [sorceress] otherwise why should I keep falling more and more in love with you? Why should I start being jealous of the people who loved you in the past? No, not jealous, really—rather sad because I wasn't there, because I wasn't ten other people loving you in ten other ways, at ten different times of your life and mine . . . being made one with you in tenderness and passion and sensuality and understanding.

Well, I am not ten other people and I am here and now, not then and there. But here and now I love you very much and only wish I could love you more and better—could love you so that you would be well always, and strong and happy; so that there would never be that discrepancy between a tragic suffering face and the serenity of the nymph's lovely body with its little breasts

* Laura Huxley, *This Timeless Moment*.

and the flat belly, the long legs . . . that I love so tenderly, so violently.

Well, I must go to mail my letters and try on my suit and act the part of a respectable literary gentleman who doesn't sit in cafés writing love letters, of all people!—to his wife."

The first time I read this, I cried. I so often feel like that about John. There must be many of you that feel the same, dyads that almost weren't, but were blessed to touch.

—ANTONIETTA LILLY

Introduction

In *The Center of the Cyclone*, Chapter 18, John and Toni meet. In *The Dyadic Cyclone*, we continue this history of our joint efforts.

We officially met on 21 February 1971; each of us has adapted (within certain limits) to the other. The scope of shared experience since then has certainly been as powerful for each of us as it had been at any time in our individual past lives, before we met. We have led such an active life together that Toni, in response to an interviewer's question recently: "Do you ever get angry with John?," answered, "I really never get angry with him, but I do find myself yearning for trivia occasionally."

Since the meeting described in *The Center of the Cyclone*, we have moved from Toni's Los Angeles home to another one in Malibu, in Decker Canyon, where we have organized workshops. At the beginning, they were for anyone who applied. Later, we tended to gravitate toward a group of young doctors. As our relationship matured, we found that we wanted to work with those who were trained in more advanced matters dealing with life on this planet and how to successfully carry it out.

At Decker we also have a separate building that contains two of the isolation tanks for use by ourselves and our visitors. The isolation tank, which I developed, is a method developed in 1954 for solitude, isolation and confinement studies at the National Institute of Mental Health, Bethesda, Maryland. At that time I was asking the question: What happens to the central nervous system and the mind of a man isolated in the absence of all stimulation? I was an eager young scientist pushing forward into regions of the unknown: the nervous system (working with animals) and the mind (working on myself and a few other subjects). I spent ten years working with the tank without any aids (such as LSD), and found many new spaces for myself.

Later, from 1964 through 1966, as was told in my books *Programming and Metaprogramming in the Human Biocomputer* and in *The Center of the Cyclone*, I took LSD in the tank at Saint Thomas and found many new spaces, unexperienced before. The mask that was used in the early work in fresh water was eliminated: in Saint Thomas I used flotation in shallow salt water.

At Decker the tank technique has been simplified still further, and is now easier and safer to use. An Epsom salts ($MgSO_4 \cdot 7H_2O$) solution of 53 percent by weight in water gives us a density of a solution to float in of 1.30 gms/cc. The Epsom salts solution is ten inches deep; if necessary, one can quickly sit up: one's seat lands on the bottom of the tank; as the upper portion of the body comes out of the solution, the lower portions sink. Lying supine with arms extended at one's sides, one can comfortably float; one's feet, one's hands and one's head all float at the surface of the solution. The air above the solution is kept at about 93° as is the water. There is complete darkness and complete silence.

In spite of the bad reputation of the so-called "sensory deprivation" experiments, this tank method has rarely led to panic, fear or intense pain. By means of the technique that we now have, practically everyone can safely float in the tank. (We do not allow certain kinds of medical cases to use the tank. For example, if there is danger of seizures we do not encourage use of the tank except under careful chemical control of the seizures. The tank is contraindicated for certain kinds of mental cases.)

Toni and I have each spent a good deal of time in the tank and have had many basic experiences. Somewhat over 200 subjects have used our tanks.

From October 1973 to November 9, 1974, I did a long series of experiments on states of being, in and out of the tank. I spent a large fraction of that year in "Samadhi."* This series was abruptly terminated by an accident on a bicycle going down the mountain road at Decker Canyon. The chain came off the sprocket and jammed the rear wheel, throwing me onto the road. I ended up in the hospital for nine days and in a hospital bed in our home for a period of twelve weeks. Some of our experiences of that year and their sequelae are recounted in this book.

Though our life is somewhat orientated to tanks, far-out explorations and a search for the outer limits of the mind, we do many of the ordinary things that other people do. Toni does her gardening. She makes hooked rugs while she is standing by on some of my inner explorations.

We love high altitudes. We find that at high altitudes we stay in high spirits a lot more easily, even as the Tibetans have found in the past. When we found Dr. Franklin Merrell-Wolff living at 6,000 feet on the side of Mount Whitney, he confirmed this experience in his own case. Many years ago when he made his breakthrough into an enlightened state, he found that living at high altitude aided him in staying in those states. I refer you to his book *Pathways Through to Space.*

Both Toni and I love to ski, especially in the Sierra Nevada

* I use the term "Samadhi" in the sense of a general domain of states of being in which the levels of consciousness are more extended than the ones generated by the belief systems usually operative (see Chapter 18, Appendix 4) in the consensus reality. In this domain one's belief systems and the metabelief operator are creating/experiencing/operating in a nonordinary reality including e.r./i.r./e.t.r./N. (Cf. Table 1. Levels of Consciousness, in *The Center of the Cyclone,* pp. 148–149, Julian Press edition, and pp. 158–160 in the Bantam edition.) This domain includes 24, 12, 6 and 3 of Table 1 and includes the subdomains of the external reality (e.r.), the internal reality (i.r.), the extraterrestrial reality (e.t.r.) and the Network (N) of Creation. The belief systems are analyzed in my books *Simulations of God: the Science of Belief; The Human Biocomputer;* and *The Center of the Cyclone*

mountains of California and the Rockies of Colorado. One year I taught Toni to ski at 9,000 feet at Mammoth, on the last snow of the season. After that we went to northern California in early summer and skied Mount Lassen and on the mountains beside Crater Lake in Oregon. The next winter we went to Sun Valley with a good friend of ours and skied Dollar Mountain together. Each of us took lessons and perfected our techniques further.

I feel that Toni is a unique, strong human being. She is probably the most tolerant and developed woman that I have met in my life. She has a maturity of viewpoint, a finish and élan, a joie de vivre, a steadfastness and a groundedness that I have seen in no other woman. She is very capable in human relationship. Male or female, businessmen, politicians, scientists, doctors, actors, mystics, children—all enjoy her warmth and enthusiasm. During the year of experiments with the Samadhi domain, when I pushed most others beyond their limits, Toni stood by and kept our planetside trip together.

Toni:

"John is about as unique and creative a person as I have ever met in my four decades of living. He meets every condition of living, loving and working in a way I usually cannot foresee— very rarely predictable. His breadth of scope is immense and eternal; some of the time he becomes childlike and completely *uncool;* at other times, he can become precise and gemlike with an intellect that is probably unmatched in our generation. As we used to say about intellectuals in high school, John has a combination of the kid on the block with the biggest chemistry set, an Irish dramatist and F. Scott Fitzgerald with the sea flowing through his veins. When he is inspired there are very few men or women who can match his agile intellectual gymnastics. His access to vast fields of knowledge is matched by his capability to make connections among them all. His originality is a joy and his humor a delight. To me he is *more fun than anybody.*

"I find that he is one of the very few philosophical scientists. It is a rare combination, but one that seems so complete and natural. When philosophy is combined with science and topped with humor, I am interested. When most of the other possibilities, all of the mysterious intangibles, are recognized in some form, I am completely involved. These characteristics along with his willingness to be vulnerable are truly unique.

"Our souls touched when we met and these last five years have been very full ones for me. In this book I give you my impressions of what some of that has been like, here in this garden of earthly delights."

Chapter Zero

Coincidence Control Develops the Dyad

In one's life there can be peculiarly appropriate chains of related events that lead to consequences that are strongly desired. After such experiences, one wonders how such a series of events developed; sometimes there is a strong feeling that some intelligence (greater than ours) directed the course along certain lines which It/He/She was/is programming. In such a series, life becomes greater than one expected, planned/programmed/realized as possible.

The actual events (at the time of occurrence) may be experienced as negative (punishing), positive (rewarding), and/or neutral (indifferently objective); the real experiences themselves may involve pain/fear/anger, joy/delight/love, and/or a state of being of objectivity/neutrality/dispassionate-appraisal. One's own participation in the events seems, later, somehow predicated on *being taught something that one needed to know* before the next events unfolded.

For example, there are days in which all events planned for the day, for the next week, for the next few months, line up, almost automatically resolving former conflicts of hours of meetings, deadlines, financing. Someone (A) telephones, asking for a meeting a week hence: one writes the date into the engagement book. A crisis develops negating that date. Within a few hours person A calls and asks for a change of date because some factor changed in his/her life apparently unrelated to one's own. Thus one is given the time to resolve the crisis.

In our dyad such transformations of our calendar happen, not one at a time, but in multiple interrelated simultaneously operating configurations involving our many different projects (writing-editing-rewriting books, making motion pictures, running a busy household, giving lectures, being interviewed, meeting with friends, creating new scripts, etcetera). Each change in plans interrelates with all else happening to keep a constant flow of that which is apparently important actually taking place next. (As I write this, three of these rearrangements took place in one hour, affecting today and next month's plans.)

In reality, of course, a good deal depends on the happiness/work/reasoning of the dyad. If our basic belief that the dyad is greater than either of us individually (see Chapter Four, "Coherence in the Dyad") is functioning fully, events line up. If, at any point, this belief is in abeyance, events do not (apparently) line up.

Several years ago, I enunciated a format (a principle) for such concatenations of events, somewhat as follows.

There exists a *Cosmic Coincidence Control Center* (CCCC) with a Galactic substation called *Galactic Coincidence Control* (GCC). Within GCC is a *Solar System Control Unit* (SSCU), within which is the *Earth Coincidence Control Office* (ECCO, sometimes mistakenly shortened to ECO, as in Ecosystems and in Ecology [the *study of* the Earth (Coincidence) Control Office]). Down through the hierarchy of Coincidence Control (from Cosmic to Galactic to Solar System to Earth) is a chain of command with greater and greater specification of regulation of Coincidences appropriate to each level in the system. The assignments of responsibilities from the top to the bottom of this system of control is by a set of regulations, which, translated by ECCO for us human beings, is somewhat as follows:

To all humans:

If you wish to control coincidences in your own life on the

planet Earth, we will cooperate and determine those coincidences for you under the following conditions:

1) You must know/assume/simulate our existence in ECCO.

2) You must be willing to accept our responsibility for control of your coincidences.

3) You must exert your *best capabilities* for your survival programs and your own development as an advancing/advanced member of ECCO's earthside corps of controlled coincidence workers. You are expected to use your best intelligence in this service.

4) You are expected to expect the unexpected every minute every hour of every day and of every night.

5) You must be able to remain conscious/thinking/reasoning no matter what events we arrange to happen to you. Some of these events will seem cataclysmic/catastrophic/overwhelming: remember, *stay aware, no matter what happens/apparently-happens to you.*

6) You are in our training program for life: there is no escape from it. We (not you) control the long-term coincidences; you (not we) control the shorter-term coincidences by your own efforts.

7) Your major mission on Earth is to discover/create that which we do to control the long-term coincidence patterns: you are being trained on Earth to do this job.

8) When your mission on planet Earth is completed, you will no longer be required to remain/return there.

9) Remember the motto passed to us (from GCC via SSCU): *"Cosmic Love is absolutely Ruthless and Highly Indifferent: it teaches its lessons whether you like/dislike them or not."* (End of Instructions)

With respect to the coincidences used to train Toni and myself, I tell the following:

Toni first saw me in the hot bath at Esalen Institute in Big Sur one night in January 1969. She was at Esalen visiting our very dear friend Alan Watts, who died suddenly last year. Alan was giving a weekend seminar.

I did not know she was there nor that she existed.

As is related in *The Center of the Cyclone*, Chapter 5, "A

Guided Tour of Hell" (citations for *The Center of the Cyclone* refer to Julian Press edition, unless otherwise noted), I had arrived at Esalen on a trip with Sandy Unger. I had just been through "the guided tour of Hell" under Sandy's supervision. We were on our way to a Psychopharmacology meeting at the University of California at Irvine. We stopped at Esalen on the way south from Berkeley and Palo Alto.

We attended Alan's seminar and separated. I went to the baths late at night to be alone and meditate on my recent experience. I wanted to see if I was capable of remaining at Esalen to work on myself, or would feel it necessary to return to the Maryland Psychiatric Research Center in Baltimore with Sandy. While I was in the bath, two other persons interrupted my solitude. In the dim light I recognized Alan's silhouette as one of them, but could not recognize the obviously female person with him. I resented, somewhat, their intrusion into my solitudinous meditation and remained silent. As Alan knew, many persons go at night to the baths at Esalen to be alone and to meditate. Alan did not interrupt me. He and the woman remained silent.

Toni:

"I remember that night in the sulphur baths* at Esalen after Alan had finished his evening session. We went to the baths together.

"There was no light except that of the stars. As our eyes became accustomed to the dark, we saw a silent figure sitting in the far corner of the bath near the wall away from the sea. I felt some vibrations signaling silent concentration.

"There was a flowing energy in the water among the three of us in the bath. I felt Alan's unusual silence, his acceptance of an unspoken agreement to remain silent. I, too, felt the vibes in this direction. After we left, Alan remarked that the other person in the bath was John Lilly. I had read his book on dolphins with some interest."

* These are concrete block tanks, about two feet deep and six feet on a side, with water from the hot springs (at 105° F.) flowing through and out over the cliff to the sea below.

Thus did Toni and I make a first "contact" in 1969. Apparently, *Earth Coincidence Control Office* (ECCO) was preparing the coincidences to line up later. The coincidence of our first face-to-face meeting was deferred until 21 February 1971, two weeks after my return from seven months in Arica, Chile. Once again Alan Watts was involved.

With a friend, I attended a lecture given by Alan at the Beverly Hills High School auditorium. After the lecture I left the room and saw Alan in the hall, surrounded by a large number of friends and admirers.

Toni:
"I had no knowledge at this juncture that John was in the audience nor that he was invited to the party afterward. I also did not recognize him out of water and in daylight. I later was told by Virginia Dennison, a long-time friend of Alan's, that it was she who had invited him to the party."

My friend and I talked with some of her friends. Somehow (I did not know how) we were invited to a party for Alan at a house in the hills near Hollywood. We decided to attend. She obtained directions; we started to drive in her car.

On the way, we stopped to eat supper. We resumed the ride and a tire blew out. It was very late (11:30 PM): there were no service stations open in the immediate neighborhood. By the time we found a solution to the tire problem it was 1:00 AM. We almost decided to go home, that the party for Alan must be over. If we had taken that course, I would not have met Toni: ECCO left it up to us to push beyond the coincidences of the flat tire and the late hour.

The next events are recorded in Chapter 18 of *The Center of the Cyclone* (pp. 228–229) Bantam edition, and pp. 214–215 of the Julian Press edition:*

The meeting took place at a house in the hills near Hollywood at 1:30 A.M. I had been invited to a party after an Alan Watts

* John C. Lilly, *The Center of the Cyclone*, Bantam, 1972, 1973; and Julian Press 1972.

lecture at this house. The car I was riding in had a flat tire—
hence the late hour. Alan had left the party—in fact, there were
few survivors. As I walked in the front door I noted a dark-haired
woman sitting on the floor in the large entrance hall. After meeting the host and the few remaining guests, I went over to her.

As I moved closer, I felt and saw her aura of love and beneficent
influence. Her face is striking and unusual: there is an eaglelike
quality to her gray eyes and classic nose—a sharp penetrating
dispassionate, analytical quality, with awakedness and lively
interest showing frankly and directly. I felt her centered,
grounded, trusting, confident self sitting there watching me approach her from across the room.

I sat down with her, looked directly at her looking directly at
and into me. Instantly I knew her and she knew me. We went
into a sparkling cosmic love place together. I asked her name,
age, attachments and all the necessary "48" information—she
did the same.

I felt we had been together in previous lives and said "Where
have you been for the last five hundred years?" She answered,
"In training."

We both found this same feeling—our lives had been a training
for each of us to meet the other. We were to meet to do a work of
some sort together—work yet to be defined.

Four days later I went to a party at her house. We began to
realize our new reality, a real together reality. We have not been
apart for more than a few hours since.

Thus was our dyad born on 21 February. That night I found
that which in Chile I had lacked and desired more than the
continuance of my experiences there. I felt complete and whole
meeting with Antonietta. All the travail and hardship since
January 1969 suddenly made sense: ECCO's longer-term coincidence control patterns now began to show their power in
earnest.

The dyad's cyclone formed from two individual cyclones, and
became a stable entity greater than either of us, Toni or me.

In *Center* (Julian Press ed., p. 215), I wrote further:

Once Toni was asked by a friend how she'd changed since we'd
formed our dyad. She told about grieving (joyfully) for her

former self, saying, "She wasn't such a bad sort alone; now that she's in the unity of the dyad, she's completed, us."

The ruthless nature of cosmic love (baraka) has been reshown to us in our dyad. Cosmic love loves and teaches you whether you like it or not; it has an inevitability, a fullness of taking over, a fateful joyous quality that spreads and brings others to you, teaching through you. Each of us feel this strongly, now.

This meeting with my soulmate, with all of its overtones of joy, acceptance, and happiness, heralded the beginning of a new attack of ego (Karma). As Oscar had said in Arica, "You have dealt with most of your ego. There are just a few grains of sand [and I added, "of diamond hardness"] in the perfect machine— now all you have to do is clean that machine and it will run smoothly in Satori."

In joining up with Toni, I discovered that the sand was once again in myself. Luckily both of us were strong enough so that we could work on this together. This mutual cooperative venture, to clean up our machines together, is in the essential nature of our dyad.

Little did either of us know that at the time of writing the above last paragraph—these statements were presaging some deep tests of each of us and of the dyad.

This book (*The Dyadic Cyclone*) gives the story of this "mutual cooperative venture . . . in the essential nature of our dyad." (We each very nearly lost the other several times; through each one's effort and the help of ECCO we have survived for five years to date.)

Our "work yet to be defined" (above) is now clearer, more defined. (See above *Instructions to Humans* from ECCO; *Simulations of God: the Science of Belief*; and the text and appendices of this present book.)

BEYOND "REPRODUCE!": SUPRASELF DYAD*

We, in this dyad, each have already reproduced.
You have children made, as have I, each with another, not us.
You can no longer become pregnant.
With you I cannot impregnate.

* John C. Lilly, *Simulations of God: the Science of Belief*, pp. 273–274.

We can love, fuck, ecstatic union.
After many such, what then?
Are we here for sensation's sake?
Can we go beyond, through us and sex?
Where is "beyond"?
Far out spaces, greater beings-entities than us, beckon and call.
Together can we go to them, or is it each of us alone?
Let us try, together, to so go.
Let us face our hindrance, evasions, blocks,
    and soar, together.
The hindrance of body ecstasy tied here convert
    to spirit travel energy there.
The hindrance of planet earth, mother ties to her bosom,
    use constructively.
The evasion of loss of independent self, convert to dyad greatness.
Together fusing into one to travel as two-in-one.
No rivalry, no control for each separate over other,
    one directed by each of two, fused.
A dream, a fantasy? Poetry?
No.
A program, a metaprogram for a Supraself dyad.

(Written on 15 December 1969: about one month before the first contact between Toni and myself at Esalen Institute, Big Sur, California, and one year and two months before we met on 21 February 1971.)

Chapter One

Emersion from the Influence of an Esoteric School

The book *The Center of the Cyclone* recounts much of my inner reality and external reality experiences. Toward the end of the book, I relate a period spent with an esoteric master and the beginnings of his school in Arica, Chile. In order to be in the school, I had to revise my belief systems. The metabelief operator (see Appendix Four) that I was working under said in effect: "This vehicle has been educated in several of the Western sciences: at Cal Tech and medical school, in psychoanalytic school, in the Catholic Church, in the isolation tank, etcetera. In each case, you took on the belief systems of each of those disciplines. There are several disciplines that are interesting and make claims that you should investigate. On the suggestion of Baba Ram Dass you have studied the yoga anthology *Yoga Sutras* of Patanjali, an Indian philosopher (c. 200 BC). You have yet to experience what it is that Patanjali is discussing. It is time to immerse yourself in one or several of these belief systems from the East."

As the story is related in *The Center of the Cyclone*, I then went to Chile to join the esoteric school.

I met Oscar in Chile. I was impressed with his energy, his discipline and his understanding. Here was a man whose belief systems were completely alien to my previous experience. I decided to study under him in a new course especially designed for fifty-four Americans, of which I was one. I became deeply involved and had the experiences that I went to Chile to find realized. At that time it was possible to study under the personal guidance of Oscar. I describe these experiences in detail in *The Center of the Cyclone*. That book ends with my return from Chile and the meeting with Toni and presents the point of view that my experience in Chile was very positive.

I left Chile before the end of the training. At first Oscar expressed grief that I was leaving his group. He quickly adapted to my decision to leave and expressed the wish that I rejoin him when he came to the United States, later. I agreed to do this.

Leaving Chile I had a very strong ambivalent feeling that I could not continue in the new format that Oscar introduced in January 1971. Just before I left, he had introduced the concept of the group as dominating all individuals. He instructed each of us to go into three days of prayer in solitude, each in our own home. His directions called for lying prone with the forehead on the two hands on the floor doing a sequence of prayers that he gave us in detail. He said that this was the most comfortable position to maintain for the required period of nine hours a day for the purpose of praying.

Within the first fifteen minutes I found that this position was incredibly uncomfortable. Pressure on the hands and on the forehead led to cutting off the circulation to the forehead and to the hands, resulting in pain. I assumed other positions of prayer. His instructions were to pray for guidance as to whether one should be a member of the group or not. By the end of the three days I was given my answer: I must leave Oscar and return to my own work.

Previously, I had spent five days alone in the desert; on 22 October 1970 I wrote out several pages of notes analyzing Oscar and the school. The notes are reproduced without any editing whatsoever in the appendices to my book *Simulations of God*, published this year. These notes were written on the last day of my five days in the desert. (See p. 239 in *Simulations of God*.) I quote from the end of these notes:*

> To assume "God," to assume "prayer," to assume "connection"— all seem shorthand for states of consciousness, for experiences inside, for solitude-isolation trips. These words short-circuit and oversimplify what is real and what exists. Maybe he's [Oscar's] right and I'm wrong—but maybe we are both right. He, with his education and background, uses these terms to express real experiences for him—I block because I've explored these concepts to their depth and found them arrogantly shallow: for me. With similar experiences (I hope I can have them!) *I can re-formulate in a more scientific and operational language what happens and how to get there. I must do my own work* (as always), *and study the results from my own knowledge* and not lean on Oscar or his theories as be-all and end-all. Otherwise I may as well quit this trip right now. I need time and no pressure from Oscar: he pushes: with solitude-isolation and with programming. He's a programmer! He's enthusiastic and a bit arbitrary—doesn't explain to me what he's doing [what] I'm doing. He's the Qutb, the Master—the traditional geheimrat professor of Europe and the East. He's to be educated about me, an American of independent mind and means. I have never uncritically accepted anyone's teaching or knowledge: I won't start now with Oscar.

One may well ask why these notes were not published in *The Center of the Cyclone*. This is an important point. When I returned from Chile I still had an attachment to Oscar. I still had attachments to members of the group around Oscar. I was still entranced by my experiences in Chile. Yet I had left Chile.

I met Toni and recounted my experiences in Chile, told her of my attachment to Oscar, that he was coming to the United States with the group after they had gone through another two months of work, which he was devoting to attempting to achieve "group Satori."

In March, he wrote me an exuberant letter in which he stated that the group had achieved Satori (Level 12 in the nomenclature cited in *The Center of the Cyclone*). In his second letter he asked me to meet with him in San Francisco on his return.

* John C. Lilly, *Simulations of God*, p. 245.

Toni and I went to San Francisco and met Oscar and his wife Jenny with three other members of the Chilean group, including Joseph Hart. At this meeting, Oscar was his enjoyable complex multilevel self with a good deal of humor. He obviously enjoyed his meeting with Toni. He suggested our coming to New York, where he was opening up the first course in the United States, in the fall of 1971. In order to understand what I had been through in Chile, Toni decided she would take the three months' training offered by the group in New York. We drove East and met again with Oscar and the group at Bayville on Long Island.

In spite of having left Chile early, I was still operating under the illusion that I was considered a member of the group (at least by Oscar). Oscar did not disabuse me of this point of view in his discussions with me, personally. At Bayville there was an encounter with him in which he said that he would have to ask the group if I could rejoin. At this point, things became rather dramatic.

Oscar called me into his room in the motel in Bayville and very intensely said that it was impossible for me to rejoin the group, that in their meeting he felt that they could tear me to pieces, like a tiger. Later rumors about what really happened in this group meeting made Oscar out to be doing a bit of politics.

He had gone to the group and proposed entry of his wife Jenny into the group, but did not strongly advocate my rejoining the group. I talked with many different persons in the group and found that they had had orders not to talk to me. However, several did talk with me secretly. I had many good friends in the group. I was startled and quite hurt to find that as a whole they were rejecting me. I went through a good deal of grief and finally managed to overcome my entrancement itself (the term entrancement is meant in terms of "infatuation" and "blindness" resulting therefrom), and analyzed my ambivalence (i.e., wanting and not wanting to rejoin).

Meanwhile I had written the manuscript for *The Center of the Cyclone*, praising Oscar and recounting my experiences. All in all the account came out mostly on the positive side; the negative was suppressed. The analytical notes from the Chilean desert were not included. I gave Oscar a copy of the manuscript. He read it and reported that he was delighted with it. (He may not have been so delighted had the notes from the Chilean desert been inserted.)

In the meantime, the training had started for the new group of seventy-four students at the Essex House in New York and Toni joined. I stayed on the periphery of both groups and found that there were definite instructions that people in both the groups were not to communicate with me. I attempted to communicate with my former friends, but there was a concerted effort on their part not to do so.

I was available to them, living in the Essex House with Toni, but my availability was not made use of for the whole three months.

At one point I was asked to lunch by Steven Stroud, one of the Big Sur people who had gone to Chile with me and who was one of the more dedicated members of the original group. At lunch he made me a proposition. I was in the state of wanting–not-wanting to rejoin the group. His proposition was that if I would withdraw from publishing the manuscript for *The Center of the Cyclone*, I could then be a member of the group. This was the final straw that broke my ambivalence and my entrancement. I informed him that the manuscript was well on the way to being published, that it would be very inconvenient to withdraw it and I did not see that this was necessarily a realistic bargain. I refused the proposition and withdrew my request to rejoin the group.

During this period I saw Oscar socially several times. We found each mutually entertaining but did not resume the deep relationship that we had developed in Chile. His new mission was tied up with the group that he had selected, recounted above and in *The Center of the Cyclone*.

In retrospect, it can easily be seen that I was not the only one that was eventually rejected by the group, by Oscar. Several self-starters left. Claudio Naranjo was the first to be summarily removed from the group while still in Chile. Several others were dropped in Chile. I was the only one that left in Chile on his own initiative.

Apparently my leaving could not be forgiven by Oscar or by the group. I remember the day (in Chile) that I announced to various members of the group that I was leaving.

During our Sunday exercises in the desert (the so-called pampas exercises as given in *The Center of the Cyclone*), several members of the group came up to me in sorrow that I was leaving. One or two came up with great rage. I was startled at the high emotional level at which these people treated my leaving. To me at the time it was a very logical step. I had received my answer in the three days of solitudinous prayer: I had reached the end of that particular trip, had completed my objectives with Oscar; I was more or less satisfied with my analysis and conclusions. It was with difficulty that I understood their emotions. Apparently they had become very much attached to me as a member of the group and were disappointed that I was leaving. Somehow, some of the people felt that this decision cast a reflection on them. What I considered to be logical and intuitively revealed, i.e., terminating, they considered to be betrayal.

I believe it was these feelings that generated the ultimate rejection in New York. I hold Oscar as a personal teacher who had introduced me to extremely valuable experiences through techniques, methods and ways of thinking that I hadn't had before I went to Chile. For this I felt eternally grateful to Oscar. I liked him personally but I found the politics surrounding him too much for me. In my own tradition I have established bonds with my teachers with the hope that in the future I can return to them when need arises. With Oscar this turned out to be impossible. Two years ago, when I had a need of talking to Oscar, I found that the group surrounding him prevented any contact with him and I had to do without his counsel and proceed on my own. I have not seen him since that New York period. I do not even know if he received my messages.

Since that period, various members of the group have come to call on Toni and myself. One who expressed his rage in the Chilean desert apologized for his behavior and asked my forgiveness. I said to him that there was nothing to forgive, that I understood from whence he was speaking and from whence came his negative emotion.

As my emotional entrancement and ambivalence died out and as my objectivity with regard to the group increased, I realized that somehow I am not built nor have I been trained to come under the sway of any group. I gradually realized that I am an explorer who at any time can become a student in order to learn more, in order to sharpen my own philosophy of exploration and my own techniques of exploration; but this student must also graduate when he has learned enough for his purposes. I reserve some of my entrancement for my dyad. This frees me up to continue my explorations.

My own childish nature, hidden in the layers of sophistication, of education, of explanation, surfaces freely in the dyad. For me, it is inappropriate for this childish nature to surface in other ways. With Toni I give free rein to my childish nature when we are alone. Slowly but surely, the young child in me is becoming educated, immersed in the security of Toni's love; he still has difficulties in surfacing at the behest of a group.

To give you a specific example of the kinds of things that occurred in New York, Toni recounts her experience with the Arica group. You can now see the background that led to her experience and my state of mind during her experience. I needed to go to New York and spend that three months outside of the group to resolve my own loving attachments to that group and attain a higher degree of objectivity in regard to my human relationships with them. It is a lesson well learned and I am very appreciative that Toni gave me this opportunity by taking the training with the group (New York #1, as it is called). It was during that year that I realized that each independent self-starter, as I call them, taking that training, left the New York group on his own initiative. Other people took the training on the basis of my experience in Chile, recounted in lectures afterward. Other persons have taken the training on the basis of having read *The Center of the Cyclone*.

I wrote that book in a state of positive transference for Oscar and for the group reflected in the book. Apparently I laid the groundwork for my more objective analysis of that positive transference in the notes in the Chilean desert. In all fairness, I should have published those notes in *The Center of the Cyclone*.

In my state of entrancement, I failed to do so and only later was I able to publish those notes after the entrancement disappeared. Thus does one's objectivity suffer from attachment. In the words of Patanjali, "Pleasure leads to attachment; pain leads to aversion."

Through these experiences I learned that attachment and aversion are both the result of lack of objectivity. To achieve the state of High Indifference described by Merrell-Wolff, one needs to experience the depths and heights of attachment and pain. Objectivity comes, then I experience High Indifference.

Apparently, as long as I am in this human vehicle I will be unable to stay in a state of High Indifference. One's brain contains special survival circuits generating pleasure and generating pain in order that the organism that one inhabits can survive on this planet. It is only through close brushes with death, through the education that intense pain brings and through the education that intense pleasure carries with it that one can ultimately achieve the state of High Indifference beyond Bliss, beyond the hells created on this planet (in one's self and through others), that one can finally give these up and leave the vehicle to go on somewhere else beyond human conception and human imagination.

I do not believe that any teacher, any master, and guru, while still in this vehicle, can remain one hundred percent of the time in the highest states of which I have had experience. He cannot do this until he has the dyad as well as the means to remain in the highest state while operating outside consensus social reality, as did Sri Aurobindo, a yogi, teaching in India (see Chapter Fourteen).

Recently I was sent a book on kundalini yoga by Gopi Krishna. I had read his autobiography several years ago, as suggested by Dick Price of Esalen Institute. I was impressed by Gopi Krishna's experiences, both positive and negative in raising his kundalini. I was unimpressed by his latest book. He makes judgments that are all too human. He uses Alan Watts' autobiography as an example of someone who was on the edge of attaining enlightenment but did not achieve it because he neglected kundalini. He pushes his own methods as if the be-all and end-all for achieving the ultimate states of being. Despite his contentions, his writings do not reflect speaking from a position of the higher states of being. He judges all too humanly.

Merrell-Wolff states in *Pathways Through to Space:*

> It is a mistake to think that the Dharma of even the God-Conscious Man is without problems. As God-Conscious, His impulse is His Dharma, and thus there is no emotional conflict. But the question "What does that Dharma mean in practical action?" is quite another matter. Absolute solutions of relative problems, outside of mathematics, do not exist. The Higher Consciousness is certain on Its own Level; It does effect an enormous clarification of insight on the subject-object level; and It always manifests as an intent to effect the highest good of all; but in all dealings with human beings unknown variables are involved, even from the perspective of high Adepts. As a consequence, *Illumination by no means implies infallible action in the subject-object field.* So there always remains the practical problem, which we may state in the form of a question, "What course in action best manifests the inwardly recognized Dharma?" Naturally, for the solution of this problem, the Illumined Man who has, in addition to his Illumination, a broad rational understanding of the science of ethics is also best equipped for making lofty intent to manifest as wise action.
>
> Another important point which should be remembered is the fact that rarely if ever is the personality of the God-Conscious Man enveloped in the full Light of the Higher Consciousness at all times. Generally the period of the envelopment is brief, sometimes of only momentary duration, and in many cases it happens but once in a lifetime. Much of the time, even in the cases of Men who have known a high order of Illumination, the consciousness sinks more or less into the subject-object field, with a corresponding obscuration of the insight. The lesser impulses, which have their ground in the subject-object man, are not completely transformed in one moment, although the purification of them proceeds progressively. There remains, therefore, a practical need for discrimination among the complex of all impulses that may arise. He who has had even no more than one moment of Illumination does have a modulus for such discrimination, and that gives Him a decisive advantage over other men. But nevertheless He has not transcended the need for discrimination in practical action.*

* Franklin Merrell-Wolff, *Pathways Through to Space.*

There are at least four areas of human experience and human action, which we must distinguish. First there is the planetside trip, one's relationships with others, one's daily life. Secondly there is the experience of transcendence, of Illumination, of far-out domains. And thirdly there is one's written report of Illumination, far-out spaces and so forth. And fourthly, there are reports by others of one's experiences and of one's writings about these experiences.

Most of our knowledge of the religious leaders of the world, Jesus Christ, Buddha and so forth are by disciples, followers who were experiencing positive transference to their teacher and who revised the direct writings and the direct accounts of the experiences of the transcendent states. An Illumined Man cannot fully express His Illumination in his accounts of the experiences nor in how he handles his earthly responsibilities. His Illumination may or may not be reflected in how he carries out his everyday life. His Illumination may or may not be reflected in how he writes about others and their ways of life. An Illumined Man, in his vehicle, not in a state of Illumination, may be as human as anyone else. His judgments may be as bound to his "common sense" as any person who is not Illuminated. Paraphrased here, Albert Einstein defined "common sense" as "that set of biases and prejudices which one accumulates before one is eighteen years old." The Illumined Man must analyze his own Unconscious Programs in order to achieve action and decision and judgment in consonance with His Illumination. Illumination does not automatically guarantee a full analysis of the Unconscious, resident within the human vehicle. Until such analysis is carried out rather completely, the coherence with Illumination is missing and the large gaps show.

By direct personal experience with Oscar I know that he had achieved Illumination in the sense that Merrell-Wolff defines. I deduce from Gopi Krishna's autobiography, *Kundalini: The Evolutionary Energy in Man*, that he too has had experiences of Illumination. I know from reading Merrell-Wolff's writings and from meetings with him that he also has had the direct experience. In comparing my own experiences with those of Oscar Ichazo, of Gopi Krishna, of Merrell-Wolff and of others—such as

Sri Aurobindo, Ramana Maharshi, Ramakrishna, Yogananda—
recounted in their autobiographies, their writings and the writings of their followers, I deduce that my experiences fall into this same category.

My Western education in science, in psychoanalysis and through experiences with close brushes with death (before I was aware of these writings or before I had met some of these men), place me in the peculiar position of being an explorer rather than wishing to inhabit these regions continuously during this lifetime. As I show in Chapter Seventeen of this book, and as I hope to show in a much longer book analyzing a year spent in these states of transcendence (irrespective of the consensus reality around me), there is a basic necessity that is neglected in most of these writings and by most of these men. This necessity is the analysis of one's impulses, of one's survival programs placed in one's unconscious during one's lifetime, having to do with trauma incurred on one's planetside trip. The Western yoga demands analysis of one's self as one is, not as one wishes to be. Transcendence by wish is possible and has been demonstrated by many people but such transcendence cannot be permanent. Self-analysis, analysis of the memories stored deeply within Self, is an absolute requirement for a successful integration of experiences of Illumination, Enlightenment, Samadhi, Satori with one's planetside trip.

There are many, many people (in the United States especially) who believe that transcendence is a stepwise process given by some divine source to favored individuals. Ideally this may be true. There may be individuals who have experienced that which is right for transcendence by having the right parents, the right peers, the right education. If such people exist, I have yet to meet them. If such people exist, I have yet to find writings that give proof of this. The travail of pain, of fear, of rage, of wisdom through excess is still necessary for an adequate self-analysis and for an adequate integration of one's freedom within to act from a state of High Indifference continuously and without letdown. No one that I know of, including myself, has yet achieved this, here in the United States. I keep hearing of the next guru coming from the East, from Tibet, from Japan, from Afghanistan, from Arabia, from India, from China, and yet when I meet them I see definite limitations imposed by the earthside personality. I also see unquestionable evidence of Illumination experiences stamped in each of these persons.

There are those who feel that total transcendence and integration leads to a holy aura, to a charisma, to an esoteric influence upon others, to a divine influence that somehow magically will transform others into a state of Illumination. Examples of Jesus Christ, of Buddha and of other ancient figures are constantly brought to the fore as proof of these achievements. With this I cannot agree. It seems to me that such ancient divine presence on the earth is a projection of followers entranced by charisma, entranced by apparent miracles giving free rein to their idealizations in their imagination, in their writings. Apocryphal stories spring up around any figure who has experienced Illumination and who collects followers. There is a tendency in these accounts to ignore those parts of that particular master that are all too human.

I am willing to revise these concepts at any time that I can directly experience such an idealized divine person. Until that time I will continue my explorations and my analyses of these phenomena insofar as I am able, without entrancement and without aversion.

I do not wish to accumulate followers. I do not wish to be revered. I wish to encourage others to investigate, to explore, to self-analyze, to self-transcend, to expand their consciousness and to improve their planetside trip within the consensus social reality as it is, not as they wish it to be. When and if I have Illumination experiences I am grateful. I do not know their source. I do not understand them yet, and I cannot take on the belief systems of others that so readily explain these phenomena as manifestations of a God that they define in their belief system; their God is too small. It is my metabelief that if there is an Intelligence in the Universe, it is so vast that man, Illuminated or not, is a small puny animal, inhabiting a very small planet in a very small solar system, in a small galaxy in a very small part of a truly vast and immense Universe beyond the imagination, beyond the intellectual grasp, beyond the emotional attachment of us, the human species. Our explanations, our beliefs about God, our experiences of Him, are not the province of a few privileged self-styled men of God. If any of us are in communication with this Intelligence, then all of us have the potential of consciously establishing that communication. It is not only for the elite few using esoteric methods and impressing followers with ritual and their own experiences.

I believe that anyone who sets about it can experience the phenomena described. If he/she has a sufficient discipline, sufficient time, sufficient education, sufficient analysis of self, he/she can have these experiences under the proper conditions. *Literally in the mind there are no limits, except those placed upon that mind by itself. Enlarged inner limits lead to vast experiences within.*

Thus did I emerse from the bonds I established with an esoteric master in his school. Thus am I giving you my present limits as I conceive of them.

In Toni's chapter on her Arica experience, one can see the detail of her relation to various planetside episodes that occurred in New York during her three-month stay. In reading this account, one must remember that Oscar was no longer as available to the students as he had been to me in Chile. He was already becoming more remote, doing less teaching and turning more of the teaching over to the forty-four survivors of the fifty-four entrants who had formed the original group in the school in Chile. By this time all self-starters had left the group. The group of survivors was convinced they were "right"; none of them had done self-analysis to any great depth. Toni recounts her experiences with this group with great candor. Many similar episodes happened in Chile, which have not been recounted by me or anyone else, in print. Even in Chile, Oscar was surrounded by palace politics, which in my own explorations I either tried to minimize or ignore. Thus has it been and probably always will be around a teacher working in the depths and heights of the unrealized human potential.

At this point I am reminded of my first trip to Arica, Chile, during which I spent many hours alone with Oscar Ichazo. My notes after that trip generated the following passage in Chapter 10 of *The Center of the Cyclone* (p. 154, Bantam edition; p. 144, Julian Press edition):*

> Thus, in that one-week trip to Chile in May of 1970, I was able to see something of the framework of the training that Oscar was proposing to give. Even though I couldn't see the full panorama, I had glimpses into spaces that I wanted to go as well as spaces to which I had been and wished to return.
>
> I had some doubts that I kept to myself. I did not like the idea of being in a closed group, esoteric or otherwise. I have pursued my own path, learning from whomever and wherever I could. In my experience, the politics inherent in many group decisions lower the quality and the effectiveness of the action. The experienced, wise, energetic, intelligent individual functioning in a loose coalition with others in a wide network is far more effective than he is in a tightly organized group, or so it seems to me.

Thus I entered into Oscar's course and beliefs starting 1 July 1970, immersed myself in them for seven months in his controlled environment in a foreign culture (in Arica), and re-emerged from his direct influence on 7 February 1971 in the United States. Powerful continuance of interpersonal attachment-aversion continued until dissolved in New York in November, 1971. This experiment (1 July 1970 through 31 December 1971) I count as a successful one; (1) the dyad of Toni and I survived its first onslaught successfully; (2) I came back to the "intelligent individual functioning in a loose coalition . . . in a wide network"; (3) I learned that my explorer's paradigm is workable, useful and teachable to others. This paradigm, reproduced from the Epilogue of *The Center of the Cyclone*, is as follows:†

> In the book I illustrate a general principle of living and being. It is a principle I wrote out in the *Human Biocomputer*. Here I revise and enlarge it. In a scientific exploration of any of the inner realities, I follow the following metaprogrammatic steps:

* John C. Lilly, *The Center of the Cyclone*.
† *Ibid.*

1. Examine whatever one can of where the new spaces are, what the basic beliefs are to go there.

2. Take on the basic beliefs of that new area as . . . true.

3. Go into the area fully aware, in high energy, storing everything, no matter how neutral, how ecstatic, or how painful the experiences become.

4. Come back here, to our best of consensus realities, temporarily shedding those basic beliefs of the new area and taking on those of the investigator impartially dispassionately objectively examining the recorded experiences and data.

5. Test one's current models of this consensus reality.

6. Construct a model that includes this reality and the new one in a more inclusive succinct way. No matter how painful such revisions of the models are be sure they include both realities.

7. Do not worship, revere, or be afraid of any person, group, space, or reality. An investigator, an explorer, has no room for such baggage.

I used this system many times in my life; in the early isolation work, in the tank work with LSD, in the Esalen experiences, in the Chile work. Each time I made what reconnaissance I could, entered the new area with enthusiasm and as openly as I could, took on the local beliefs as . . . true, experienced the region intensely, and finally moved out again, shedding the beliefs while critically examining the data and reprogramming my theories.

In my own way I have found that deep understanding is the best path for me into the unknown, the "highest" states of consciousness. I fully expect to continue to pursue this path. I consider everything I have written as transitional—as the exploration deepens and widens so we will be able to do a better job of mapping and exploring and further mapping.

As of today I have found no final answers, I am intent on continuing the search. Am I just the leader of 100 billions of connected cells? If so, who elected me leader? Where did the cells come from? If I am more than just the net result of 100 billions of cells living-cooperatively, where did I come from?

Chapter Two

Experiences in New York: Toni's Account of Arica Group Training

"Memory is incomplete experience"—J. KRISHNAMURTI

After realizing that my life would forever be combined with John's, I accepted the fact that he wanted to return to New York and meet with the group that was returning from Arica, Chile, to form Arica, Inc. After John received a letter from Oscar asking us to meet him, it seemed inevitable that I was to be part of this new play. The interest in the newest guru from Bolivia and Chile was growing, and I was curious enough to be talked into investigating it.

My first impression of Oscar Ichazo, the founder of the Arica Institute, and his lady Jenny was not one of surprise. I recognized their energies as familiar. Oscar reminded me of "the kid on the block who always went to private boys' schools" and naturally would be understood and befriended by John,* "the

---

* When I was a girl, there were always one or two boys that were different from the group. They had chemistry sets, read a lot and were intellectually inclined.

kid on the block with the biggest chemistry set." Oscar had a formal approach ("not sure immediately of where the action was," in street language, but very precise and determined, once he did). People of this nature always make good technicians and Oscar certainly is that. There was also an air of mystery about him that the formalism helped create. I wondered what kind of a lover he was and decided he was in the "priest" category: belief in his theology would come first in his priorities.

John had given me enough information about his reasons for leaving the training and the group in Chile to make me quite apprehensive about what his reception would be on his return. However, I felt that when one hangs out with an explorer, this was what one did, so I went along wondering what would happen next.

When Oscar asked us to meet him in San Francisco, it was with definite instructions that we were not to tell the rest of his group, who were, by that time, leaning toward the fanatical side. Of course the information leaked out, as information will, so many of the group were angry that John was the first to see Oscar, especially since John had not stayed the full term in Chile.

We heard that the group was by that time incensed that John was already teaching some of the techniques that they felt should be taught by the group as a group. So the political ploys were very familiar ones:

1) John should not do that. He didn't stay the full ten months and join the temple.
2) He's not doing it right. "The hand is placed this way and not that way."
3) The manuscript that he wrote, for *The Center of the Cyclone*, contains some of the training, so he should not be allowed to publish it. It's too dangerous . . . unless it is under their supervision.

I agree with don Juan in Carlos Castaneda's *Tales of Power* when he says,

> "It doesn't matter what one reveals or what one keeps to oneself, everything we do, everything we are, rests on our personal power. If we have enough of it, one word uttered to us might be sufficient to change the course of our lives. But if we don't have enough

personal power, the most magnificent piece of wisdom can be revealed to us and that revelation won't make a damn bit of difference.''*

Meanwhile, back in San Francisco, it seemed to me that Oscar was wooing John back to the fold. There was a quality to the wooing that made me sense Oscar was still very much hurt by John's leaving the student position. The Bolivian guru was very much sought after and was busy forming the group into an organization.

Oscar's sense of timing is great even though his limited English is/was a handicap. He is an imaginative storyteller and never lacks for listeners. His lady Jenny is a very South American woman in the sense that her strong views are hidden and acted on behind the scenes only. I believe South American ladies have a much less prominent place in society than we do, generally, and feel they must survive by manipulating their various planetside trips more from the background. Jenny's former husband Marcus was living with Oscar's second wife in Chile. Marcus was heading the Arica (Chile) Annex, or home office, as we would say, so Jenny had a lot invested in Arica, Inc.

Oscar and I hit it off immediately, I felt. Because of my past experience with gurus of various kinds, I met him as a man, an entertaining one at that, and most gurus love the change. We laughed a great deal, but alas, Jenny was not at ease with me. I took her to lunch (American style) at John's suggestion, to try to become friends, but it just would not come together.

The group shut John out more and more and it really was fascinating to see *groupthink* forming as intensely as it did. He was defined as definitely out of the group after he refused an offer to rejoin if he would withdraw his book. *The Center of the Cyclone* was then published. Some of those people that ordinarily would never have behaved in such a mindless way were acting like robots. Even a few of John's closest friends—those who loved him—would turn away when they saw him, lest they have repercussions from the group. (This reaction lasted until 1973 when some began to seek us out to explain.)

The overvaluation of what they had to teach as a group was

* Carlos Castaneda, *Tales of Power*.

at a fever pitch. They were fanatically serious at that time (they were saving the world). One knows from history how humorless that trip tends to be (from Mohammed to Hitler, etcetera). My Mediterranean disposition gravitates toward laughter; I found the humor in this situation—and part of it really was funny.

The programming—as John would say—was also anti-couple. It was kind of the religious concept "divide the dyads and be stronger as a group." So the trips going down from Arica teachers had the flavor for me of martyr, Messiah, religious zealot, spiritual storm trooper, madonna, generally groupiness, one "mini mouse" super-secretary, and variations on these themes. Definitely a boys' club with women playing submissive, subversive roles.

I have always been skeptical of any system that uses fear— whether that be a fear of a hell, fear of the destruction of the earth, fear of rising Kundalini* asymmetrically or whatever. The Arica group uses—incidentally—prophecies of destruction of the earth in ten years. (It's still ten years I see from Oscar's interview in the December 1973 East-West Journal; it's been four years since I first heard him use that number.) Arica also taught that one can experience crystallization of one's ego in the big toe for all eternity; bringing fear into the eternal. This Oscar told us in one of his lectures during the three-month training at the Essex House.

This group also did not seem to be free of the "spiritual buccaneering" that is common in similar situations. When money is needed any person with a possible surplus of money is fair game to supply the dollars needed. I hesitate to make any judgments pro or con; the obvious difficulty of many members of the group to earn money outside the group effort put me off as to their motivations when it came to people with money. In one case, a lovely woman in the training group contributed a little over a million. Her hope was spiritual help for her retarded son. Arica has her to thank for getting through some tight financial spots during their beginning.

On the positive side, many of the members for the first time

* Gopi Krishna in his *Kundalini: The Evolutionary Energy in Man*, gives an autobiographical account of the unpleasant results of arousing Kundalini on one side of the body rather than both sides.

felt they belonged to an extended family and had something to do (finally) that would make a difference. Chanting and meditating together with the support of an extended family environment is powerful indeed. Man has always huddled together with others for warmth, protection and just plain comfort. (My daughter, Nina, for example, felt great after a few hours of communal singing at the local Yoga ashram. She is only lately able to do that without identifying with all the other negative and political situations involved with belonging to this particular group.) There is the peculiar belief system that you must wait in line for enlightenment; this line has gates and gate guards. This seems to be one basic operational belief that is relied on by most organized groups of this kind.

The type of training that I experienced during the three months was a combination of Gurdjieffian, yoga, high school gym and some tantric yoga. Toward the end of the training, we sat in front of the school symbol for twenty minutes a day, with a strobe light impressing the symbol on our whatever. The techniques could and have changed since that time (1971). A big factor, of course, was the break of one's normal pattern by focusing approximately fourteen hours a day, six days a week for three months, on the training.

There were many breaks into different states of being, in levels of consciousness. Some persons would not admit, after spending all that time and money, a thousand a month for three months, that they had not experienced the expected state of "permanent Satori," which Arica guaranteed. There was also fear that they would not be accepted by the Arica group for further training (the next carrot in front of the donkey).

A humorous incident happened about midway through the training, although at the time, I didn't laugh very much. One day the "dragon lady" (my nickname for Jenny, Oscar's lady) came into class and demanded that Corinne Calvet leave the training.

Corinne was a funny sort of old-time-movie star. She had talked Oscar into giving her a scholarship, which wasn't hard to do at that time. Oscar was fascinated with anyone having to do with films and remembered Corinne's movies. She was part of the Hollywood period that had conditioned his and my generation. Corinne has a great French sense of humor—if the climate is right; sometimes she can be provocative with her demands for "center stage." Teachers who are intent on giving you "the message" find that quality difficult. Jenny, apparently not too keen on having Corinne close to Oscar, was watching her activities very carefully. I enjoyed Corinne's humor; we soon became close schoolmates.

One day (soon after our daily gym exercises) we started Kiné rhythm, a Gurdjieffian-like movement-mental exercise using a small rock in which one places one's "consciousness." The rock is held in one hand and is moved in certain patterns alternately, using each hand. One also visualizes a pattern of movement in the head and a set of moving sensations in one's body, each coordinated with the other movements.

After about fifteen minutes in planetside time, I looked up and saw an "apparition" coming through the door. It was the dragon lady—who (from the expanded state of being I had moved into) appeared as if a true Kali,* spewing fire and destruction.

Everyone became still in suspense, waiting for what was to come next. Jenny went up to Corinne and asked her to come down to the office with her. From Corinne's face I could see and feel that it was as frightening a call as she had ever experienced —reactivating old memories of encounters she had undergone with the gestapo when she was in Paris during the Nazi occupation.

They both left. After about twenty minutes, Corinne returned in a state of extreme shock. "I've been kicked out," she whimpered. The trauma she was going through exhibited her feeling of eternal fear and eternal loneliness. She proceeded to fall into little pieces—hysterical—with all of us trying to hold her together. One of the trainers called down to the office to find out what to do, and in a few minutes the dragon lady returned.

We sat in a circle (Jenny, one teacher and about eight students). Jenny in all her finery—fire and brimstone glittering away —told us that Corinne's attitude was not fitting; that she must leave the group.

I could tell by the expression and attitude of the teacher from

* The goddess of destruction; the personification of the destroying principle in opposition to the creation principle, Shiva; one of the two aspects of the energy of the Universe.

the Arica group (Bob Jolly), who was in charge of our group, that this decision was a surprise to him—Corinne being asked to leave without the participation of his teacher–group in the decision-making process. I began to plead Corinne's cause with all the fervor I could muster. In my expanded state I felt I was pleading for reconsideration of all of mankind.

Jenny did not accept my pleas; her state was one of emoting virtuous dedication to the process of immediate rejection of a lower being from her chosen Group. She was so into her trip, she became constricted in her awareness. She was smoking a cigarette. My rock, or "consciousness holder," which I had been using for Kiné rhythm exercise, was on the floor where I had left it, close to her. My rock was a geode (a beautiful cuplike rock filled with gemlike crystals) that John had given me.

Jenny ground out her cigarette on the crystals, using my "consciousness holder" as an ashtray.

In the expanded state I was in, need I tell you of my discomfort? In no time at all, the group had two loud hysterical ladies on their hands. I remember screaming like a banshee. I demanded to know whether this was a democratic group decision or an authoritarian trip, with her as dictator? Was *she* telling us that Corinne was out? I also very quietly advised her to be sure of how she intended to respond because it would be repeated. Her answer was that the decision had been given her by "a higher source," implying that her decision was a Revelation, not to be questioned. Her performance was quite impressive. I had the uneasy feeling that the decision was all too human and that the method she used was old-fashioned South American aristocratically oriented politics.

A month after finishing the training, John and I went on a United States-wide tour of interviews on radio and television for the newly published book *The Center of the Cyclone*. We became rather fatigued from the travel and the many hours of giving—undergoing midnight radio shows, etcetera. I picked up a rather dangerous virus. All that hotel food, no sunshine—I missed sunny California—and pushing the body unnaturally in the tour and the training, caused me to have a close brush with death in the hospital for a six-week period (see Chapter Eight,

"Illness in the Dyad"). I pushed the river too far for too long for my particular body.

In conclusion I would like to say that I think those three months were also the beginning of Oscar's and Jenny's American training; it was a mutual exchange. I am appreciative of that opportunity to be taught and to teach in such an intensive mode.

I believe that most mental-physical-spiritual techniques and tools are neutral. Do particular styles of presenting those tools or techniques appeal to me or not? I think the average United States Westerner is drawn to the styles of presentation in which he/she has been raised. In the United States we value our personal initiative and our personal integrity. We learn what gurus give us as best we can and combine their teachings with our own knowledge, our science and our democratic ideals. Among most persons in the United States there is a past history of fighting and winning against aristocracy and its dominion over the individual self: no would-be kings or queens survive long in our culture.

It is all very well to say that "ego"* questions dogma fed one.† Described this way "ego" must be dropped when in a school such as the Arica Institute (thus killing curiosity). Using this view at the expense of the individual self causes arbitrariness to appear in the form of the new group "ego."

Can a group not reflect the group leader or leaders? I don't know the answer; however, I did feel that Oscar's and Jenny's influence or style was felt by the "temple" members, who then

* In Chile, Oscar's own definition of ego as "that which keeps one out of Satori," apparently was misinterpreted in New York by the teaching group. They mistook the symptoms of such anti-Satori programs (e.g. the "questioning" aspect of ego) for the disease and said to the students, "Thou shalt not fight my teachings," instead of analyzing anti-Satori programs.

† As is shown on page 168 of *The Center of the Cyclone* one must distinguish self, ego, and essence. The self makes the choices to either move from ego programming or to essence programming. Contrary to the psychoanalytical definition of ego, in the school in Chile ego was defined as any program that keeps the self out of essence programming. The training group in New York did not make these distinctions. They define ego as any expressed disagreement with their orders, thus leaving no room for self and its decisions; as if they and they alone were speaking from an essence position.

56 *The Dyadic Cyclone*

influenced the teachers in a pyramid type of structure, similar to the Catholic Church's own hierarchy (Pope, Cardinals, Bishops, Priests and Nuns), not Gnosticism,* which the Catholic

* *Encyclopaedia Britannica*, 1960, Chicago, Illinois: GNOSTICISM, a movement of religious syncratism [sic] (or fusion of different and previously independent beliefs), which maintained itself side by side with genuine Christianity as the latter was gradually crystallizing into the ancient Catholic Church, and which bore the strong impress of Christian influences. . . .

Among the majority of the followers of the movement "Gnosis" was understood not as meaning "knowledge" or "understanding," in our sense of the word, but "revelation."

These little Gnostic sects and groups all lived in the conviction that they possessed a secret and mysterious knowledge, in no way accessible to those outside, and not based on reflection, on scientific inquiry and proof, but on revelation. It was derived directly from the times of primitive Christianity; from the Saviour himself and his disciples and friends, with whom they claimed to be connected by a secret tradition, or else from later prophets of whom many sects boasted. . . .

In short, Gnosticism, in all its various sections, its form and its character, falls under the great category of mystic religions. . . . All alike boast a mystic revelation and a deeply-veiled wisdom. As in many mystical religions, so in Gnosticism, the ultimate object is individual salvation, the assurance of a fortunate destiny for the soul after death. As in the others, so in this the central object of worship in a redeemer-deity who has already trodden the difficult way which the faithful have to follow. . . .

And as in all mystical religions, so here too, holy rites and formulas, acts of initiation and consecration, all those things which we call sacraments, play a very prominent part. . . . Indeed, sacred formulas, names and symbols are of the highest importance among the Gnostic sects. We constantly meet with the idea that the soul, on leaving the body, finds its path to the highest heaven opposed by the deities and demons of the lower realms of heaven, and only when it is in possession of the names of these demons, and can repeat the proper holy formula, or is prepared with the right symbol, or has been anointed with the holy oil, finds its way unhindered to the heavenly home. Hence the Gnostic must above all things learn the names of the demons, and equip himself with the sacred formulas and symbols, in order to be certain of a good destiny after death. . . .

Marriage and sexual propagation are considered either as absolute Evil or as altogether worthless, and carnal pleasure is frequently looked upon as forbidden. Then again asceticism sometimes changes into wild libertinism. . . .

Gnosticism itself is a free, naturally-growing religion, the religion of isolated minds, of separate little circles and minute sects. The homogeneity of wide circles, the sense of responsibility engendered by it, and continuity with the past are almost entirely lacking in it. It is based upon revelation, which even at the present time is imparted to the individual, upon the more or less convincing force of the religious imagination and speculations of a

Church was based on. It had a South American aristocratic political feel for me at that time.

I am partial to a jnana-yoga approach where you analyze both mind and body, perfecting the individual anti-satori and satori programs without the group pressures. One other example of "groupthink" occurred about halfway through the training.

I suggested to Oscar that he invite Kurt Von Meier (a long-time friend of mine from California, who calls himself a native American shaman, though non-Indian) to address the group. He brought some *Amanita muscaria* mushrooms (which are legal) to New York. (Oscar had experienced *Amanita* effects with Indians of the Altoplano of Bolivia.) We sat down with Oscar and smoked some of it the evening before Kurt's lecture. The following evening Kurt lectured on the *Amanita* as a source of religious inspiration in Christianity and other faiths. Gordon Wasson's book *Soma* shows that it was used in India and Siberia; others have traced its use in the early Christian era.

Kurt's lectures are delightful: he weaves verbal, mental tapestries, intricate beyond anything that I have heard before. Later, it turned out that Kurt was the only outside lecturer that Oscar invited to speak to the students of New York #1 of the Arica Institute.

This freedom from outside influence led to what we call *groupthink* (see Irving Janis's *The Victims of Groupthink*). During the training an article appeared in *Psychology Today*, copies of which we circulated among the group. I felt that they were fast getting into *groupthink*. I suggested Kurt to Oscar, feeling the group had better get some outside influences brought to bear on their thinking and feeling processes. This was more or less ignored. The "top management group" attempted to keep the groupthink concept as their own.

I would venture to guess that some of the beautiful youngsters

---

few leaders, upon the voluntary and unstable grouping of the schools round the master. Its adherents feel themselves to be the isolated, the few, the free and the enlightened, as opposed to the sluggish and inert masses of mankind degraded in matter, or the initiated as opposed to the uninitiated, the Gnostics as opposed to the "Hylici . . ."

that have taken the training, across the country, have by now influenced it enough so that such egos are no longer visible to the new member. These new ones have little or no contact with "The Crown of God," as the temple members were called then.

This personal view of my experience with the Arica Institute, I hope, explains my basic philosophy about groups, tribes, families, communes, etcetera. . . . Not too much changes. The Arica Institute in its various forms could be a religion/corporation (I feel it is both), for the basic patterns of each are there. Each person joining either a religion or a corporation has a limited range of realities from which to choose. I share with you a glimpse of my impressions as molded by my metabeliefs (beliefs about beliefs).

Chapter Three

Origins Before This Dyad

Two of my previous books *The Center of the Cyclone* and *Simulations of God: the Science of Belief* end with an account of Toni and I meeting and a discussion of our particular dyad. In each of these cases I saw that there were some deep general principles operating between us and in each of us. In this account we pursue more in depth what it is that has led to our attraction, our living together, and our sharing of life on this planet.

Looking at us individually, from the standpoint of the consensus reality, we have had similar, though not identical, histories. Each of us has been through two previous marriages and has a daughter from a former marriage. In addition, I have two sons from my first marriage. Each of us terminated our own past two marriages on our own initiative.

We both grew up in a strong family environment; each had an older brother who died and has a younger brother who is surviving today. Each father was/is a strong, self-starting individualist. Our mothers were loving family-oriented women.

In addition to our marriages each of us has had several love affairs other than with our spouses and has been willing to learn from every love relationship each of us encountered; from positive as well as negative experiences. We each learned about entrancement, the seductive aspects of beauty and sex and the problems inherent in projection upon a partner during entrancement. Each of us has carried forward a model of an ideal dyad and has realized the blinding qualities of such models projected onto someone who did not fit it very well. Somehow or other each of us has learned to be more objective, more "clinical" as it were, in our appraisal of mates and possible mates. Toni and I find that we have each (almost secretly) developed an ideal of what it can be to live happily with a mate. Each of us has found that it is necessary to have a home that is adequate to take care of work, family and friends.

With my medical and scientific background applied to the dyad, I have found a clinical detachment is necessary at times in order to avoid getting lost in the usual emotional morass of male/female relationships. Toni has achieved a similar detachment from the usual altercations, conflicts, discussions and emotional involvement that beset many couples. I don't wish to say that we have the ideal relationship. Each of us has a fierce temper. We sometimes express ourselves quite loudly to each other for a short time. Each is capable of deep grief; each of us has, whether real or not, survival programs that dictate certain kinds of reactions to social, financial and sexual situations.

When we find ourselves with emotional problems, emotional difficulties, either owing to the basic survival programs being turned on in the brain or because of some unknown factor, each of us is willing to step aside and analyze in one's self what it is that gave rise to that particular storm. We have reached the point where we can treat with humor a good deal of this material, realizing its ultimately trivial nature and its totally unimportant place in the current situation. Real problems having to do with other persons, either male or female, are discussed as candidly as we can and yet with a certain degree of diplomacy necessary for smooth operations in the here and now. Each of us realizes that action or talk coming from one of us in a fatigued state of being is trivial and to be discounted by the other.

We have each been trained by our own past deep dyadic relationships. This training is invaluable in telling each of us not only what is possible and real, but what is impossible and unreal.

We have found that expectations of performance (that is *operational* performance in the here and now current situation of one by the other) is the main source of conflict. If one member of a dyad carries a secret picture of expectations of performance of his or her mate and the mate fails to live up to that secret picture, the dyad is in trouble. One solution to this kind of difficulty is illustrated by Fritz Perls' Gestalt Training Program, which I took at Esalen. I paraphrase Fritz: "I am not on this planet to live up to your expectations, nor are you on this planet to live up to mine. I have my trip; you have your trip. If we can work out a mutual trip with joy and sharing, let us do so; if we cannot do this, let us say goodbye."

This kind of philosophy may look to those who have maintained a very long marriage and a long, happy family life like the epitome of iconoclasm (the destruction of accepted idols, images or icons). For those in a warm, happy family life this philosophy is iconoclastic ("as if destroying their idealized image"). For those who have yet to achieve a warm, happy family life, Fritz's philosophy is necessary in order to proceed to try to find that particular person with whom each can have a warm, happy life.

In addition I proceed, as does Toni, on the philosophy that there are no mistakes, there are only correctable errors. However, there are no errors, there are only alternative programs. If one person does not work out in one's dyad, then one should as cleanly as possible and with the least fuss accept the fact that one must go to an alternate program, that is, seeking that person with whom one can live happily. Hanging on to a set of programs that are obviously leading to years of negative struggle, trying to achieve something with someone with whom one cannot achieve it, is a program which leads to unhappiness and to the accumulation of negative karma (consequences) for many years beyond the humanly experiential years.

I was brought up in a family in which the ideals of the

Catholic Church dictated that the couple remain together irrespective of any conflicts, difficulties in the external world,
financial difficulties, social difficulties, or biological difficulties.
This dictum insisted that no matter what happened, the couple
could not be divorced: both must remain in the same house
and bring up their children together.

This was the ideal upon which I undertook my first marriage.
I watched my parents in their struggles to maintain a relationship; they used amazingly intricate and secret maneuvers to
maintain the relationship (at least superficially). I also watched
them suffer from the Catholic Church's dogma about not using
birth control. I saw my mother's run-down physical condition
worsen as a consequence of pregnancy after pregnancy and
spontaneous abortion after spontaneous abortion after the birth
of her first three children. Biological fatigue developed to extreme
limits.

As a youngster I saw my parents move into separate bedrooms
and knew they never made love from that point on. I watched the
resulting conflicts when father sought the company and the
solace of other women. I experienced father's and mother's rages
as a consequence of the secret maneuvering resulting from this
situation. As a youngster I made vows to myself that I would
never be placed in such a situation.

Little did I know then the powerful forces that drive people
into such situations. Little did I know that I would later involve
myself in an almost identical kind of relationship with my first
wife. She and I attempted to keep our marriage together for a
period of twenty-two years. My second marriage was a dyadic
relationship during which we shared the same house for some
seven years.

In each of my marriages there was a good beginning year in
which each of us worked very well together in our mutual
endeavor to create a successful marriage. In each case during
the subsequent years there was a long period of mutually working together and successfully carrying out what we intended to
do. In each case unresolvable conflicts developed, with the
necessity of appealing for outside help for the marriage.

In each marriage I finally came to the conclusion that I could not live up to my own expectations of myself and of my own performance with the particular spouse and that I also could not live up to her expectations of my behavior in the dyad. With a good deal of anger, shame, grief and self-judgments, I initiated divorce proceedings in each case.

In the case of my parents, I found that they were maintaining a home, in spite of the unresolvable conflicts in their dyad, for their children. In my first marriage this was my ideal also. I was brought up to believe that one's own inner strength was what was necessary to create a home and to keep it going. I was brought up to believe that marriages are broken up because of sexual temptation on the part of the male. That the male is somehow wrong, that his sexual drives, his "penis orientation" as it were, lead him into traps with women other than his wife and that his "instinct" to impregnate dominates his existence far and above any loyalties to children, to wife or to his home.

In this particular belief system, love, compassion, loyalty and trust are said to be undermined by sexual proclivities. In this belief system women are understood not to have the sexual drives that men have. For most of my young-adult manhood I was afraid that I would be betrayed by my own sexual nature.

I came to my first marriage at the age of twenty-one, totally inexperienced in sexual relations. Previous to this time I had been completely out of contact with the sexual experiences of my own age group. My first wife was similarly inexperienced. On our wedding night we were both rather surprised to find out that sex was all so easy and not nearly so terrifying as each of us had projected. Each of us was rather surprised and said, "Oh, is that what it's all about—so simple, so easy."

Within the first year of my first marriage my wife was pregnant with our first child. My wife resented the fact that she had become pregnant. Since we were married in the Catholic Church and there was a lot of family pressure for grandchildren, we did not take the path (which is readily accessible today) of abortion. (I am glad today we continued: I am very grateful that I have a son who is a dedicated man in his own right.)

All during that marriage I was an intense, dedicated young scientist, continuing my education at Cal Tech, going through medical schools and entering into the war research program of the Office of Scientific Research and Development (the Committee on Medical Research) at The Johnson Foundation of the University of Pennsylvania.

It is hard to portray the intensity of my research proclivities during this period. With great dedication and a fierce protection of my time away from my family, I would spend hours on weekends and at night in the laboratory working out technical problems.

Upon graduation from medical school I entered into the war program. It is hard to recapture the patriotic zeal with which that young man was pursuing his path attempting to help the war effort. He was dedicated to saving lives, not killing. On that basis, he did not volunteer for military service. He insisted that what he do during the war be strictly defensive: medical and physiological research.

He became involved in the study of explosive decompression in an effort to prevent the bodily damage from this cause that was taking place in pressurized aircraft. He pursued studies of bends at high altitude and the problems attendant upon anoxia experienced by pilots. He devised several new instruments for measurements necessary for the analysis of anoxia and of bends. These pursuits meant a lot of travel, for the Air Forces and the Committee on Medical Research. These activities kept him away from his family a good deal of the time.

When the war ended he dove deeply into the studies that he really wanted to pursue—those of the physiology of the brain. His second son was born during this period. His wife wanted this child, and created it more in an atmosphere of acceptance of pregnancy and with the desire of carrying the child to term.

During the next few years, deep conflicts occurred in the young researcher and in his marriage. His research dedication, his unresolved inner conflicts, his unreal expectations of his wife, his parents' Catholic-oriented expectations in which he no longer believed, led him into a blind alley. He needed outside help and sought it for his wife and himself. His medical colleagues found a psychoanalyst for him.

Because of my medical training I was able to take a training/

research psychoanalysis that was also a therapeutic one. I spent five to seven days a week, one hour per day for three years reviewing my inner conflicts and the events of the previous years.

My wife spent a similar amount of time with another analyst of the classical tradition. My wife did not think that she needed analysis and was quite angry, feeling that she had been forced to undertake it. Her analyst reported to me afterward that he had never had such a case, that she had been angry every single hour, five days a week for three years.

During my own analysis I found a professional appeal in researching my own mind and that of others. My analyst gave me the option of taking a complete course of psychoanalytic training. I then undertook the full professional training of the Institute of the Philadelphia Association for Psychoanalysis and the Philadelphia Psychoanalytic Society and completed that training under the Washington-Baltimore Psychoanalytic Institute.

The difficulties of our marriage were not resolved by the analysis. Some of the difficulties in my own personality were straightened out, but not all of them. In Washington we lived together and, in the new environment, continued to bring up our two children. I continued my research in neurophysiology and took on new research in solitude, isolation and confinement, establishing and using the new tank method. The incompatibility in the marriage continued. The internal dyadic stresses built up even more than they had before. I mustered my courage to the sticking point and finally left my family. The divorce proceedings were rather bitter and I was tempted to give my wife everything and leave completely. In the settlement I gave her the house, money to pay the mortgage and alimony (which still continues sixteen years later). I moved from Washington to the Virgin Islands and spent a year alone.

I fell in love with a married woman, who subsequently obtained a divorce so that we could marry each other. Within the first year of our marriage she became pregnant and my first daughter was born. The dolphin research program was started. (The history of this period of research is recounted in *Man and Dolphin*.)

As the requirements of this research developed, it was necessary to start another laboratory, this time in Miami. My wife preferred Miami and Coconut Grove to the Virgin Islands as a place to live and bring up a family. She became my executive assistant. I found that dividing my time between Miami and Saint Thomas was not productive. By chance Gregory Bateson was able to take over at the Saint Thomas laboratory while I set up and operated the Miami laboratory. My wife had social ambitions; we joined several social clubs in the Miami Beach, Miami area.

Then the social whirl started. I found a very deep conflict between the social life and the research life. It was necessary for us to raise the money to support the laboratories, both through government funds and private support. Raising the money turned out to be an onerous burden for me. I found that I was not spending as much time doing the research as I was in raising the money to support the research of others. Slowly but surely a series of conflicts with my wife developed, which neither one of us could handle.

When Gregory Bateson left the Saint Thomas laboratory to go to Hawaii, I found myself spending more time in Saint Thomas and less time in Miami. The relationship with my wife had become intensely emotional, negative and nonproductive; she refused outside help. My Board of Trustees objected to her being in the Institute. Her maneuverings became very unpleasant to the scientific staff and finally I had to fire her. She then started a series of maneuvers that became highly unpleasant and rather dangerous.

Meanwhile, through my experimentation in Saint Thomas with the isolation tank and LSD, I arrived at a new unfolding of my essentially idealistic ethics in regard to dolphins. I didn't want to hold them as prisoners any longer. I decided to close both laboratories, leave my marriage, leave scientific research and go to the Esalen Institute to find out what it was in my own personality that led to such difficulties in my personal relationships.

I made a settlement offer to my wife. She did not accept the settlement and insisted on going to court. The court awarded her less than my offer did. Currently she is appealing this judgment. We were separated in 1967 and in 1976 the case is still in the courts.

I give this history to show that I have not been very successful in my marriages; similarly in my love affairs—there had not been any deep-lasting relationships.

With a history like this, and in viewing this history, I am a bit shaken by the fact that I made such bad choices in the past; and yet if I hadn't made these choices, at age sixty I might still be compromising and might never have found Toni. All through this past history I was trying to find peace and do productive work at the same time. My own belief systems were divided up into such peculiar compartments that I could not bring them together and integrate them adequately for both my family life and my professional life.

My basic problems resulted from blindly taking on the Catholic Church's belief systems in my youth, from attempting to negate them at about the age of twelve, and from not really succeeding in doing so. Pressure from my parents led to my being married the first time in the Church and deferring divorce for many years.

Even more basic considerations, however, are as follows: When one is a young male, one may tend to project an idealized image upon the first woman with whom one falls in love. Without the experience of many loves, one is not very clinical about the first love affair, which may end up in marriage. One does not examine the relationship between that woman and her mother and between that woman and her father. One does not pay close attention to the relationship of the woman to her brothers and/or sisters. One becomes entranced, literally *in-trance-ed* in regard to the other person, projecting idealized images upon the other that do not fit. One then wakes up several years later, finding that time has passed and that the idealized images do not fit and that what is left is not what one wants or needs. Practical, cold-blooded, clinical assessment is not part of "falling in love." If one defers sexual experience from the time of onset of sexuality, at twelve or thirteen, to twenty-one, one is passing by a valuable period in which such experience is going to be of benefit to one in one's later life in selecting a marriage partner. The old-fashioned virtue of remaining a virgin until marriage is nonsense. It is denying to a person the right of learning—the right of learning through experience—that which is necessary for the proper selection of the other parent of one's children, of the other grandparent of one's grandchildren.

In this account, I have left out much of importance in the generation of the "me" of now. At a certain point one owes discretion to one's wives, children, lovers and to one's self. At this time this is all I can say. Possibly at some future time there can be a deeper analysis, given in a disguised form, in which I can tell more of the inner/outer realities as I experienced them, without hurting others.

Chapter Four

Coherence in the Dyad

"Coherence Theory: The theory of truth that every true statement, insofar as it is true, describes its subject in the totality of its relationship with all other things."*

In another way: Coherence theory states that the truth of any statement depends upon the truth of all surrounding statements within that context, within a whole. In this view, the truth is generated by the interrelated consistency of statements within the particular semantic structure. In any whole, each part is related to all of the other parts in ways that add up to, are multiplied to, something greater than the sum of the parts.

Thus, in a dyad, the dyad structure of two people living together is far greater than each of those persons living alone. The truth of their living together is in the context of the dyad, not in the solitudinous self of each member of that dyad. The truth of the dyad is tested in the context in which the dyad is embedded, i.e., in the social consensus reality as well as in the

* *The Random House Dictionary of the English Language*, N.Y.: Random House, 1973.

solitudinous dyadic relationship. The dyadic whole is greater than merely the added sum of the two individuals. The importance of a dyad can be measured probably more exactly by an approximate equation as follows: The usual belief system says, if we have a female individual "A" and a male individual "B" that a dyad is expressed by "A" plus "B." This equation does not express a possible sufficient measure of the complexities of dyadic relationship. The complexity of the relationship of two persons probably can be better expressed by using a higher function of the relation, such as, "A" times "B" raised to the second power $(A \times B)^2$. To make this more general, any group complexity, such as in a loving, intense family, is more like "A" times "B" times "C" times "D," etcetera, raised to the nth power where n is the number of individuals in that group. To express true complexity of a group is an immense theoretical problem yet to be expressed adequately and efficiently. Intuitively one can sense the true complexity of a group's coherence without yet being able to express it densely.

The dyad (male and female) is a very strong unit. At one time I read in depth the literature of those who had crossed oceans, either alone or in a dyadic or triadic situation. I found some interesting correlations. All else being equal, a man or a woman crossing an ocean alone may or may not have survived, depending upon whether he or she had the ability to project positive interpretations upon his or her difficulties. Those who tended to project terrifying, fearful, self-destroying images, when alone, usually ended up dead.

In the pursuit of the solitudinous sailors, I found accounts of many couples (of the order of ten times the number of the solitary sailors) who had crossed oceans successfully. I met some of these couples and found that they either were or had become an integrated dyad in the face of the necessities of ocean sailing. The drama in their crossings was of such a low key that they did not think it worth reporting in a book, in contrast to many solitary sailors who have dramatized their voyages. The male–female dyad seems to be a very stable way for humans to operate when faced with the unknown in the physical world.

What are some of the requirements for this kind of dyad?

First of all, it is necessary for such a couple to share with each other candidly, and with no holds barred, all negative feelings and positive feelings having to do with what they are trying to accomplish and what they are doing currently. If this can be done in a graceful and diplomatic way, much of the usual friction found among unhappy couples can be avoided.

The survival programs necessary for the comfort of each member of the dyad must be worked upon and not taken as a hidden agenda within the dyad. If the couple does not know how to survive without the usual accoutrements of civilization, it is wise for them to take to the wilds, go camping together, and in so far as is possible, live with the minimum possible requirements so that they know how far down the scale of civilized living they can go and survive satisfactorily. Too many couples battle over nonessentials as if these were necessary for survival.

I have seen many persons of the younger generation take off for the woods and live for a year or so with the minimum possible necessities in order to train themselves as to what is necessary for their planetside trip. This is done either as a solitaire or as a solitary couple, a dyad. I have seen parents bringing up their children by taking them into high mountains for a summer vacation and insisting that they subsist on the minimum possible standard, carrying their own food, their own shelter and their own clothing on long treks into the High Sierras or the Rockies. This training is obviously basic to eliminating a lot of the illusions attendant upon living in cities and participating in elaborate civilized rituals as if these were necessary for one's personal survival. With direct experience of the wilderness, not only a willingness but a joy of going into the wilderness periodically, one can survive the rigors of civilization far more happily and with less investment in those things that are not necessary to one's happiness and security.

Coherence in a dyad can be obtained by these methods. The truth of relationship in a dyad can be brought out very strongly by facing the dyad with challenges, the challenges of nature, the challenges of the sea, the challenges of other species on this planet.

The external reality test of a dyad comes in confrontations

with nature. Until the dyad is firmly established and accepted by each member as a more efficient way to live on the planet, it is not wise to have children. A happy family life is predicated upon a very strong dyad. Love of teaching the young is absolutely necessary to raising a strong and happy family. Families that go into the wilds together learn that teaching the same procedures, the same techniques and the same way of life needed in the wilderness to their children leads to a family unity that is hard to obtain in the city streets.

The above are some of my belief systems in regard to dyadic coherence and dyadic strength in the external reality. In Toni's and my dyad I have tried to enunciate these factors and to live them out as far as this is possible within our particular limits. We lived together first in a small house within a portion of residential Los Angeles. The first two years I was trained in Toni's techniques of living in a small house with a continual flow of interesting people coming through the house in a very active creative environment with many younger people present. I found that in order to write *The Center of the Cyclone* and *Simulations of God*, I had to retire from this environment into a small motor home parked in the street outside the house. This gave me the necessary solitude for integrating and creating those books. We then took trips into the High Sierras and up the west coast of the United States to different wilderness areas. Toni discovered that when I was above approximately 6,000 feet, I automatically went on a high. She began to appreciate the benefits of the two of us going alone into the wild (under rather civilized conditions). I then introduced her to skiing on snow—the first time at an altitude of 9,000 feet.

Toni had a history of being an expert water skier and thoroughly enjoying it. Snow skiing was a very strange new use of her acquired techniques and talent in water skiing. The addition of high altitude added a stress that she did not have when she was skiing at sea level. She protested and then finally took hold of the challenge and learned how to ski on snow. Trembling in fear, she finally went to the top of a mountain and came all the way down, under the guidance of an instructor, neither falling nor hurting herself in her first long trip down a mountain. We then took several ski trips together and went summer skiing on the side of Mount Lassen and The Watchman at Crater Lake in Oregon. These experiences added new dimensions to our dyad.

We also spent much time at altitudes above 10,000 feet, camping and experiencing contacts with wild bears in the High Sierras.

After these experiences together we decided to move out of the city. We bought a house at 1,300 feet, two and a half miles from the sea, and during the intervening years we put our energies and time into creating a home that we both enjoy and in which we can adequately live, teach, rehearse and hold workshops. Several younger people have been drawn to us and come and go through the house at frequent intervals. This home is sufficiently remote from the city to give us a feeling of the wild; the coyotes come down from out of the hills and we can hear them at night. A far ranging mountain lion, a California cougar, apparently took one of our cats. Recently a coyote came within 200 feet of the house late at night.

Toni has a garden in which she accomplishes her earthly labors. We walk up a nearby mountain every morning to an altitude of 300 feet above the house.

Since we are fifty miles from the center of Los Angeles and near the Pacific Coast Highway, many of our friends in their transits from Los Angeles to San Francisco, and vice versa, stop in and spend the night. There is an active flow of very interesting people through this house. We have loosened our bond with the city and yet we are close enough to the city so that we can do our business there when we need to without having to be immersed in the city twenty-four hours a day. The profound stillness renders us an incredibly refreshing sleep every night.

Good sleeping conditions are absolutely necessary for the biocomputer. The dyad requires rest, profound rest, after the multiple activities of the day. Any couple who does not get this rest has difficulties merely owing to the accumulated fatigue in each of the biocomputers. Sleep is necessary to dump the programs of the day and to clean out the biocomputer for use the next day.

Working on the house, working on the grounds, working in

the garden, generates, somehow, a sanity that is hard to get without these activities. The human body evolved on this planet in close contact with the earth. Breaking these bonds with the earth leads to peculiar types of insanities found in cities. Breaking the bonds with the earth causes "the paper reality" of civilization to encroach upon one's consciousness to a point where one believes that the paper reality is *real*, rather than a convenient construction of man. Instead of the paper reality being the proper servant of man, it becomes his master.

The survival of a dyad in our civilization requires adequate attention to the paper reality. Cooperative efforts between two people in this area can strengthen the dyad also. Cooperative appreciation of the talents of each member of the dyad by the other member is very necessary in this area. The challenges of proper bookkeeping for a family, shared within the dyad and fully using the talent of each in this area, shortens up the necessary time spent in satisfying the requirements of organized human society. Coherence in the dyad in this area necessitates candid critical appraisal of the expenditures of money and of the hidden ways that money can be spent within the dyadic structure.

Most dyads have problems in the areas of money, sex, power. Each of these must be examined within critical honesty and the basic dictating programs—the belief systems of each partner in the dyad—must be critically examined. Toni and I have not completely examined all of our belief systems in these areas. We are going at this slowly and carefully and diplomatically. Each of us has seen the collapse of our previous marriages owing to lack of communication between us and our partners in these critical areas of human endeavor. We confer openly on the basis of which funds are to be expended. We try our best to bring any hidden agendas out in the open if we find them operating within ourselves.

We also work on sexual problems raised between us or between us and others in as candid, honest and diplomatic fashion as we can. We examine our beliefs in this area between us and have developed satisfactory ways of operating in this particular area.

Power in the dyad is epitomized by the question that we ask

each other—"Who is programming whom?" In addition we ask, "Who is entranced by whom?" Why was entrancement experienced with that particular person? We examine our social relationships with others on this basis. At times we must protect our individual initiative and at other times protect the initiative of the dyad in the face of opposition from outside. We always ask the critical question, "Why in a particular situation were we taken in by the proposals, plans and expenditure of funds by this or that particular person?"

In our way of life we have many experiences with far-out young individuals. My writings have given rise to an attraction to us by many people who read my books, assume that they can come to our house, do their particular drama, and that we will act as therapists for them. This leads to many humorous situations. We have worked out ways of dealing with such situations with the help of those who stay with us and those who work with us. Some individuals act as if we were public property and they attempt to use our home as their own personal theater for a display of their particular dramas. Somehow people attempt to lay their trips on us. We are slowly but surely developing countermeasures for this kind of happening.

Each of us is learning that compassion is not pity, and that the ultimate compassion is teaching the lessons that are necessary for others to learn and learning from the lessons they are teaching to us, whether consciously or unconsciously on their part.

Being exposed to the younger generation and their teachings, I find, provides a very huge reservoir of energy for Toni, for me, and for the dyad. The young are willing to teach. They are teaching in a new way. Those who are willing to learn from us have a vast reservoir of new creative talent.

Our policy is to try to increase the self-initiative of the hesitant youngsters. To show them (through tank work and thorough participation in their projects) that they have within themselves that which is necessary in order to be successful on the planetside trip in their own inner intellectual discipline and in their spiritual strivings. We attempt to open up their initiative and our initiative in new areas. There has been and is mutual success in this undertaking with enough of the younger generation so that we are vastly encouraged and somewhat optimistic of the fate of the younger generation.

We realize that we are dealing with a very selected sample and that this is not general enough in the United States. We hope that those youngsters who have been in contact with us will have lasting benefits and will become free-floating teacher-students on their own.

The essence of the methods we use could be subsumed under the word "teach-back" in which teaching is a mutual process. Sometimes we are teachers, sometimes we are students, and this oscillates back and forth in a continual interplay.

After *Simulations of God* had been wrapped up and was in the hands of the publisher, and the bound galleys were available, our friend Burgess Meredith, and the jazz musician Charles Lloyd decided to give readings of the Prologue of *Simulations of God* to college audiences. We heard the tape of the first presentation, at Santa Ana College. This inspired us to start working on a theater piece.

Burgess showed us that narration with music is a powerful way of presenting ideas to an audience; these combined arts moved the audience to understand the ideas. The music and narration combination turned out to be a powerful force in transmitting the feelings as well as the meanings to the younger audiences.

Quite spontaneously, Toni's daughter, Nina, and I decided to create a dance/music/narration piece based on some ideas from *Simulations of God*. One morning I wrote the narration. Nina selected another dancer and started translating the narration into body language for the dance. Nina selected a creative young musician Dean Olch to do the music. With two other musicians, Dean began composing the music for the theater piece in cooperation with the dancers.

At first I attempted to be an old-fashioned director of this piece. I was quickly taught by the youngsters that this isn't the way this portion of the new generation operates. I then sat back and watched, withdrew my directing tendencies and I awaited the group's unfolding.

By coincidence there was an opportunity to do the piece for the Garden Festival of Los Angeles organized by Warren Christiansen, a friend of Nina's. We designed the piece to fit in a one-half hour slot in this festival.

I felt the piece would never come together. At the first performance it came together so beautifully that I was overwhelmed by the high feelings that this excited in me, in the audience, in the dancers and in the musicians. During the first performance in public in front of an audience at UCLA, I suddenly felt the creative potential that is present in these youngsters. They have a new discipline that I now respect far more than I ever would have if I hadn't gone through this experience.

Toni operated as producer of the piece, and with her usual smooth, diplomatic facilitation of relationships within the whole group made it possible for our dyad to put energy and money into this project. Some of the rehearsals were done in the living room of our home; some were done at dance studios. Toni watched my particular performance with the younger people and gently pointed out where my problems lay in my relationships with the others. She analyzed my need for precision. She analyzed their needs for a looser connection and I was finally able to let go of my perfectionism and allow the unfolding of the true creative talent in these other persons.

I was then able to encourage their initiative and to help them out when they were into real difficulties in which they needed my help. I found that they would gently criticize my timing of the narration; that they would ask for revisions, where needed in their view of the piece. When I wished to stop and give them the basic philosophy behind it, they listened intently and went ahead and created that which was appropriate to that particular philosophy. I pointed out the necessities of feedback in order to integrate the group. They organized the feedback and satisfied the requirement in spite of great difficulties in getting the whole group together for a sufficient number of rehearsals.

The developing coherence in our dyad made all of this possible; I was able to accept Toni's criticisms and her "fair witnessing" of my behavior and modify it accordingly. (I do not wish to say that I have perfected this particular mode of operating, but I am continuing this kind of work and learning from it with Toni's help.)

The feedback from the three public performances of this piece have been very gratifying to everyone concerned. The costuming of the whole group was organized by Toni (through the cooperation of her good friend Mary Taylor), who also enhanced her daughter's performance by facilitating all of the different requirements necessary for the project.

Nina has turned out to be a young genius in the organizing of groups and eliciting performance from them (including myself), which I didn't think was possible at the beginning. Her disciplined performance as a dancer is very striking. The way that she integrated her dance with that of the other dancer was truly surprising and very moving.

Audience feedback showed us that we had created something that put the audience through a new experience they had not had before; those who came up after the performance were obviously extremely moved by it and somehow had had almost a religious experience during the presentation. (In each of the three performances the audience was deeply moved—they were silent throughout the entire presentation and for a long interval at the end before applauding.)

In Appendix Five of this book we give you the script—as it was finally derived from the interactions within the group—the narration, the dance directions and the music directions, all of which we wrote down as we proceeded. We also give you the philosophy upon which the piece was based (as it appeared in the brief explanatory material that had been distributed to the audience before the performance).

Chapter Five

The Transpersonal Supraself and the Dyad's Own Security

In the two books *The Human Biocomputer* and *The Center of the Cyclone*, the concepts of something greater than human operating in one's life are presented. In these books specific instances of these operations are given. The term "transpersonal" means something beyond the human unique ego or Self. There is a publication called the *Journal of Transpersonal Psychology*, which is devoted to the studies of this aspect of Self. The term "supraself" I introduced in *The Center of the Cyclone* as covering those experiences in which the Self listens to, is taught by and is immersed in inner realities—beyond those of the Self functioning in the external reality or in its own internal reality.

In a description of the operational domains of the realities available to humans, I have written (in the above two books) of the external reality (e.r.) and the internal reality (i.r.). I have in the last two years added a third domain, the extraterrestrial reality (e.t.r.). These realities are defined as follows:

In the ordinary everyday consensus external reality, the Self functions mainly at the boundary between i.r. and e.r. The operations of the body are considered to be in the external reality, the operations of the mind in the internal reality. The Self metaprogrammer (*The Human Biocomputer*) functions in the internal reality (i.r.) and uses the body in the external reality (e.r.). In the isolation tank, the external reality (e.r.) is attenuated to the point where the Self metaprogrammer can inhibit the few remaining clues as to the existence of the e.r. and immerses itself in the i.r. The Self metaprogrammer immersed in the i.r. then can have "transpersonal" or supraself experiences.

The supraself is considered as an autonomous metaprogrammer; in addition, the supraself metaprogrammer can be seen to program the Self or the Self metaprogrammer in such a way as to move it into the extraterrestrial reality (e.t.r.). (In the less precise older language: "The Self can imagine and live in nonordinary realities, created in the mind.")

The supraself metaprograms and the supraself can be detected as functioning when the Self metaprogrammer (the Self) is functioning with respect to the external reality or to the internal reality. The transition to the extraterrestrial reality (e.t.r.) is experienced when the Self or the Self metaprogrammer gives up or allows the supraself or the supraself metaprogrammer to take over and program the Self. In the farther reaches of the e.t.r. the Self loses its identity and becomes the supraself or the supraself metaprogrammer. In most people this process of allowing or of identifying with the supraself metaprograms is apparently not experienced as frequently as the immersion of the Self metaprogrammer within the internal reality. The experiences are said to become transpersonal or beyond the Self when the actual identification of Self with the supraself occurs.

These terms are operational, that is they are used in mapping descriptions of real experiences. They are not dogmatic doctrine to be followed. These concepts are aids in describing experiences. Once one has such experiences and examines them, the concepts can be used to create new experiences. The language, originally descriptive, becomes injunctive or directive.

In ordinary everyday life one can feel the operation of the supraself, the supraself metaprogramming, directing one in a subtle unconscious way. Once one has had experiences of identification with the supraself, these daily operations become more and more conscious, i.e., supraself metaprogramming becomes part of everyday ordinary life to a much greater extent in the conscious sphere than it is in, say, childhood. Advanced consciousness, in the way that we are using the term, develops throughout one's life as one begins to make distinctions of the above sorts.

My own experiences as given in *The Center of the Cyclone* and in *The Human Biocomputer* necessitated the development of this terminology in order to be able to talk about and to teach what I have learned in these regions. The three domains (external, internal, and extraterrestrial) do not define all the phenomena capable of being experienced. There are domains beyond the extraterrestrial reality. After the fusion of the Self with the supraself and transpersonal experiences are beginning, one finds that one can go still further. At this point one loses one's identity totally and one becomes "all others" in the universe. As I state in *The Center of the Cyclone* (Chapter 17), one joins the network of Creators in which the individual Self fuses with the network of those who are doing the creation continuously at very high levels. Here there is no more of one's Self or of one's supraself. One is the ultimate creative process. This region I symbolize by the Network (N). In *The Center of the Cyclone* I called this region "plus three." I find "the Network" a more satisfactory term than "plus three" of the Gurdjieffian numbering system.

During the last five years with Toni, I have experienced these regions a number of times. Each time I have experienced a little more consciousness of my supraself and of its fusion with other supraselves. Each time there is an increasingly clear loss of individuality, each time the "state of being" of unity with the cosmos has been increasingly powerful.

While writing my latest book, *Simulations of God: The Science of Belief*, I felt that it was being done through connections between me and my supraself; I stepped aside and "allowed" the ideas to come through from supraself and its connection with the Network.

When one can achieve connection with one's supraself in a conscious allowing way and can allow for the connection of that supraself to the Network (N), then one is maximally creative within the limits of what I call one's vehicle (the body and the brain). In the state of connection and of realization of the supraself by the Self it is as if something is writing or dictating through one's Self. As it were, the conscious functioning Self that operates with other people steps out of the way and allows the supraself to dictate the book or to do the work. I suspect that the above kind of functioning is similar (if not identical) to the state of grace of the Christians, to the practical Satori of the Buddhists and to the lower levels of Samadhi of the Yogis. (For the latter classification, see Table 1, page 148, *The Center of the Cyclone,* Julian Press edition, 1972).

The higher states of grace, the higher levels of Satori, the higher levels of Samadhi seem to correspond to the experiences of immersion in the Network. (For example, "fusion with the Universal Mind" is one description of such a state of being.)

Those who have not been in these domains may not respond directly to the descriptions of the experiences nor to the operational language resulting therefrom. Those who have been in these domains may come back and attempt to teach how to experience these domains to those who want to go there. One finds that most persons living in the consensus domain (e.r. plus a limited i.r.) who have not experienced other domains may either call one a holy man, a psychotic or a seditious propagandist. This widely spread attitude, this opinion, generates esotericism and the esoteric schools.

In our current United States society there are a large number of people who have experienced these domains using LSD, mescaline, peyote, or during close brushes with death, under anesthesia or in coma and, more rarely, through personal work resulting in enlightenment experience. Thus it is now becoming safer to write about such experiences, to describe them and to help these people to understand their experiences.

In my own case, I have found that it is safe to go through these experiences isolated in solitude from one's contemporary society. In the tank, one can safely move into the internal reality, experiencing one's Self-metaprogramming directly. One can then move under the behest of the supraself and allow supraself-metaprogramming to take over one's mind. Once this occurs one can go into the extraterrestrial reality (e.t.r.) and finally into the Network (N) and beyond the Network. After such experiences, on emersion from the tank, one can censor the account in the light of one's practical judgment about the social results of giving the account to one's contemporaries in the external reality. Used judiciously the tank technique can allow one to make the transition from the internal domains to social domains. One's own discipline in regard to one's own social domain allows one to adjust the balance between what the remembered experiences were and what one reports to others.

In our dyad this is a heavy program. Toni appreciates and respects my experiences in these regions. She also is far more aware of and has more respect for social consequences of communications on the planetside trip than I. Her connections to her family, to her garden, to her house, to her friends, to what I call her "village," gives her security, which she reflects in her relationship with me.

With this dyadic security, I feel free to pursue such explorations. Toni recounts experiences she has had in these regions in the past. During the period when this was legal in the early 1960s, she was in LSD therapy under the control and auspices of an LSD therapist. For example, she recounts an experience in which she joined the deep pulsations of Creation of the Universe with its pulsing, flowing, changing energies (at the boundary of the extraterrestrial reality [e.t.r.] and the Network [N] in the preceding terminology). On return from these domains she described the experience "as vast pulsating changes in the energy field," which she calls "large squiggles encompassing small squiggles." She suddenly realized, "Oh, that's all there is to it!"

These experiences enabled her to appreciate firsthand what it is that I am describing. Before we met, her practical Self had been educated sufficiently in these regions to satisfy her Self metaprogrammer. She respects the vast forces, the suprahuman nature of her own experiences. Thus she feels secure during most of my explorations of these regions. She furnishes the basic platform from which I can launch from the dyad into these domains in the tank.

For example, recently I went into the tank at about 11 PM in the evening to explore the boundaries between the external reality (e.r.), the internal reality (i.r.) and the extraterrestrial reality (e.t.r.). I went into the tank in a particularly receptive frame of mind and was willing to allow my supraself to do its own thing. In this particular case, the supraself was allowing my Self to continue conscious functioning during the experience.

John:

"The experience starts with my physical body lying quietly at the surface of the Epsom salts solution in the dark in the silence. The feeling of flotation is deep and profound. Gradually a deep pulsation starts at a frequency of about one every two seconds, a slow sine wave motion. These deep pulsations are so strong that my self feels that there may be a very large earthquake taking place. I raise my head above the surface of the water and listen. I feel the sides of the tank with my hands. The water itself is not moving. The sides of the tank are not moving. With this check on the e.r., I lie down again; the pulsations continue. The frequency of the pulsations goes up until finally there is a very high-pitched roaring sound. There has been a smooth transition from the very low-frequency vibrations to higher- and higher-frequency vibrations.

"I am then programmed down back into the lower-frequency vibrations. It is as if I am going from far-off resonance to a closer and closer resonance with some sort of a huge carrier wave coming from the e.t.r. As the frequency of the vibrations decreases, I realize that these are 'beat frequencies,' that my inherent oscillator has changed its frequency more toward the critical frequency coming from the e.t.r. (The 'beat frequency' is the difference in frequency between my oscillator and the carrier frequency from the e.t.r.) Slowly but surely I move toward the e.t.r. carrier frequency and the vibrations slow down until there is only one every minute.

"At the instant that I approach resonance with the e.t.r. carrier, the walls of the tank disappear, my physical body disappears. I realize my 'Self' as a point of consciousness within another body that I call 'my simulation of the physical body.' Somehow the water and the tank are still there but the walls of the tank have decreased to about one foot in height, above the water at the exposed surface of the floating body. The 'external reality' around the tank opens up, the room disappears and the lawn outside the tank house appears continuous up to the edges of the tank.

" 'I' lie there and realize that there are other 'human beings' wandering around on the lawn. They are all nude, men and women, apparently visitors to our home. One of them, a rather nice-looking young lady, comes over and looks into the tank and sees me lying there. She doesn't say anything. I see her rather beautiful face, her breasts and her body, which is bending over the tank. She is staring at me. She then walks away. 'I' get up out of the water and move into the house where I know that Toni is watching television. The house is very much the way it normally is in the evenings, dimly lighted. I see Toni's body lying on the pillows in front of the television set. I call to her. 'She' gets up out of her body and comes over to me. We have a conversation in which I tell her about getting out of the body, about the other people out in the yard and the woman who looked at me. 'She' gets up out of her physical body; 'she' has a body like the one that I am in, in that it is separate from the physical body. Her mobile body is unclothed; her physical body is clothed. We discuss some very personal things, which I do not want to report."

In considering this experience afterward I realized that this is the first time that "I" have been able to hold on to the earthside external domain (coordinates) in such an experience. I have been trying for several years to keep "myself" on this planet when having experiences in the e.t.r. domain.

In spite of reading Robert A. Monroe's *Journeys Out of the Body*, I had missed the whole domain of experience in which he describes very similar, if not identical, kinds of happenings. I had not consciously programmed before this particular tank episode to have such an experience. However, deep down inside

I have wanted to have experiences like Monroe's. My previous experience in this domain had always skipped this particular kind of experience. (I was trying to go much further out and succeeded.) It is also the first time that I had a "body" in these regions. In general, "I" tend to travel as "a point of consciousness." Apparently since living with Toni, I trust our environs more than I have at any previous time in my life. Previous to this, I had always skipped the "e.r. domain," the region around the tank and the region having to do with this planet.

This experience convinced me that I could now trust our environment, that I could now trust our dyad and was willing to allow the supraself to program me into such experiences in my own "e.r. neighborhood." Toni's insistence that the transpersonal and the personal can be experienced here and now on this planet finally convinced "me" that it was safe to do it this way.

Apparently our supraselves have become linked strongly enough in the dyad so that one can program the other. The dyad itself has now become stronger than either of the individual Selves within it. A dyadic supraself has developed (or has allowed connection to each of us) that does more and more of the programming without the previous dichotomy of two individual selves. (The belief structure now allows this concept.)

Long ago, in 1970 (see *The Center of the Cyclone*, Chapter 17, "State +3: Classical Satori; The Essence as One of the Creators"), I realized that there were many transitions of the Self, the supraself and the Network. Coming back from Network fusion, I was simultaneously billions of Selves, millions of Selves, thousands of Selves, tens of Selves, then two Selves, finally one Self. This recent experience showed me that there are many more dimensions to supraself relationships than I had realized. (Expansion of belief limits into new domains has taken place.)

In the above account I purposely have not used the terminology of "astral projection." There is so much literature, so many accounts and so many theories of the so-called "astral plane" that I find the region quite contaminated in the literature with a lot of theory and programs with which I do not agree. I now know what people mean by experiences "on the astral plan" as direct experiences. I do not yet agree with the multiple divisions and sort of very heavy theoretical considerations with which people have loaded the firsthand experiences.

One can explain such an experience by saying that it all existed within one human biocomputer, namely mine, and that this is a particular way of constructing one's simulations and moving among one's simulations. If one uses this explanation, I did not leave the tank at all and the whole construction above was in my own mind securely fastened in my brain. Most Western scientists, psychiatrists and psychologists would take this point of view. They would say it was a beautiful construction of John Lilly's imagination. All I say to such people is "have such experiences yourself and then see if this explanation is adequate for you."

I prefer not to try to explain such experiences on the basis of our currently limited Western scientific, psychiatric, and psychological point of view. I feel there is far more here than these theories can account for. I suggest that those who are really interested in experimentation in this region "do tank work and have these experiences." This is the one way we can develop a *consensus science* rather than a *doctrinaire attitude*, which generates put-downs toward such experiences in others.

I feel that medical and psychological personnel can explore personally such experiences in order to better understand their patients. Instead of tagging them with diagnostic labels such as "paranoid" or "schizophrenic breaks," loss of rationality, delusion, illusion and so forth, I suggest they pursue the experience themselves. In my experience with others (bright, intelligent people of all sorts) each can have such experiences under the proper circumstances. They can be reassured that the environment is sufficiently safe and that others before them have had the experiences. (The "others" are not mentally ill or locked up in institutions.)

In our new handbook The Deep Self,* which deals with the tank work, we present the firsthand accounts of people, other than ourselves, who have gone through these experiences.

---

* In preparation.

Thus, in our dyad, Toni and I mutually respect each other's experiences in these regions and find that they are very refreshing and quite entertaining. It adds a series of dimensions to our dyadic relationship, which gives us a stability and coherence that was rather rare in each of our previous lives. It is through experiences such as the above that we realize that we are connected in very subtle ways to one another and that our dyad is greater than either of us alone. (Refer to Chapter Zero.)

Chapter Six

Creativity, Physiology and Internal Science in the Dyad

The usual male-female dyad expresses its creativity through the creation of children. The creative act starts out as a biological one and gradually moves to a family-social creativity; caring for, reacting to and helping children to grow into the consensus reality successfully. In the United States today most dyads are either producing children, raising children, or retired from these primarily biological activities. Toni and I seem to be past this era in our lives. Our children are all grown-up and need only peer attention now and again.

Other kinds of creativity keep us busy. My main activity is writing books with Toni's help. During writing I find I must be alone. Toni respects this need. She helps me to set aside the time without interference, without interruption so that the books can be created. To write fast and create rapidly it is necessary for me to have adequate sleep and adequate rest, adequate exercise and adequate diet.

We sleep together in the same bed. This seems to be absolutely essential in our dyad. Neither one of us can obtain the deep sleep apart that we obtain together. There is a basic biological and physiological comfort in having the warmth and the closeness during the night that can be obtained in no other way, in our experience.

Sleeping together seems to be the basic platform upon which all else is done. We each respect the necessity of adequate sleep and rest in the other.

I find that the tank, the isolation tank, is an absolute necessity in order to recover during the day quickly and easily from overloads brought about by too much activity, too much exchange with other people, too much travel into Los Angeles and back. If I am worn-out during the day, instead of taking a long nap, I go into the tank for a half an hour. The tank not only allows me to deprogram that which has been going on previously, but permits me as well to recharge my biological battery in the midst of busy activities.

For example, recently I was shoveling gravel and installing a new antenna system from seven o'clock in the morning till five in the afternoon. I was physically worn-out—in that delightful state of muscle fatigue but so worn-out that there was an inability to remember where I had left the tools. There was a pressing engagement that was to take place at 6:30 that evening —a rather important conference with several other people about a motion picture. I realized that I must somehow recharge the brain and the body.

I went into the tank, floated and allowed the previous activities of the day to gradually disappear from my mind. As the day's residues slowly but surely disappeared, I went into a Void state in which the blackness, the silence and the floating were the only contents in my consciousness. I did not go to sleep. I entered an abstracted state in which there was no body, no external reality, only the floating, the darkness and the silence. By objective outside time, I did this for only thirty minutes. The inside time in the internal reality disappeared. (There were no signs of e.t.r. or N.)

I came out of the tank completely refreshed, full of energy and ready for anything that was needed. That evening with four other people I created a whole script outline for a motion picture.

This alternation of high mental and physical activity with

recovery in the tank, seems to be the key to my particular creativity.

Each of us in our dyad has a great respect for the necessity of the correct food. We do not necessarily agree on what that is but we respect the differences between the diet that each of us has devised over the years for one's self. My diet is usually a very severe one. I take large amounts of vitamins in the time-release capsule form and large amounts of protein, preferably animal protein. Toni likes more variety than this. She is an excellent cook and prepares many novel and exciting dishes for herself and our friends. I restrict myself to tasting these and insist on taking my own particular diet.

Each of us has discovered that we need a certain amount of physical exercise every day. In order to get the brain going in the morning, we walk up a hill near our house lifting our weight 300 feet together. Toni walks this rather slowly. Most mornings I run ahead of her and then rejoin her still down the hill. This form of exercise furnishes the central nervous system with activated circuitry that goes on for the rest of the day. The central nervous system needs activation in the morning: the feedback circuits need to be activated in the lower levels of the spinal cord and of the brain. Once started they maintain this activity and furnish the cerebral cortex with this energy for hours after the initiation. However, to maintain such activity one also needs rest, vitamins and protein.

One rather fatiguing factor that I have found in life is the frustration effect if I am faced with too much talk, too much chatter, too much of what I call "triviality." I wear myself out fighting it. This requires that I leave a particular group for a period of time in order to allow this kind of activity to cease in my own mind. Toni respects this necessity in me and when I disappear from a group she allows it to happen with graceful tolerance. She has a much higher threshold for such fatigue effects and can stay with a group for much longer periods of time than I can.

At times, like anyone else, we need entertainment in which we are observers rather than participants. Toni watches television. I can only stand television when something that is of great interest to me is being shown. Most of the television entertainment to me is dull. I prefer to read a good book, listen to shortwave radio or see a good movie. Some movies that I ordinarily would not look at Toni encourages me to go see. Most of the time I find this rather rewarding. I watch the movie through her eyes and see what it is that she finds in it.

She also looks through my eyes at people, at movies and at television every so often. This dyadic interlock goes on rather continually. There is something mysterious here that I do not understand.

Looking through each other's eyes, feeling as if one were in the other's body participating in activities, occurs daily. As with many couples who are close, we find this to be quite an automatic operation that takes place below our levels of awareness. Only in retrospect do we realize that we were doing this. In the analysis of difficulties with others or between ourselves, this is a very valuable trait. In doing it we try not to lay our own trip on the other. We try to step aside and allow what is happening to pass through one's Self without the impedance of the intrusion of one's ego.

After long creative periods at home we find that we can be reactivated by travel, by giving a workshop, by giving a lecture elsewhere. We give lectures in two ways. I may do a solo trip or we both may be on the stage and have an exchange with the audience. In workshops we divide the load between the two of us. This is a very efficient method of operating. One can rest while the other is talking. One can answer questions that are appropriate to the knowledge of that one while the other listens. Thus we educate each other on our basic ideas.

We have many talks together, which are very rewarding. I talk over new ideas with Toni. She talks over her new ideas with me. Each of us tries to find the automatic scripts, scenarios and programs within the Self which tend to come up all too autonomously. We apply the analytic methods that each of us has learned in the past to such scenarios and scripts and treat these diplomatically, tolerantly and with humor. My energy is heavier, more direct and yang than is Toni's. She is more diplomatic and careful than I am. Her energy is yin-oriented.

If we lose contact with each other in a large group, or during each of our negotiations (each with his/her offspring), we may have a highly emoting exchange. One of us may become quite angry, directing negative energy at the other. The receiver of the energy then has several alternatives:

1) Wait and listen.
2) Become loudly angry in turn.
3) Become angrily silent.
4) Ask: "Where does *that* script come from?"
5) Stand by until the energy dissipates.
6) Do an energy transform in Self, allowing the entering anger to become free energy for any new possible– probable alternative that may appear.
7) Do 1–6 above in any order that seems intuitively appropriate.
8) Make true the belief that the dyad is greater than either and that something has provoked a hidden isolated unconscious belief system as yet to be unearthed.
9) Help unearth and analyze in the light of no. 8, the hidden agenda-belief system.

Chapter Seven

Bodily Limits vs. Mind Unlimited in the Dyad

In three of my previous books, the concept of an unlimited mind in a limited body was presented.* The following is a paraphrase of a statement I have made several times:

"In the province of the mind, what one believes to be true, either is true or becomes true within certain limits. These limits are to be found experientially and experimentally. Once discovered these limits are further beliefs to be transcended.

"Within the current mind, the body imposes definite limits. These limits are to be found experientially and experimentally. These limits are to be expanded by physical exercises. When so expanded, the original limits, one finds, were transcended and new limits established. The newly expanded bodily limits help to expand the mind limits."

These basic statements apply in the dyad as well as to each individual in the dyad. The above "metabeliefs" (beliefs about beliefs) can be used in the dyad as supraself- and supradyad-metabeliefs to expand the limits of the dyad itself. If the meta-

* John C. Lilly, M.D., *Programming and Metaprogramming in the Human Biocomputer; The Center of the Cyclone;* and *Simulations of God.*

beliefs can be transformed from strictly personal metabeliefs into dyadic metabeliefs, the dyad itself can expand its accomplishments.

Before meeting Toni, I was able to expand my own beliefs about beliefs, and I was able to extend my bodily limits through the proper physical exercises. Some of the details of this history are given in *The Center of the Cyclone,* pp. 99–100, and Appendix Three in *The Dyadic Cyclone.*

This system of metabeliefs can be extended beyond the dyad. Toni and I have introduced this set of beliefs about beliefs to many people at workshops, at meetings in our house, at lectures and among our friends. It is very gratifying to both of us to see the expansion of minds and the improvement of bodies through these rather intriguing statements.

We have each been through various regimes that expand the mind and its basic beliefs and its beliefs about each of our bodies.

When I was a student at Cal Tech, I spent two years doing judo and jiujitsu. Toni has gone through a course of aikido. We have each been through Ida Rolf's course of Rolfing for many hours. (Ida's program restores structural integration to the body. Rolfing allows one to determine which childhood traumas are responsible for certain weaknesses in the adult body, and frees one then to compensate for and eliminate them.) Toni is a proficient water skier and I am a fairly proficient snow skier. In our daily lives, daily shopping, etc., and on our vacation trips, each of us share the driving under rather difficult conditions on mountain roads and on freeways; our house is fifty miles from the center of Los Angeles and we do a lot of business there. We do daily exercises together and separately. Toni works in her garden and I do various kinds of construction and repair about our house.

These activities keep us in fairly good physical condition. We are not professional athletes and we are not professional teachers of bodily skills. Our main emphasis is in the expansion of basic beliefs about the limits of mind and, somewhat, about the limits of the body.

We participate with younger people in their dance programs, helping them in the various ways that we can. We have many opportunities to observe how far the body can be pushed in dancing, in music, in drama, in carpentry, in the skills necessary in construction of electronic equipment and in formal exercises such as hatha-yoga and similar activities.

We have rather a unique opportunity to check out the mental and physical skills of each other in mountain driving, practically daily. We live at the top of two and a half miles of a twelve-percent-grade mountain road, paved, with many turns. Most days we drive from 1,300 feet altitude to sea level, over this stretch of road. If any fundamental mistakes are made in this performance one either hits the rock wall on one side of the road or goes over the edge and drops into a deep canyon. This consistent daily reminder of how close we are to the edge of death through lack of skill or lack of attention keeps us on our mental and physical toes every day. To go shopping, to go to the bank, to visit friends, we must negotiate this rather difficult stretch of highway. We have to be able to handle this road late at night when we are tired, or early in the morning when we are just waking up, or during the day with various conditions of good feeling, bad feeling or fatigue.

I highly recommend this exercise for its demonstration of bodily limits and the interaction of the state of being of one's consciousness with one's physical condition. It furnishes a daily measure of where one is currently. Hundreds of thousands, if not millions, of people do this sort of exercise daily, most of them not realizing that this is probably the most highly developed and dangerous form of meditation that man has ever developed on this planet.

Since we live in southern California and there is an abundance of good sunlight the year round, we spend as much time as we can, either in the nude or with the minimum amount of clothing, depending on who is present, exposed to that sunlight. Each of us has noted that sufficient sunlight also changes our state of mind, our state of being, in some very fundamental way. Our bodily limits are expanded by adequate sunshine. When either because of necessity of other work or because of a rainy period we are unable to get the sun, we notice a very slow but detectable deterioration in our bodily and mind performances. Once we can get back into the sun, we find that it gives us a lift in a very particular way that nothing else seems to be able to do. It is as if the human animal is so constructed that it periodically needs ultraviolet and infrared radiation of its blood and in its skin in order to stay in the best of health. There is some very fundamental biochemical research needed here to find out what these changes involve.

We find upon arising in the morning, that no matter how we feel, whether we have had adequate rest during the night, or whether there was not enough sleep, if we can walk up our hill (a rise of 300 feet), the day is started out in a much more energetic way; the energy derived from this exercise of lifting ourselves this far every morning carries over into the rest of the day's activities. If for some reason or other we miss our walk, somehow that particular day is much slower. There isn't so much energy available for other projects. We also find that this exercise renders a by-product: it keeps our legs in good shape for skiing activities or walking in the mountains. Luckily, both our hearts are in very good condition; this exercise makes sure that they maintain good shape. Each of us has a good pair of lungs and this exercise also makes sure that these function adequately under all other conditions.

The physical physiology and psychology of sexual activities in each of us have become less pressing with the years. Each of us has had enough experience in this area with others so that somehow or other sexual impulses are no longer to us the be-all and end-all that they used to be. Each of us is used to and understands the traps that sex and entrancement can bring about. In the older Freudian theory of these matters, Freud promulgated in his *Three Contributions to the Theory of Sex* the theory that the basic impulses could be transformed into sources of energy for mental and physical disciplines. He called this process "sublimation." At one time I was deeply immersed in psychoanalytic work and applied his theories both to patients and to myself. It seems to me that sublimation is a result of strenuous disciplines both in the mental sphere and in the physical sphere over many years. I agree with Freud that if these impulses are repressed and not allowed expression at certain critical phases in one's life, one then becomes a slave of these impulses expressed in hidden and covert forms. However, if at these critical phases these impulses are satisfied to their upper limits, then later, after many years, one automatically enters into a phase of greater and greater transformation of the sexual energy into other uses. I agree with Freud that this cannot be done by a mere operation of willpower. I prefer the mode which is too simplistically expressed by the phrase "wisdom through excess," and self-analysis.

In our dyad, each of us has a history of learning about these impulses through the help of other people, and for periods of time trying out various means of satisfying these impulses. We have each learned what is basic to our sexuality. We respect the demands of sexuality and no longer try to restrict it into repressive computerized repeating tapeloops kinds of activities and thought. We have each studied Tantric yoga and its teachings in regard to transformation of this energy into so-called higher states of being. These studies and practices have taught us that as one has more trips around the sun, these transformations become easier; the disciplines of the mind and of the body change from urgent reproductive needs into the ability to defer such actions more easily and with a greater degree of discrimination. Each of us has learned to value more the qualities of mind and spirit in people; to value the qualities of mind and spirit more than the sexual attractiveness of a given person. We neither demean nor worship sexual attractiveness; we place it in its proper context—within a mental and spiritual framework within which it is possible to effect transformations, without exerting the old-fashioned willpower in regard to these essential qualities of human beings.

About sexual energies and their programming, Toni says the following:

> "Did you ever think that math or physics could be sexy? I recently realized that they can be powerful tools in what could be called metasex.*

* See Marco Vassi's *Metasex, Madness and Mirth* (Penthouse Press, Ltd., May 23, 1975), for an expanded view of sex and metasex.

"This point was made clear to me when our dear friend Heinz Von Foerster, the cyberneticist, was visiting recently. Heinz has the most remarkable quality of portraying meaning through mathematical concepts. He can apply new general principles to experiences, which create pictures of them with refreshing accuracy.

"Heinz and John were in deep, or a better term would be, dense, conversation about all sorts of fascinating concepts about teaching and learning. Heinz made the point that in John's books he mapped 'domains' instead of 'pathways.' The difference between the two approaches in my own thinking and experience suddenly became clearer. I could go "meta" immediately by using this concept ("going meta" is the process of getting out of the programs into the metaprogrammic level).

"Meditating on it further produced all sorts of other breakthroughs automatically. In other words, in the new metaprogram I meditate on domains and not on the pathways; this procedure expanded the possible, allowable set of programs automatically.

"For example, in the past I allowed my first experience with orgasm to program and imprint specific tapeloops in my sexual pattern or rhythm. During my life, different partners changed this patterning in one way or another. Some programs seemed to me fairly invariant across partners; this of course was a belief to be transcended, as John would say. The older I became, the more I realized that transcendence of the belief was possible and true. If you have ever had an orgasm in your toe, for example, it certainly frees up your beliefs about sexual body-geography. The meditation of precise construction in one's sexual mapmaking can lead you to enter new (or expanded old) domains. Such maps will or will not be powerful, depending on your beliefs about the power of your own maps and metamaps.

"It is possible, I believe, for all of us to expand, when in an awake state, our moments/eternities in this mystical state.

"I appeal to your best thinking. Instead of getting out of your head, use this metaprogramming to program yourself into desired states, and free you from habitual, undesired repeating states.

"Jnana-yoga, a way of wisdom, can lead to new sexual experience beyond one's 'expected fixed patterns.' "

In our experience in the young male and in the young female, such beliefs and metabeliefs about sex are hard to find. Among the modern younger generations there is a good deal more freedom in the sexual sphere than when we were young. Each of us was brought up in a family in which the children were expected to restrain the sexual impulses until they were older. In each of us this brought up conditions in which we were able to develop discipline separate from sexual activities and proclivities. I am not saying that this is right or wrong, I am saying this is the way that we were brought up.

There seems to be less of this parental control in the modern world. There is far more experimentation in the sexual sphere among the young. As far as we can find out, this leads to a good deal more freedom to transform this energy while persons are younger, than when we were at that same age. The wisdom of experiment and experience in this area seems to be training the youngsters to be able to select a mate with more freedom than we were able to do on our first tries.

Each of us was married at a rather young age to our first spouses. We are unable to judge the younger generation from the platform on which we were raised. Most of the youngsters who are attracted to us are in a much more free state than we were at their age. In spite of the fact that they have fewer limits than we did, each of us is able to expand those limits at a later age. Thus we have a certain degree of understanding, though I am sure it is not so full as these youngsters will have in their turn when they reach our age.

Thus I feel that, in the future there will be an expansion of conscious understanding of these processes way beyond that of my particular generation.

For example, one young lady recently told us that she had read all of the pornography that was available and had gotten thoroughly bored with it. It may well be that pornography will become in the future merely another form of literary presentation and if it is not well done, it will disappear. What used to be surprising and shocking in this area is now becoming merely boring. The new freedom to write about and to publish material about sexual activities has overshot its mark. I suspect that in the future sex will take its proper place as a part of human life, neither repressed nor made to seem flamboyant. It is already viewed in this way by a very large segment of our younger generation. It looks as though sexual crimes result from sexual repression. With the new freedom to treat sex as a natural function, sexual crimes should decrease and finally disappear.

Thus as the belief systems in the consensus social reality are modified and become more in consonance with our true nature, as we examine those belief systems and transcend them, it may be possible for most of humanity to become enlightened, Illuminated, informed, educated and sophisticated in terms of what man really is, rather than what some powerful people of the past have tried to make him/her appear to be.

The yoga of Western science, especially in biology applied to our own species, tells us what we biologically really are. Through this yoga we will realize that we have placed arbitrary limits upon a biology that does not recognize those limits. As we also perfect the yoga of our minds we will remove the strictures, the highly artificial, man-made strictures that exist upon our minds. We will all realize Union in the highest sense of this term—spiritual Union with that which we can become through freeing up our mind from the strictures laid upon it in the past. The true wisdom of the body will be transformed into the true wisdom of the mind, which will then be transformed into the true wisdom of the spirit. Defeatist and negative doctrines of the past will die out and disappear.

Realistically these are my hopes, these are the hopes of our dyad. Such hopes presume a sufficient spread of metabeliefs suitable to our species, agreed upon metabeliefs, which will give freedom in the bodily, mental and spiritual realms throughout our planet. Apparently there are enough teachers now throughout the world to exact this goal. There is a sufficient number of followers of these teachers to expand the human species to its full potential.

Of course, all of this postulates that we will not destroy ourselves in our international and planetwide conflicts—economic, martial, political conflicts, which at times look overwhelmingly large and almost impossible to solve. It is no longer possible, without destroying the whole human race, to foster beliefs that are parochial, nationalistic, racial or shortsighted, else the human race will be terminated, not worthy of its place upon the planet earth.

This do I believe, and I hope that my species will transcend and create, rather than destroy, this beautiful planet.

Chapter Eight

Illness in the Dyad

Some of the major crises of any dyad, of any couple, of any marriage, are the times when one or both members of the dyad have a physical illness. The crisis may or may not involve the possible death of one of the couple. The crisis may involve a long period of lack of verbal communication between the two members of the couple. High fever, coma, medical intervention, hospitalization, surgical operations, periods of anesthesia and recovery from it, plus the expense of the medical and hospital care, all can lead to a testing episode of the strength of the dyad and the strength of each individual in the dyad.

Several times during the last five years we have faced such crises.

The first of these episodes occurred two months after Toni took the Arica training in New York. John was faced with the possible loss of Toni through death.

Similarly, later, Toni was confronted with John's near-death. In each of these cases, the non-ill member of the dyad stood by, gave support when needed and waited out the crisis while medical help took over.

Toni's illness became more serious immediately after a tour, a very densely packed schedule of talks, TV appearances, and late radio shows in which we were cooperating with the publisher in the publicity for *The Center of the Cyclone*, which had just been published, in early 1972.

Toni, along with her illness, developed a virus just before we were scheduled to give a workshop together in Topanga Canyon, near Los Angeles. During the workshop Toni developed a high fever and became too ill to continue; she returned home to bed. This was our first real test of our dyadic relationship. Up to this point we had not been apart more than a few hours at a time. The requirements of the workshop and the requirements of the illness caused us to be separated for many hours over several days.

When this workshop was finished we had another one scheduled at Esalen Institute in Big Sur. Toni decided to try to travel, so we drove to Big Sur and started the new workshop; it was during this time she became too ill to go on and required hospitalization. Her past history of colitis made us aware that there was a very great danger of recurrence of this disease. We obtained the help of a doctor in Carmel. She was put in a bed in the Carmel hospital while John continued the workshop in Esalen.

John had to arrange his schedule in the workshop so that he could drive the forty miles to Carmel and back every day. It gradually became obvious that Toni was too sick to communicate. When John sat beside her bed, she could barely talk and would lapse into some state in which she was unavailable to him. John faced Toni's possible death with agonized grief. He realized that the decision had to be hers as to whether she returned from the edge of death or went on and died. He felt impotent in the face of this powerful adversary who had Toni in its grip.

Previous experience with his own near-death several times before had taught him that anyone at the edge of death made their own decision as to whether they would return or not.

Several times as he sat beside Toni's bed, he prayed that she would be allowed to return and that she would decide to return. He asked the Guardians to give her permission and to teach her how to come back. Her pain was quite profound and her consciousness was busy solving the problem of the illness. External manifestations of her will to live were lacking.

The hospital was unusual in that it contained very nice rooms and many gardens. Her medical care was of the best. The hospital personnel were cheerful and most helpful.

For approximately two weeks the outcome was uncertain. Finally one day Toni came out of her removed state, looked at John and said, "I'm coming back. I'm going to be well."

John saw on her face that this was the truth and that her desperate washed-out look was disappearing. The next day she began the long climb back to rebuilding her body and recovering. Her recovery took several weeks, rather joyful weeks, finally.

We both learned new lessons from this experience. Lessons of patience, of standing by, of making sure that the hospital and the doctors were doing the best they could and not interfering with the other member of the dyad's choice to live. And also not interfering with the wish to die if that was the way it was going to turn out.

Over the years John had seen too many interferences with patients in hospitals, well-intentioned interferences but, nonetheless, interferences. John's medical experience had finally arrived at the point where he realized that the participation of the patient in an illness is incredibly important, that the patient has very personal experiences inside which tell him/her whether or not he/she can reenter the body, the vehicle, on this planet. As was narrated in *The Center of the Cyclone,* John had gone through several episodes in which the Guardians had kept him informed of the state of the body while he was out of it. During times of medical or surgical intervention he returned to the body, checked out what was happening and then left it again.

These episodes taught him that a very large portion of any illness is not under the control of the medical personnel; it is under the control of the individual and the individual's relationship to those greater than any of us.

He had learned that coma is only a medical term describing the state of the body; it does not tell one what is happening to the person inside. John found that in his particular case he remained conscious but did not necessarily stay in the space dictated by his body. He was experiencing Supraself.

As he sat by Toni's bed, he reviewed his own case and allowed her the same freedom to either go or come back that he had found in himself. He did this at great cost in terms of grief and deprivation of the dyad. He realized our fragility, our mortality while in the body. He also realized his eternal connection to Toni in the other dimensions. He realized that if she did die, he would eventually rejoin her. He took heart from this fact and was able to be patient.

Over the years, each member of the dyad has discovered that tranquilizers, sleeping pills and pain killers impair the consciousness of the ill person while in the body. The domains in which one can continue the struggle is out of the body with the Guardians in some other space. If one comes back to the body while the body is drugged, it makes a very difficult communication problem with the other member of the dyad by the bedside.

One's Self, as it were, is perfectly clear but one's body is drugged. One struggles to use the body to express what one is really feeling, where one has been, but the drugs make this almost impossible. One's speech is slowed down almost to the point of total absence of its use. This fact makes it very difficult for the non-ill member of the dyad to communicate with the other's Supraself or Essence. The usual communication is rendered laborious and totally unsatisfactory. Where possible one then employs other means of communication, directly Essence to Essence (dyadic Supraself connection). It is in this communication that one consents to the other to either come back to the body or leave and go elsewhere.

As John sat beside Toni's bed he allowed his own Essence to communicate with her Essence in these higher levels. He knew then when to let go of his attachment to her and her attachment to him, so that she would be free to make her own decision in these spaces.

He had to review everything he knew about our virtual immortality as well as our bodily fragility and mortality. Day and night he meditated and waited for the decision of Toni.

When she finally decided to come back, and did come back, his joy was great and his grief was terminated.

Toni:

"My memory of this illness is that being at the very doors of the great transition was dreamlike. After examining the possible approach of the interface between *as if* life or death, something else, it seemed, decided that right then was not the time to cross over.

"The gradual decline of my physical self was nurtured by my own curiosity. 'Something' seemed to become clearer as I became weaker.

"After the long illness, the turning point came after an unbelievable night of pain while I was still in the hospital. A night where all my pain systems were activated. I had an intense reaction to the medication they were giving me. This reaction came on in the form of a blinding headache. Along with the body pain, I was one throbbing, pulsating conscious point of pain in a timeless inner reality and for a few hours of external reality time.

"I finally understood the words, which I first read as a young girl, in Dante's *The Divine Comedy* (*Inferno*):

'It was purification of a sort through this fire of pain.'

"I remember a part of me still able to stand away and examine the rest of me that was quivering in the midst of it. Dawn finally came with a realization that I was to go no further and the direction now was back. When John came to see me that day I could tell him that I would get well. It was a moment of knowledge and I am grateful. This timeless moment is etched in my memory and can be recalled in meditation occasionally.

"John's constant vigil was a light so that I could see my way back."

Chapter Nine

Introduction to Our Teachers

John's Teachers

In introducing our teachers, it is most important to note that we do not have space to list all teachers and the lessons learned from them. Let me explain why I have chosen the few that I have mentioned here.

In my (John's) own particular case, I have listed only those who contributed knowledge and wisdom in the positive realm. I have left out all of my negative teachers, those who taught me never to take that trip again. I have left out my first two wives and my lovers for reasons of discretion, and in order not to stir up energies which reverberate in the social structure. In making up my own list, I was appalled to find how many of them had died. What they have taught me still lives within me and somehow their deaths are a loss to this planet.

What are the characteristics of the teachers that I have selected here? What is the character of their teaching?

First of all, the underlying thread seems to be that these men taught with a sense of humor. Second, they were teachers who had knowledge that I didn't have and which I acquired to my uppermost limits.

I have been beset all of my life with a sense of what I consider to be true. This means *true,* not "as if true."

Even as a little boy I had this very peculiar sense of the *true* behind appearances. There was a part of me that knew the substance, the essence of knowledge, of people, of the universe. I would not accept "the usual nonsense," as I called it, that was offered me in school, in scientific school, in medical school, in the psychoanalytic studies, in the study of biophysics, in my government service, with study of the previous knowledge about dolphins, in the work with the dolphins, in the work at Esalen Institute, in the Arica school in Chile, in the media, in the motion-picture industry in the Los Angeles area, and among my current friends.

This sense of truth, in a way, was backed up by a sort of a pigheadedness, a refusal to take on what I considered to be false, superficial and not worth studying, in other words "as if meaningless."

As I look back over my life, there are many things that I should have studied but did not; these include: the law, politics, more about the history of our civilization, and business as practiced in the Western World. Here I am not complaining; I am merely outlining my areas of maximal ignorance.

It is very difficult as a student to select the proper courses that are going to be useful in one's future life. A student speaks from ignorance.

Over the years I have learned to respect my ignorance and to talk to those with knowledge attempting to fill in the edges of my own ignorance. This is not easy to do. When one speaks from a platform of ignorance, one is a fool.

I have been through two rather bitter divorces. Had I known more of the law, possibly I might not have entered into these divorces with such a lack of expertise. I might have been able to work out better arrangements between myself and my ex-wives. Much was done in each case with an inner sense of virtue misplaced.

Because when I was younger I devoted so much time to

pursuits other than my family, I am left with regrets about my two sons and my daughter. I have the feeling that if I had been cleverer and armed with more knowledge and more of the common sense that I see in others who manage to maintain family stability, I may have done better.

With Toni and myself in the dyad there is none of that which went on previously in my life in my dyadic relationships. Though it seems to be rare in couples, we each have a regard and a respect for the other's knowledge and ignorance. Toni is a rare human being, a rare woman in my experience. Every so often I attempt to project on her attitudes and feelings from my past. She quickly detects this and either moves away from it or calls it to my attention in a gentle and compassionate way.

Along with the name and identification of each of the teachers listed, I either paraphrase or quote the lessons they taught to me, lessons that polished the scientist in me and lessons that made it obvious that the inner realities are part and parcel of science, even though the natural scientists play the game as if the observer is not part of the system, not a participator within the system.

When I was sixteen I wrote a short essay for the school paper and entitled it "Reality." This paper appears in Appendix One of my recent book, *Simulations of God: The Science of Belief.* At that early age, I had laid out already a blueprint for my future life, a blueprint of the kinds of teachings in which I would be highly interested. I wrote that I would be interested in the mind and brain of man. This paper can be analyzed sentence by sentence and I can tell you how many years were devoted to the problems posed in each of those sentences.

For example the word *"res"* means "thing" in Latin. In Anglo-Saxon, "thing" means "a law court." *Res* in its original meaning in Latin was also a "law court." I have been in law courts four times in my life and I now realize why these are considered the basis of reality in human intercourse. These lessons I do not go into in my list of teachers.

I have arranged the list in chronological sequence, according to the years in which they taught me. Some of them cover such a long range that they overlap others. So, may I present my teachers.

Saint Paul Academy, Saint Paul, Minnesota—1928–1933

RUSSELL VARNEY, science and military teacher: Classical physics and the novel controlled experiment are worth pursuing.

JOHN DE QUEDVILLE BRIGGS, headmaster: Defining the whole man —the scientist and the writer: *mens mentis in corpora sano.*

HERBERT TIBBETTS, master: Express what you know to be true, *now* in writing (*Reality*), and on film (*Academiana*).

RICHARD C. LILLY (father), banker: In complex negotiations never lose your temper. You may act "as if" you have lost your temper, but make sure that inside you are in control of it. When sizing-up people, use your intuition to its fullest extent and trust it more than the credit rating of that particular person. Banking in essence is a paper reality, but never forget that it is the people who create the paper reality. You can never get anything done in any large institution unless you have friends in the proper places. The business of the world is best done through goodwill. That is the fundamental meaning of credit. Perfect your arithmetic so that it is very fast and accurate. Perfect it to the point where you can think in terms of arithmetic and do calculations fast enough mentally to stay ahead of your competitor. The game of poker is the training ground for good bankers. If your business or your profession is your be-all and end-all here, retirement will be a disaster. Choose a business or a profession where you are not forced into retirement when you reach a certain age.

DAVID M. LILLY (brother), diplomat-industrialist: Hindsight possesses 20/20 vision. Life can be lived now with logic, common sense and sanity. Use gentle humor and a firm hand when giving orders. People need their grass cut. Build lawn mowers to satisfy that need.

Cal Tech—1933–1938

HARVEY EAGLESON, professor of English, and House Resident: "God died in 1859, and the pile of dirt on his grave has been increasing to the present": Sigmund Freud, Hiroshigi, the Art of Teaching; living alone; discipleship and advice.

DR. McMINN, professor of English: "Your poetry can express itself if you step aside and let it flow."

HENRY BORSOOK, professor of biochemistry: "The knowledge you have is limited. You can expand it in Medical School. The knowledge you need is locked up in medical schools."

ERNEST WATSON, professor of physics: Good experiments in physics are under the guidance of adequate operational theory. The crucial experiment rarely needs statistical support. The crucial experiment is repeatable only by those with adequate technique and theory knowledge. Understanding comes only with experimental experience.

ROBERT A. MILLIKAN, president and organizer, 1923 Nobel Prize winner in Physics: The whole man in science functions in such a way as to generate support for science in general and in his own area in particular. Genius makes use of its own new and inventive science. Science is (in the essence) man's best thinking applied to man's problems of existence: the most efficient speed for an automobile is to be found and the car driven at that speed with minimal accelerations–decelerations; to build a fire, create the maximum numbers and maximum lengths of chimneys with the wood. Dress appropriately for your expected audience. Live in consonance with family, students and colleagues.

ARNOLD O. BECKMAN, teacher, businessman-scientist and philanthropist (he taught me inorganic chemistry in my undergraduate years at Cal Tech). "Chemistry is merely a machine such as a hopper with a crank on the side of it. You simply put the data in at the top, turn the crank and the answer comes out at the bottom." Scientists need instruments. We construct instruments for their uses based upon the best science. The availability of critical instruments determines the future course of science. Whenever possible, contribute one's energy and money to the furtherance of the scientific education of the young.

FRITZ WENT, professor of plant physiology: Plant growth can be controlled through regulation of light-dark cycles, humidity, minerals, nitrogen, grafting and genetic manipulation. Why can trees and vines pump water higher than thirty feet (1 atmosphere) even when cut? Photosynthesis is the key to efficient use of solar energy; solve how this process is accomplished and we can feed the world population efficiently with least effort and least expenditures of energy.

Fʀɪᴛᴢ Zᴡɪᴄᴋʏ, professor of astrophysics: Novae and supernovae occur frequently enough in our galaxy to call our attention to the fact that it is possible that they could eventually cause our demise.

Eᴅᴡɪɴ P. Hᴜʙʙʟᴇ, astronomer who defined the red shift: The red shift is proportional to the star magnitude. The more the red shift the farther the star from us. The universe, from our viewpoint, is expanding uniformly at a constant rate. (Spectrographs have monitored the movement of the galaxies in the Universe away from each other and away from our solar system by showing the apparent alteration in the color of a star in relation to its distance (Doppler's effect) at the red end of the spectrum of the spiral galaxy. These recessions away from our galaxy occur at a constant rate in relation to their distance from the earth, i.e., the universe is expanding at a constant rate.)

Aʟʙᴇʀᴛ Eɪɴsᴛᴇɪɴ, physicist: Common sense is that set of biases and prejudices acquired before the age of eighteen years. I find it difficult to believe that God plays dice with his creation. There can be no absolute frame of reference in space-time: the limiting velocity of signals in the universe is c, the velocity of light, of electromagnetic radiation and of gravitational waves. Mass and energy are interconvertible: the rest mass, m sub zero (m_0), of a particle of matter has a potentially realizable energy equal to the rest mass times the square of the velocity of the resulting electromagnetic radiation.

The solution of the problem of the nature of the universe lies in developing the unified field theory connecting electromagnetic waves and gravitation.

Space-time is curved in the vicinity of large masses; the universe may appear closed as a consequence of its mass distribution. Examine the basic assumptions-postulates-axioms upon which a given science rests; manipulate these systematically and create new sciences. Live alone, walk and think with colleagues, work with graduate students, live for your science and its advancement.

Sir James Jeans, mathematician and physicist: The universe and ourselves are mysterious. We are here to solve the mystery of existence.

Medical Training—1938–1942

Will Mayo, M.D., of the Mayo Clinic, Rochester, Minnesota: Your choice of medical school is important. In the first two years you will have acquired the knowledge of human anatomy. This will be your most important course as an M.D. In the first two years you should get clinical experience. The only medical school that has the best anatomy course is Dartmouth. The professor is Frederic Lord. Dartmouth also starts clinical work in the first two years. Go there for your training, then go to the University of Pennsylvania for studies in human physiology, etcetera.

Chuck Mayo, M.D., of the Mayo Clinic, surgeon and friend: Surgery is the failure of medical science to solve the problems of growth of tissues including neoplasia (cancers). Aside from gross damage requiring sewing, etcetera, surgery must become obsolete as we learn more of biochemistry, gene control, and the real laws of tissue regeneration and neoplastic process.

If you must do surgery, remember the whole person always; treat your patient with gentle compassion and do thorough workups. Make a friend.

In surgery, make minimal-sized incisions; large incisions are *tissue damage* syndromes; the smaller the incision the less the healing time; and the less the recovery time. Inconvenience yourself rather than the patient; develop your sense of feel in your hands and your techniques to be able to work blind inside the body cavities with assurance.

Follow-up every patient with friendly concern. Learn from your mistakes; you are allowed very few as a professional.

ROLF SYVERTSEN, M.D., professor of anatomy and histology: "If you wish to go skiing every weekend in May on Mount Washington, it will be necessary to make some adjustment in your study of anatomy. If you wish to ski you must work evenings in the anatomy laboratory. I am not open to bargaining.

"Your attention to detail is rather rare in a medical student. Most medical students would have ignored those small valves that you found in the left ventricle of the heart." (After I had spread the intestinal tract out across the anatomical laboratory in order to measure its full length, Syvertsen suddenly entered the dissecting room and gave me a long lecture on the sacredness of the human body and said that this was not a way to treat portions of it. In my defense I said, "The textbook says that the gut tract is 28 feet long when extended. I wished to find out if this was true or not.")

H. CUTHBERT BAZETT, professor of physiology: In training human physiologists it is necessary to insist upon the dictum of the British scientist J. B. S. Haldane: If you are to do research on human subjects you must first do the experiments upon yourself. This procedure will assure that you will appreciate the limits within which one must work. This method will also give you insight regarding your own motives, and assure that you will devise the least damaging, least uncomfortable, most efficient, and least dangerous methods. Often times, the right crucial experiment done upon yourself correctly does not require further subjects for the area.

The observer, working on himself, generates results and data to be submitted to others, equally or better trained for consensus science control. But he does this only after he, personally, has integrated the data and transformed his language for appropriate presentations in the consensus reality.

Biophysics—1942–1953

DETLEV W. BRONK, biophysicist and director: Young researchers need space, apparatus and colleagues. Aside from this let them alone. Supply each one with a salary at a low level, a laboratory of their own, a machine shop, a darkroom and allow them to operate at any hour of the day or night. The duties of a scientist include writing scientific papers and lectures for the laity. Support of science is through private foundations preferably or through government grants and contracts. The initiative of the individual scientist is an important asset in science.

BRITTON CHANCE, biophysicist and friend: It is possible to do at least three things simultaneously. One can carry on one's laboratory work, talk to a visitor and settle his problem, and write scientific papers. Scientific techniques need to evolve to develop new science. One needs a knowledge of analog computers, digital computers, electronics and software in order to progress in modern science. It is best to arrange for other scientists to receive Nobel prizes rather than one's self. A Nobel Prize can be a distraction from one's work.

CATHERINE DRINKER BOWEN DOWNES, authoress: Writing is a hard profession. Adequate research is an absolute requirement. One can integrate a family and the writer's profession. It is worthwhile for us to study the best people that man has produced and write their lives in an understandable and expert fashion. The most interesting objects for research are human beings.

Psychoanalytic Years 1949–1958

ROBERT WAELDER, Doctor of physics, an analyst's analyst: In your own psychoanalysis, no one but you makes the rules for feeling, thinking, acting. We are not here to test Freud's theories, to review other cases, to discuss science and philosophy except inasmuch as these are part of you. I listen, I think while you talk and think out loud. Eventually I will learn enough about you to make a few suggestions. Before that I will say little or nothing.

John (angrily): "How can you analyze me? You overeat, are overweight and smoke lethal cigars."

Waelder: "I did not have the opportunity of being analyzed by an analyst as clever as yours."

John (laughing): "Okay!"

LAWRENCE KUBIE, analyst and friend: In the future, psycho-analysis must eventually base itself on a much more sophisti-cated and advanced science of the brain than was known by Freud and by current analysts.

SIGMUND FREUD, doctor of medicine and lone seeker: Established medical research and teaching restrict one's horizons. Uncon-sciously our past dramas determine, within certain limits to be found, our current and future feeling, thinking and behavior. Hypnosis, classically, abrogates the freedom of inquiry into the depths of one's own mind. Rigid theories ruin minds.

"No, science is no illusion. It is an illusion to suppose that we can get anywhere else what science cannot give us."

C. G. JUNG, psychoanalyst and "cosmologist": The Unconscious is vaster than Freud's theories of it. Somehow, inside, we tune in to the Universe outside.

Two Sons and a Daughter—1937–1975
(Mexico, Colorado and Maine)

JOHN C. LILLY, JR., filmmaker and anthropologist: The Indian cultures of Mexico have a tremendous variety and a particular sensitivity to investigators from the United States. To secure adequate data on their lifestyles and their religious beliefs, it is necessary to live with them for a number of years, until they trust you and until you have learned enough about them to be easy in their presence. It is necessary for us to work fast, to record these cultures before the encroachment of the machine civilization changes the pattern beyond recognition. Among these Indians the use of psychedelic plants has been ritualized, regulated and made a way of life worth recording.

CHARLES R. LILLY, scholar: The origins of one's self and of one's family are worthy of research and study. Tracing one's ancestors is a rewarding pursuit.

CYNTHIA OLIVIA ROSLYN LILLY: A subjective description by a particular observer is that the newborn female baby is obviously
female, even as the newborn male baby is obviously male. One
sees this in the face, in the movements of the body. In the case
of the female, the total acceptance of the world as it is, and in
the case of the male, the restless exploration and modifications
of the world as it is. "I will love you even if they hypnotize me
and tell me that I do not." Growing up as a young lady is very
difficult without daddy in the immediate environment every day.
Divorce as organized in the United States is a cruel process for
children. The creation of competition, of agony, between the
members of a couple in the name of the law is somehow vitally
wrong. Except in cases of grave physical need, alimony, as it
exists today, is often a degenerating influence upon a woman.
It is an invitation to cease all efforts to earn one's own living
and to become very clever at increasing the amount of alimony.
No woman that I have ever heard of, who is on alimony, learns
to take her own place in the world of humans; the only exceptions are those who are physically or mentally handicapped in
an obvious direct fashion. Alimony generates mental illness and
reemphasizes any tendencies in this direction. In the new world,
a woman must be educated in such a way that in her older age
she can earn her own living if she wishes, or can remarry if she
wishes, or not marry at all if she wishes. Men have sought
knowledge and means of self-support for thousands of years;
the time of woman is coming.

National Institutes of Health—1953–1958

FRED STONE, administrator: The seasoned communicator within
government knows networks of communication whose existence
he cannot share. However, he can use these networks as long as
he steps out of the credit line at the end. "Tell me what you
want done and it will be arranged, but do not ask me how it
was done, and give credit to the man whose name I will give
you at some later time." Within any government agency there is
a very strong network of loyal, trustworthy people of high
integrity. It is these people that you must find in an agency to
get the job done.

Dolphin Laboratory
U.S. Virgin Islands, Saint Thomas—1958–1966

ORR REYNOLDS, scientist–administrator: Find the effective researchers and support them. Projects have no meaning except as a means of communication between the scientist and administrators. Seminars lasting several days are the most effective means of communication between scientists. Once one finds effective young researchers, pay attention to their ideas. They may seem very far-out to you, but if these are effective people they will turn up something new, inventive, interesting and important in science. Large government operates in such a way that one can accomplish far more within it than one knows at any given time. However, this requires certain kinds of talents in dealing with the complex communication system in government. Step on the fewest possible toes but hold your ground.

GREGORY BATESON, anthropologist: In order to understand man in greater depth, we must understand the other species on this planet. Otters, wolves, octopuses, and dolphins are worthy of our study. Rituals and playing "as if" are very important components of animal behavior. When you find an apt student with talent please don't spoil him or her. If you do effective research, the support for it will come. The first priority is to get started in the research.

CONSTANCE DOWLING TORS, actress and guide: It is possible to love unstintingly and to break loose from the bonds that have been placed on one's love in the past. When one is free and open, one's belief systems can be changed by those one loves and respects. In special states of consciousness it is possible to share directly without words many specific events that have occurred in the past, that are occurring currently and that will occur in the future. One does not project the negative upon those one loves. One creates beauty in one's self, in one's environment and among one's friends.

Esalen Institute, Big Sur, California—1968–1971

IDA ROLF, the originator of structural integration: The body has stored within it all of the evidences of past traumas to the body.

In order to release these patterns built into the muscle–central-nervous-system feedback, one must experience pain at the site of the original trauma. The buried tapeloops of the past trauma suppressed from the conscious mind are thereby released. This release creates energy that is now free flowing and no longer bound into the original pattern.

RICHARD PRICE, cofounder of Esalen Institute: There is nothing more important in this life than perfecting one's self—in body, in mind and in spirit. Aiding others to achieve this aim is a way of life worth pursuing. So-called "psychosis" is merely doing your own thing irrespective of the wishes of others; it can be a transformation of self, achievable by no other means. "If you wish to be a dolphin, live it out and I'll live it out, too, with you, to the limits of our imaginations." If you wish to enter the kingdom of heaven, become as a little child. There are ten thousand trips that people wish you to take. Take as many as you please, but be sure that you integrate them and construct your own trip. Surround yourself with effective people who believe in their trips and everything else will take care of itself. There is no need to be arbitrary or tyrannical when dealing with one's associates. Assume that each person is willing to take the responsibility for his own being, his own states of being.

FRITZ PERLS, originator of Gestalt therapy: One should have a Rolfing session for each year of one's life. "Reality is the concernful." You have your trip and I have my trip. We have our trip only if we so choose. If not, that's okay too.

ALDOUS HUXLEY, gentleman and scholar (from conversations and his writings): Curiosity and interest are merited by all things human. Projection of current scientific trends into the future may prevent a future social horror. Fiction is a powerful social force to acquaint those in power with possible futures to avoid their probable existence. *Brave New World* is a blueprint of one such possibility to be avoided.

All phenomena of the human inner reality are worth investigation. Your researches into the neurological substrate of motivations is important for each human being. Your research into the phenomena of physical isolation, solitude and confinement is fundamental to human reason.

ALAN WATTS, author and philosopher: (Alan was born forty minutes before I was.) "The coincidence of our births almost makes me believe in astrology, but not quite." Introducing me to his wife Jano the first time, he said, "Here is a man who is more ruthlessly rational than I am." (This remark was made after I had spent three hours with him on the Surgeon Story, which is a long and involved intellectual puzzle. To solve it, one must be ruthlessly rational without emotional attachments to various types of human activities.) Formal rituals can be fun. Let us have fun together through formal rituals. Life on this planet is a cosmic joke. Let us enjoy it together. Buddhism in its many forms has much to offer the Western mind. Let us study Buddhism together.

GEORGE SPENCER BROWN, mathematician: The protologic behind logic determines the logic. Let us find a protologic and then construct new systems of logic. *The Laws of Form* is not a handbook on how to go to far-out spaces, but a handbook on how to get back once one is there. In the protologic of *The Laws of Form* the observer is a marked state (the Brownian operator). *The Laws of Form* poses a dilemma: where is the writer and where is the reader? When one severs a universe by making a distinction, who is doing the severing? Is this the Brownian operator, the marked states and voids alternating ad infinitum? Alternatively, is the one making the severance separate from this system? Is he creating (with a continuous consciousness) discontinuous universes?

(BABA) RAM DASS, mystic and friend: Patanjali states the basic assumptions, the basic belief systems of jnana-yoga. Study the *Yoga Sutras* of Patanjali for understanding of the deeper meditations. "The powers of the mind are attained through birth, through light-containing herbs, through mantra, through tapahs and through Samadhi." (Book 4, Sutra 1.) *Brahmacharya* (celibacy) is a groovy way of life if one is a bhakti yogi. It is a discipline that generates a large amount of internal energy useful in teaching. "My guru exists everywhere. You are my guru; the cat is my guru."

Arica, Chile—6 May 1970–7 February 1971

OSCAR ICHAZO, esoteric master and teacher: When a student has learned everything that you can teach him, let him go on his way. When a group has become integrated and learned everything that you have to teach them, let them all go on their way. Develop your own physical, mental and spiritual disciplines and practice them assiduously. There is no compromise with reality as it really is. Reality as you wish it to be has no place in your life. Cosmic love is ruthless: it loves you whether you like it or not. To reach the higher levels of consciousness, the higher spiritual planes, one's ego must die. After one's ego is reborn it becomes a tool in the service of one's Essence rather than the master of one's destiny. The only reason that you cannot reach higher states of consciousness and further your spiritual development is your own wish not to do so. The ego is anything that keeps you from the higher states of Satori. The injunctive use of words is the only valid use for words in achieving changes of states of being. A powerful exercise loses its power as you master it and the insights that it reveals. Without the higher states of consciousness the higher states of being, the planet earth will be finished in a catastrophic ending. Every human being on this planet must share these higher states. When one has trouble within one's own country achieving these states, one must travel and find a place where one can safely transcend the limitations of one's own culture. The United States has been and possibly will remain the chief focus of energy on this planet within humankind. God is very much larger than our conceptions of him, than our projections and our simulations of him. Western science and mysticism eventually will fuse and we will be unable to separate the two.

STEWART BRAND, inventor and editor of *The Whole Earth Catalog* and the *Coevolution Quarterly:* Pertinent information is the life-blood of the planet. Earth is the only planet we have, let's not throw it away. Man is changing the planet unconsciously; let us make this a conscious process and do a better job of it. We need new ideas. Let us find those who have them and transmit their information as cheaply and for as wide an audience as we can reach. Let us use every available means—film, sound, print, the media—to disseminate useful information. There are literally millions of people who yet do not know how to carry on their planetside trip in the most economical fashion. Let us research means to do this and transmit these means to those who need them.

Los Angeles, California—1971–1975

ANTONIETTA LENA LILLY, my best friend, love, and wife: Life is a balance game. No matter how far one pushes life in one direction, it swings back oppositely. Every human being is worth listening to, for enough time to understand. Social forms express one's empathy, patience and concern. One's village is the world; the world is one's village.

Politics is fun; it's the name for human relationships. The politics starts with three persons together.

The dyad is the most stable human relation; the triad is unstable. Saying "no" can be a graceful elegant art, as can saying "yes" or "maybe."

Beauty is from within; use, in its expression, what one has with external aids extending to one's home and garden and friends. Tools are to be used; one does not praise or blame tools; one cares for them and uses them carefully, efficiently and in the proper context.

Reality is economic; if it isn't economic, it isn't real.

The universe is a series of interrelated, smoothly flowing squiggles, lubricated with cosmic giggles.

NINA CAROZZA (Toni's daughter), dancer and teacher: It is necessary to perfect one's posture and one's grace of movement by arduous work every day. When teaching, stay on top of where each person is at any particular time and move them from that point along the lines that you feel they can follow. It is necessary to achieve relaxation in a class before one can evoke spontaneous dancing from them. Watch the energy flow and tilt it as the need arises to achieve this spontaneity. Most people like to dance but are afraid to do so. Get them past this barrier.

ANGELO FICAROTTA, carpenter and father: Creation of houses, of cabinets, of furniture is a continuous meditation and a productive way of life on your planetside trip. Automobile accidents, strokes and illness can be handled by one's self and one can heal most wounds through one's own efforts. I do not need to believe in anything but my own direct experience and my family.

THOMAS FICAROTTA, contractor: Some lawyers indulge in sophisticated extortion. Some lawyers and some judges tend to forget that we all live in a very small town known as planet earth.

BURGESS MEREDITH, actor, director, author: Loyalty to one's friends irrespective of what they do, of what they believe or of who is against them is a prime virtue. Good manners are essential to life on this planet. Work with the establishment, not against it. It will change as you change. The performing arts are a way of life. The performing arts can educate the public not only as to what art is but also as to what is behind and important to science.

ARTHUR AND PRUE CEPPOS (dyad) publishers: You don't know a book and what it contains, even if you have written it, until you have read it five times. There is an old Chinese saying, If it isn't economic, it isn't real. The Tao implies living life to its fullest as one is, not as one would like to be.

JOHN BROCKMAN, author and agent: "Kill all of your darlings," when writing a book; do not treasure any given paragraph, sentence or chapter. Ultimately words as such have no reality whatsoever. In his *Tractatus Logico-Philosophicus*, Wittgenstein said all there is to say. An autobiography can never be up to date. Everything that is said in it is passed—finished. Teasing is a fine art.

JERRY BROWN, Governor of California: The machinery of government is top-heavy with regulations, with paperwork, with excess numbers of people in it. Let us examine the government that we have inherited and remake it along simpler and more human lines. Let us question every person in authority about what it is they are doing and how they are doing it, and ask them to improve their methods—to be more economical and more understandable. No one in government is free from such analysis or the program of cooperative rebuilding of that which we must do.

BERNICE DANYLCHUK, posture therapist: With the aid of a disciplined posture therapist, one can change the basic line of one's body as it exists in gravity. "I require your cooperation. If you cannot work, please do not ask for my help." The bones of the body including the skull must be lined up so that one rests on the one below it in a direct line to the bottom of the feet. Once one achieves this alignment, one no longer wastes energy holding the body in position. No matter what one does with the body it is possible to improve these alignments during motion and during rest.

HELEN COSTA, stretch and movement, yoga teacher: The body must be stretched every day at every joint to the limits of its motion in order to expand those limits. Never overdo stretch. Do something every day that makes your heart beat faster, your breath increase its rate and depth.

GRACE STERN, yoga teacher and mystic: It is possible within one's mind to go very far out at the slightest excuse and depend upon others to bring one back. It is possible to teach an intensive series of yoga courses while at the same time keep one's family happy, well and functioning.

RUTH AND MYRON GLATT (dyad) teachers: Teaching teachers can be fun. Using audiovisual aids is the most effective way of transmitting the information to the student. The student seeing himself on TV can easily correct that which is wrong in his motions, in his techniques. Sorcery is a gentle, compassionate art.

RUTH AND HENRY DENNISON (dyad) teachers: Once you have taken care of your planetside trip, share your joy with others and encourage teachers and the young. Good cooking induces positive feelings and high states in the recipients. Travel to India and Switzerland is inspiring.

FRANKLIN MERRELL-WOLFF, author, philosopher, teacher, and mystic: States of Being, beyond the current consensus reality, are worth achieving. Illumination/Realization generate consequences/experiences that are expressible to those who can listen/reprogram Self. Teaching by example and articulate writing shows the power of Self and the power of words. There are States of Being beyond Bliss, beyond Satisfaction, beyond Nirvana: the State of High Indifference can be experienced/communicated by invitation/description/injunction. The fact that Dr. Wolff achieved High Indifference, duly reported, can induce this State in those who are prepared to reprogram Self into new domains.

HEINZ VON FOERSTER, cybernetician, teacher, and Western jnanananda: Gracious yogic manners solve problems before they arise. Communication is an invitation to participate in the game of creating. Wittgenstein (in *Tractatus Logico-Philosophicus*) reveals/conceals the structure of monologic/dialogic. Domains contain all pathways. Brown (in *The Laws of Form*) reveals monologic by hidden dialogic. Varela (in *A Calculus for Self-Reference*) clears the laws of form for self-reference. Eigen functions are useful for explicating domains of experience/representation, stable/unstable, finite/infinite, transforming/transiting the observer/agent. Inevitably, "as if" will become important in deeper levels of analysis of the observer/agent in the inner domains of experience/representation and in invitation/communication/participation/creation in dialogic/multilogic. Bright students and a happy dyad are basic necessities to a man's creativity.

E. J. GOLD, Sufi, transit guide and explorer of inner domains: By creating a remote, isolated community, one can experiment with/explore basic belief systems and transit in/out of the vehicle. Joy/humor/personal energy combined with discipline, facilitate transformation of Self/others. Games played with gusto generate new understanding of Self.

Bethesda; Saint Thomas; Miami; Baltimore; Esalen; Los Angeles; Palo Alto; Arica; and Malibu—1954–1975

THE ISOLATION TANK, in solitude as Teacher: You are your own best teacher, earthside type. The range of your own mind is far greater than your concepts of that range. Your present limits are somewhat determined by your personal set of basic postulates of your existence about your origins, your eventual destinations, by your most precious and sacred beliefs.

The truth as you know it is 99 percent nonsense and 1 percent "as if" true. Your inner experience is *true* at the time of the experience: You will remember only 10 percent, rework 5 percent and express by your limited language and forbiddings only 1 percent. Of the 1 percent you can transmit only a very small fraction for the purpose of teaching others.

Watching your own creations and their limits can be a waste of your precious time.

Creating expanded limits for your inner creations can be rewarding. When feeling the reward, be cautious and maintain a gentle skepticism.

The overvaluation space is a product of the activities of the pleasure systems within your own brain.

You cannot destroy your current beliefs. You can only bury them where they continue their influence on your feeling-thinking-doing. That which is not allowed is forbidden. To allow, examine carefully, the forbidden. Is it true, as if true, false, as if false, meaningless, or as if meaningless?

Are there influences operating upon us beyond our best science from civilizations and sciences far more advanced than ours? If there are, how can we best investigate these influences on our own? Study the problem in solitude, in physical isolation, in confinement in the external reality with the least restricting set of metabeliefs at your disposal. With this method, you may find answers within unexpected phenomena experienced under these conditions.

STATES OF CONSCIOUSNESS VS. STATES OF BEING

"Altered States of Consciousness":

There are two objections against using this phrase as scientific terminology:

1) "Altered" is a pejorative term equivalent to "castrated" in other contexts; states of consciousness cannot be castrated.

2) States of consciousness are only two in number, "present" or

"absent," "conscious" or "unconscious." A Self is either conscious or unconscious.

States of Being:

1) A conscious Self has numberless States of Being, from the usually accepted consensus states of being to more rare states, such as out-of-body states, Samadhi, unity, etcetera.
2) States of Being can be transformed, one into any other, with very short transition times, down to from ten to the minus twelfth to ten to the minus twenty-seventh seconds.
3) A person in externally described "coma" can be quite conscious in another State of Being, not necessarily tied to the body-brain-earthside coordinates.

Toni's Teachers

NINA CAROZZA: My daughter taught me about motherhood and about what caring for someone above one's self is like. She entered the world gracefully and continues to express that quality in her life. Her discipline that is part of a dancer's life is quite spiritual.

ALAN WATTS: That one's profession or work can be fun. He loved to talk and used his voice as an instrument. Some of his stories were told in the greatest Shakespearean tradition.

RICHARD OSHMAN: Business can be creative and absorbing.

WILLIE RUFF: Jazz as a musical language can be far more efficient in some dimensions than words for expressing deep feelings.

LAURA HUXLEY: Creative mixing of nutritious foods, elegantly served.

KURT VON MEIER: His lectures at schools or in his home are delightful tapestries of history, color and form. His preparation of food from his own garden, a meditation.

(BABA) RAM DASS: His joy and love of people is expressed in his bhakti yoga constantly.

RAFE AFFLECK: The simplification of line in his sculpture is a way of life.

JOE MUGNANI: Drawing the human figure tells a story about your own beliefs.

JEPPSON: Art teacher at Chouinard Art School. The Eastern thought influencing his delicate line drawings taught me about subtleties in my approach to my own work.

MARY TAYLOR: A true master craftslady in design, sewing, food and graciousness.

OSCAR ICHAZO AND HIS LADY JENNY PAREDA: South American palace politics mixed with esoteric teachings can be humorous.

JOHN C. LILLY: John has helped me dare to look beyond the consensus reality in every direction. His complete abandon and the openness of his mind are only matched by the boundless horizon of his spirit.

With his piercing gaze he will take anything apart and re-assemble it, never satisfied until he knows all the parameters of the subject of his examination. He has taught me courage and flexibility. He is a great companion, brother, lover, father and, most of all, he reflects my own humor back to me. We are each other's best audience.

JAN NICHOLSON: Our friend and secretary, whose candidness and New Zealand humor everyone enjoys—especially our cat, Pish, who loves her dearly. She talks to animals and they all respond.

KATHRYN SHARPE: Whose loyalty is as fierce as her memory. Her lovely daughters, Hannah Leigh and Mary Ann, dark and light jewels.

LOULABELLE NORCHIA: Her steadiness is a ruler against which I can test my own indeterminacy.

RUTH DENNISON: The cosmic hostess with the mostest. Her groundedness gives the airiest gurus perspective.

JANET LEDERMAN: I can teach anyone, anything, as long as they *want* to learn that thing. I can teach them that "thing," anywhere, anytime within any space.

BERNICE DANYLCHUK AND HER ASSISTANTS, LIKA YANDALL AND HELEN COSTA: They have helped me with an improved posture image of my body.

ERMA SIMS POUND, her poetry—

> How do I perceive my friend who comes to me today . . . ?
> No form rises . . . no assumption.
> Expectancy, the child, anticipates
>   the "empty space" through
>   which we slide—to meet.
>
> I give myself to *Now* and
>   experience the spontaneous form
> Through Space I am, the
> Emptiness in every form and
> Form in emptiness.
>
> Walk with me in Nakedness and
>   I will lend you my Breath
>   for Voice when you speak
>   to those still clothed.
>
> Immediately I experience, for I am born
>   a child without parents,
>   as often as there is birth.

STUART MURPHY: The mechanics of actual filmmaking is quite primitive.

SIMI DABAH: His sculpture is an expression of his grounded, centered strength.

CALIFORNIA WOMEN: Tom and Barbara Runyon give parties that are what I thought Hollywood parties were supposed to be like, until I went to a few. At the last one we went to, Robert Mitchum said something I feel was significant.

We were talking about California women in general compared with women throughout the rest of the country. From his worldly point of view (I feel he really has been around) he inferred that California women are at the forefront in demonstrating the evolution of the diversified possibilities of humankind.

I have to agree that when we lecture around the country, I find also that California women appear generally more open, creative and healthy. Their willingness to experiment with new roles and pretend to take on new belief systems, keeping intact what they know to be true and practical, is impressive. Just a few examples are:

> Jane Fonda Hayden–actress.
> Kay Cole Worden—executive.
> Nancy Hellman—artist and photographer.
> Mrs. Edmund Brown, Sr.–mother of Jerry Brown, current governor of California. Previous first lady of California.
> Natalie Solomon Krole—sculptress.
> Cris Price—comanager (with Dick Price) of Esalen.
> Patty Westerbeke—operator of Westerbeke Ranch, a growth center.
> Gay Gaer Luce–authoress.
> Joan Grof—authoress.
> Jennifer Jones Simon—actress and hostess.

MARY FRANK: Her ranch in Colorado is managed with simple elegance; her hospitality and gourmet picnics are a delight.

Chapter Ten

The Dyadic Planetside Trip: Our House and Tank Work

Toni and I have been together for five years. What is it that generates the bonds in this particular dyad?

Part of the bonding process between us is humor and states of high energy. John's self-analysis turned up an interesting split in himself. He found that a certain aspect of himself, his fun-loving, romantic "small boy-self," tended to remain hidden behind his more educated, austere, disciplined "official" self. Toni has many times caught this hidden "boy" peeking out from behind the façade of the grown man. She encourages him to "come out and play" with her "little girl" self. In this dyad the "boy" is called "Jack" (a name that was used for eight-year-old John by his drum teacher); Toni's (Antonietta's) small "girl" is called "Ann."

John places in Jack all of the characteristics of himself and those hidden belief systems that are not officially useful in the consensus reality operation, such as: certain kinds of joking, certain ideas (reincarnation, past lives, science-fiction scripts), and certain states of being ("the happy idiot," "the aroused male animal," "the angry husband," "the holy man," etcetera).

These fictitious alternate personalities have their uses in our dyad: any time we do something, say something, feel something, that is somewhat out of context-inappropriate-humorous, we conjure up "Jack" and/or "Ann." (Jack and Ann have their own communication—spoken through body language as well as verbal, vocal language, sometimes humorous, sometimes highly emoting.)

As John wrote in *The Center of the Cyclone*, when Toni and he met he said to her, "Where have you been for the last five hundred years?" She answered, "In training." Now let us ask Jack (with all of his "omniscience") what this means:

"Okay, John and Toni, here's what I feel to be true and I am choosing my language very carefully to give a certain amount of credibility to both of you. You were together in a previous life or lives, five hundred or more years ago. You missed getting together for the last five hundred years (until February 1971) and obviously you are together once again as you have demonstrated over the last five years. The last time you were together, John was insisting on being an explorer and Toni wanted him to stay at home. As you remember, five hundred years ago from your 1971 meeting, it was the year 1471. In that year, Leonardo da Vinci, for example, was nineteen years old (his birthdate is estimated to have been 1452). The Medici were coming to power in Florence. Shakespeare wasn't due for another hundred and some years. I cite these historical matters to place the time at which we apparently previously existed together.

"John has a prejudice in regard to all of this. He hardly believes in reincarnation as such; he has a very definite policy not to go into past lives. He wants to be much more involved in future possibilities of humankind rather than in reminiscing over a past that cannot be changed." (Jack is more relaxed about such matters and at every opportunity brings up the matter of reincarnation and previous lives. Apparently it was he who took over and said to Toni "Where have you been for the last five hundred years?")

"Currently John is running the show and would prefer to talk about the current life of John and Toni—what that's like—and somewhat of what they plan for the future."

John answers, "Of course the planetside trip has a past, but if one gets too involved in the past, one becomes unable to deal either with the present or with the future, and the more time one spends on the past, the less there remains for the present and the future." (A scientist commits himself to the future. He uses past knowledge to a certain extent, but he develops the future knowledge.)

About a year and nine months ago, John and Toni moved from Toni's house in Los Angeles near the west end of Los Angeles County to a house in Malibu at an altitude of about 1,300 feet above sea level and two and a half miles from the sea. From this house one can see a small segment of the sea, down through the canyon. The climate here reminds one of Arizona, so we call it "Arizona by the sea." As is typical of southern California, there are hibiscus and other flowering trees around the property. Currently I see red and yellow flowers on the trees. I see a bird-of-paradise plant in flower. I see some trees that have lost their leaves for the winter, this being February. I see one evergreen tree that died last winter because it is in a bad spot where it doesn't get much moisture. The grounds are quite hilly. There is an acre that is available for a very large garden if we wish. Toni put in twenty avocado trees last year. We hope to obtain avocados from them within the next three years. We own a total of two and a half acres and have modified the house and the grounds somewhat for our own purposes. We installed a water tank above the house on the side of the hill to give us better water pressure in the house. We put in a swimming pool, which can be heated and has some Jacuzzi jets in it, as well as air jets in the bottom. There are some beautiful incense cedars in which there resides a tribe of quail. They come back every night to roost in these trees.

The house itself is about fifty feet by seventy feet in total area, including the porches. There is a very large back porch and a small front porch. There are five bedrooms, some of which we converted to offices, and two bathrooms, and a kitchen immediately adjacent to and looking out through a rather large living room. We have installed a quadrasonic hi-fi system.

We had tile put down on the two porches and through the kitchen and one portion of the living room with carpet laid on the rest. Toni had new drapes hung and redid the walls with a special kind of wood with the grain going at a forty-five-degree angle to the horizontal.

It is John's impression and those of most of our guests that it is a very warm and delightful atmosphere in which to work and live. Adjacent to the house, but not attached to it, is a separate small building, which was formerly a laundry and currently has been given over to the isolation tank work. In this building we placed two isolation tanks: a large, white fiberglass one, sentimentally dubbed "the white whale," the other a wooden model with a vinyl liner. This building enabled us to carry the isolation tank development further than it has been done before.

There is sufficient land so that we can build another small house or work space, which we need.

In the twenty-one months that we have lived here, some fifty miles from the center of Los Angeles and in a rather remote mountain district, I have been amazed at the number of people who find us and who enjoy our company.

Originally we bought the house in order to hold workshops, which we did for the first year. We held workshops here, at Esalen and at various other growth centers around the United States.

The first workshops we gave were for anyone who applied. This led to some rather humorous situations in which people would arrive not knowing who we were or what sort of workshops we were presenting. For example, one couple arrived all decked out as if they were newly initiated into encounter groups and similar kinds of workshops. They were dressed in brand-new clothes, which looked as if they were copies of the "as if young" uniform (blue jeans and special hats). This couple showed very low tolerance for various kinds of exercises that we put people through in our workshops. For example, we exposed them to the repeating word "cogitate," to very loud noises of various sorts, in order to train them to unexpected programs and to reprogram their own dislike into curiosity for whatever it is that is going on. The man in this couple found it impossible to tolerate the levels of either sound or the patterning of the sound that was being presented to the group.

It was because of experiences like these that we finally decided to limit our workshops to either people who had previously been in workshops with us at Esalen or other growth centers, and to M.D.'s, Ph.D.'s and similarly educated individuals. Somehow or other we no longer enjoy teaching the elements to "beginners" in this area, so much as we did several years ago.

In all of our workshops we present the results of work in the tank and use the tank in the workshop itself. At one point we gave a workshop at Esalen and through the cooperation of Glen Perry, we were able to use two tanks during the whole workshop for a full week.

During the time that we have had the tanks available at our house, we have accumulated a very large catalog of tank experience. We ask each person who uses the tank for an hour or more, to write up their experience immediately after it happens. We now have something on the order of two hundred such write-ups, which will be incorporated in our upcoming handbook on the use of the tank (The Deep Self). Contrary to the written materials on so-called "sensory deprivation," which were not done in the tank, we have had very few negative experiences.

In *Programming and Metaprogramming in the Human Biocomputer* (Preface to the First Edition), I stated my position very succinctly and "densely" (meaning condensedly) to use Toni's term, in regard to the tank work.

> . . . . The interest of the author is more in the thinking machine itself, unencumbered. During those times when it is unencumbered by the necessities of interlock with other [bio-] computers and/or with an external reality, its noninterlock structure can be studied. A given mind seen in pure culture by itself in profound physical isolation and in solitude is the raw material for our investigation . . .

Thus our major interests are in those metatheoretical positions which remain as open as possible to reasonable explanation and reasonable models of the thinking processes, of the origins of beliefs, of the origins of self, the organization of self with respect to the rest of the mind, and the kinds of permissible transformations of self which are reversible, flexible, and introduce new and more effective ways of thinking.

In other words, we are interested in establishing a basic situation by means of the tank and by means of our own programming of others in which *the individual is free in the tank to do his own thing*. Often times we are approached by people who wish to use the tank asking "What should I think about, or what should I do in the tank?" My immediate answer in these cases is "My preprogram for you is for you not to ask me to preprogram you."

Some people arrive at our house expecting us to give them a preprogram. Others arrive at the house with their own expectations of what is going to happen in the tank. An amusing anecdote occurred recently when a particularly busy and highly energetic man (D. E.) arrived, didn't have much time to spend, and wanted to spend it all in the tank. So he hurried through his shower and climbed into the tank, spent an hour, came out and hurried through his second shower to clean off the Epsom salts residue. As he was going out the door, I said, "Do you have anything to report about what happened in the tank?" Very quickly, as he was exiting, he said "nothing happened."

We have seen several cases like this, a few of which we were able to question. In general it seems that these people arrive with certain expectations: they are going to accomplish certain things in the tank; there are going to be far-out trips; they are going to hallucinate; they are going to have new and unique experiences.

Some arrive already preprogrammed by what I have written about regarding my own experiences in the tank, recounted in *The Center of the Cyclone* and in *The Human Biocomputer*. When they say "nothing happened" it means that they did not live up to their own expectations of what could happen.

In general we encourage people not to expect much on their first tank experience. It is rare that they can accomplish in an initial session what they eventually will accomplish.

For instance, Richard P. Feynman, 1965 Nobel Prize laureate for his research in quantum electrodynamics, exposed himself to thirty-three hours of total tank work over a period of twelve weeks. Only after five hours of work was he able to do the things he wanted, such as moving his conscious center out of his body while in the tank.

In our forthcoming book, The Deep Self, some two hundred separate accounts of experiences in the tanks will be given.

Toni had one experience in the tank that she recounts in the next chapter as an illustration of what can happen in an unexpected way after one has been exposed to many hours of tank work.

Chapter Eleven

Toni's Inner–Outer Development Leading to a Tank Experience

At Decker Canyon, the isolation tanks had been installed only a few months, when I took this journey.

Walking to the isolation building that day, I was preoccupied with the business of setting up a new corporation of which I was going to be president. I was not sure I wanted to play such a role; I knew my pattern of seriously taking responsibility toward projects of this nature. My midyears seem to be much more adaptable to less precise relationships. Being president of a corporation seemed to be a little more precise role than I wished to play. I much prefer the "sloppy fit" and the freedom that I believe it gives me to redefine boundaries that otherwise might be too clearly confining.

My education had this looser pattern and continues that way. Formal courses have led to informal creative relations in new fields. For example, my interest in art as a young girl led me to formal experience as a student. I studied at the Art Center in Los Angeles for about a year; I then decided to study with a drawing teacher I much admired named Jeppson at Chouinard Institute. From there I went to Otis Art Institute for another few years. After a showing of my drawings, I found myself wondering "What now, bigger and better shows?" I found the art scene fun: it led to my discovery of my inner realities. The more I examined and learned of my inner realities, the more the bridge from art to what was called "therapy" appealed to me. That was the accepted religion in the circles I was influenced by at that time. In 1961, I started my own therapy with a psychoanalyst Dr. Carroll Carlson. At that time the National Institute of Mental Health authorized him (and several other psychiatrists) to use LSD-25 in clinical research in practice.

After about a year of psychoanalytic work with me, Dr. Carlson proposed that he guide me in a therapeutic session with LSD-25. I will not recount yet another "first" LSD experience, except to say that mine was *classically universal*. During this session and in the analysis afterward, I realized that I had probed this area as deeply as I had planned. I ended the therapy.

I decided to express my art, in a new form: it became transformed into a means of helping other people to experience larger domains of feeling. I became a cotherapist with Dr. Carlson's groups. These experiences gave me a new tolerance of other people's patterns of living, thinking, emoting and timing.

I was fascinated with group work, with the individuals in the many groups that Dr. Carlson was treating. It was an exciting time: he was willing to experiment with the new techniques— of which there were many at that time: Psychodrama, Encounter, etcetera. Also some already established techniques, such as Gestalt therapy. We started going to Esalen Institute in Big Sur to examine some of these new approaches to therapy. My creativity was expressed well through therapy, which offered more dimensions in new domains. My "actress," "director" and "stage designer" came out of my deeper self as new felt roles for me. My experiences of being a therapist have been deeply learning, teaching ones for me.

These more or less formal experiences led to further, informal ones. I became involved with a marvelously creative group of young people (one of whom was my daughter, Nina), called the "Company Theatre" of Los Angeles. For two very intense years,

I tie-dyed, painted, designed and sewed costumes for them and various other interested people. My house was a developing "village" of young creative people.

About this time John came into my life (see *The Center of the Cyclone*). We started giving workshops with groups. The new course of activities with John became a natural outcome of the previous flow of training-learning and lifestyle. Our new home became the new center of my inner—outer realities.

Now back to walking to the isolation building getting ready to again put myself in this box of water in the silent darkness. I want you to know that it wasn't exactly a short walk from the house to the tank building for me. All of my previous experience (including previous LSD experience) was dynamically-dramatically with me and evoked feelings I had known during those experiences. In addition, that day I had a head cold; I wondered if I was wise in going into the tank.

While I was taking my pretanking shower, all of the above background thoughts passed through me. I finished, put on my robe, walked to the isolation building. I opened the door, looked at the dark green tank container and disrobed. I opened the lid of the container, climbed over the side and closed the lid after me. I lay down and floated.

The supportive water engulfed and caressed me.

The loud silence approached.

The dancing white lights in the blackness played on my observer's three-dimensional visual display screen. I watched my thoughts go by. Ah—this time a new stranger came toward me.

Is this one friend or foe? . . .

And then, bang, panic. I shook in terror.

My congested nose precipitated me with amazing speed into a claustrophobic panic space: I couldn't catch my breath; I felt I was suffocating; I felt I might die suddenly.

The inner events piled up too rapidly. Before I realized it, I was already launched into the midst of my basic survival programs.

I might add that my Self-metaprogrammer was scrambling along with the lowly programmed systems, hopelessly identified with saving my life: they all came up with a unanimous democratic decision of *"OUT fast!"*

I scrambled from floating to a crouching position in the shallow water. I uncoiled my crouching body; my hands and the top of my head hit the lid; it opened so rapidly that the hinge broke. There was a resounding crash in the silent dark tank room.

My heart was pounding as loud as a jackhammer. I stood for a long minute or two trying to figure out what had happened. ("Can I really be so dumb as not to realize I can change my breathing and breathe through my mouth?")

Let me try to describe for you, something I call panicsville instantaneous claustrophobia, a body-shaking terror. First there were some faint memories of a childhood experience with ether anesthesia: the trauma of the ether mask over my face; someone holding me down on the operating table. Total coercion for unknown purposes; truly formidable for the young me.

Standing there alone, I realized that the ether experience had vividly imprinted itself in a blocklike form somewhere deep in my memory. This form was very busily being fed survival energy that was not available to my conscious Self-metaprogrammer, as John would say. This insight came in a second, along with a movie-framelike series of split-second eternities.

My birth experience was vividly recalled: the squeezing transit, the suffocation, the gasp of the first breath.

A deeper experience from the LSD-25 session was also invoked: I was a primordial simple biological organism imbedded in swamp mud. I knew that I had been inching along in the primordial ooze. I passed rapidly from worm to amphibian to reptile. I developed scales, finally, to help push me into the air to dry in the sun. The first conscious breath on land went through my form.

All of these past inner realities passed through me in a few seconds; "Time is surely absurd" I thought, dripping and shivering there in the tank room.

The terror abated. I became calm.

I found myself so fascinated with these discoveries in my inner reality that I got back into the tank. This time I would allow myself to breathe through my mouth if necessary.

Again the familiar patterns of floating, darkness and silence.

This time *"the stranger"* approached from a similar direction. I was able to do a Tai Chi-like mental movement and allow him to pass. My new perspective and review allowed me to see the stranger as a friend: I was able to greet him/her and allow him/her to leave without my previous feelings of panic or fear.

My tank experience that day was exhilarating. It makes me again conscious of the limitation of words: direct experience translated into words is, after all, a simulation of that experience.

John:

"We have very few reports of such experiences. Our subjects are not in therapy, are self-selected and noncoerced. Under other more pressured circumstances more such episodes might be seen."

Chapter Twelve

States of Being and Consciousness in "Coma"— The Quantum of Consciousness

In our dyad there have been few more dramatic episodes than the one that is recounted here. The episode started with the purchase of a bicycle, a ten-speed racing model from Japan, costing eighty dollars. I went to Ventura, which is about twenty miles from our home, purchased the bicycle, hooked it onto the front of our VW motor home and drove it back to Decker Canyon.

The next day I used the bicycle at our home in response to a call from Toni.

Several days before, we had installed a locking gas cap on the VW. Toni had left the house and taken the VW down the canyon. At Trancas she tried to get gasoline, found the gas cap locked and she realized that I had not given her the key. In response to her call, I decided to meet her down the road to give her the key.

I got on the bicycle, looked down at my feet with great joy and said to myself as it were "This is the first time I have been on a bicycle with such joy since I was a little boy first learning how to ride a bicycle." I went down our driveway and down Decker School Road with many turns in its slight slope and met Toni at about the third turn from the house. I handed her the key, she turned around and went down Decker Canyon road. I followed her.

This was a mistake. The bicycle had been untested. It had been freshly assembled at the Broadway store in Ventura the day before and turned out to be defectively put together. It was my responsibility to check out such devices, but this time I failed to do so.

As I proceeded down Decker School Road I passed a blue panel van coming out of a side road. I noticed this out of the corner of my vision as I went by on the bicycle. At Decker Canyon Road, I stopped as I approached the main highway, looked both ways and went on. I made the first two turns on this rather steep highway and on the third turn, the bicycle went out from under me and I hit the road.

From that point on, for five days and nights, I went in and out of consciousness and had what is technically called "retrograde amnesia" regarding the episode and for what happened externally.

The first time that I returned to consciousness I was sitting beside the road and someone on my left-hand side was arguing with me. I was struggling back to consciousness and I said to him, "I am badly hurt. I need a doctor." He said, "What is wrong?" I said, "I have lost my right eye and my brains are coming out on the right side of my head above the eye." He said, "Nonsense, you have a cut that is bleeding over your right eye and the blood is running into your right eye. Take your hand away and you will see."

I took my hand away and saw that he was correct. There was blood on my hand and on my clothes. My jumpsuit was torn and I suddenly realized that I was badly hurt.

He said, "Get into my panel truck and I will take you home."

My medical training told me, Don't move till you have assessed the damage. You may sever your spinal cord or something equally as drastic, so stay perfectly still until you know what is happening in the body—still in shock, no pain—yet. To the man on my left I said, "I am very badly hurt in my right shoulder; I can't possibly get into your panel truck. Please don't push me; I must assess the damage; I am a doctor." So the man got into his panel truck and drove off. I immediately lapsed into another universe, leaving my body sitting beside the road.

"I was in a universe in which there was total atomic war taking place on a particular planet. There were several teachers present showing me what was happening and preventing me from being damaged by that war.

"The war had been started in such a way that nobody knew how it started. There were computers on that planet that controlled the warfare. The humans had been left out in the circuitry, and the hydrogen warheads from orbiting space stations were bombarding the whole 'earth' with hydrogen bombs. I saw a flash and heard a detonation some distance away from me. Somehow or other the teachers involved had provided me with glasses so that my eyes wouldn't be burnt by the flash. I felt the concussion and saw the tornado of the blast tearing away the trees and vegetation around me. I was peering out of a cave at the time and somehow was protected by the teachers from being damaged."

At this point I was suddenly brought back to the road. The man had returned and he said, "I drove up to the house address you gave me and found that you can pay the medical bills. The reason I didn't take you to the hospital was that I didn't know that you could pay, but seeing that house convinced me that you can pay."

Just then someone who was obviously very agitated drove up in a white VW bug. This individual asked "Did you hit him?" The man answered "No, I did not; he fell from a bicycle. I have put the bicycle in the panel truck."

That person then drove off and someone else arrived in a blue VW bug. She was very excited and upset and asked the man if he had seen this accident. She had seen me, bloodied, sitting by the side of the road. She had gone down the mountain, and, using one of the fire phones had phoned the Sheriff.

Suddenly there was the sound of a loud fire truck coming down the mountain and a Sheriff's car came up the mountain. Then the rescue squad arrived. (These details of the external events were given two weeks later by the witness in the blue panel truck.)

I was going in and out of consciousness at this point. I realized that rescue operations were under way and that I would eventually be taken care of, so "I" left again.

The conglomerate of cars and the fire engine came into my consciousness very briefly.

Later it turned out that the only person who recognized me was the man riding the fire truck. Several weeks before, Toni and I had gone to the fire station to register to vote; this man had registered us.

My own inner perception of this external reality was very defective and it was only with a great deal of personal work and, later, with help from the man in the panel truck, that I was able to construct what had happened. My body in coma was then taken off to the hospital in Santa Monica.

In the meantime, I saw only a glimpse of two men with short-sleeved blue uniforms, apparently the rescue squad, who put me into the ambulance. I then lapsed into unconsciousness again, into what we now call "external coma"; I was not unconscious inside.

"I was launched back onto one more of the catastrophic planets. This time I was in another cave with the teachers, and though there was no atomic warfare, there was a heating up of the atmosphere. An incandescent gas was surrounding this planet; on the night side it was as if it were complete daylight, the gas was so bright. This effect lasted for one day. The gas then dissipated and went away. The planet went on rotating under its sun, leaving complete carnage on its surface. Almost every living thing, plants and animals, bacteria, viruses, were killed by this incandescent gas, with few exceptions. The exceptions were either deep in the sea, far enough from the surface so as not to be burned up, or in caves or in burrows. They stayed there during the time of the invasion of the gas. The few humans who survived were in caves or deep in subways, and stayed there.

Some survived deep in cellars and so on, but most of the popula-
tion of the planet was wiped out.

"The teachers then said that this had not only occurred in the
past history on earth as I knew it, but was recorded as history in
many thousands of planets throughout the galaxy. They ex-
plained that what had happened in our case was that a star that
is no longer visible, not any of those that we knew from our
knowledge of astronomy, had exploded, becoming a supernova.
The incandescence was the radiating gas of that supernova
through which our planetary system had passed. They further
explained that this was the mechanism that had wiped out the
large reptiles on our planet in the dim distant past before the
history of humans."

During this period I did not know of any earthside and
external reality, external to the body, until I "awoke" in the
hospital.

Apparently, as soon as I had arrived at the hospital, the
surgeons had assessed the damage and realized that I had a
collapsed right lung, which needed reinflation. Subsequently I
learned that I had broken five ribs on the right, on the right
side the clavicle and scapula were broken, and that I had a
concussion from a blow on the right side of the head. The tip
of my left elbow was shattered.

With a good deal of work in the subsequent weeks, I could
finally recall falling from the bicycle. It happened so fast at the
time, that it was very hard to recapture what was stored in my
brain.

Inside my own head, I finally reenacted the fall and took about
an hour for that fall to take place again "as if true." Something
had happened to the bicycle, I knew.

"My reflexes were completely reversed from what they should
have been. This was a racing bicycle with hand brakes, and I
had tried the foot brake, as was on the kind of bicycle that I had
learned to ride when I was a little boy. In doing so, I caused my
left foot to hit the pavement, throwing the bicycle out from under
me. As I began to fall, I realized that I had to get the bicycle out

of the way or I would be badly damaged. I kicked it out from under me and then I hit the pavement, trying to avoid hitting the ground headfirst, protecting my head and my hands from damage. This meant that I tried a roll in the old judo jiujitsu fashion that I had learned at Cal Tech. In performing the roll, I hit on the right side of the body smashing the ribs, and the clavicle and the scapula on the right side, holding my hand up to keep it from being damaged. My left elbow hit the pavement as I rolled. There was no pain, just a feeling of total disaster."

The inside catastrophic planetary episodes were totally real to me. When I resumed consciousness in the body, while in the hospital, I was tempted to get on the missionary podium in order to warn the world that total catastrophe could take place at any instant. We should seek caves designed as the teachers taught me to design them. We should all wear radiation-proof clothing. We should all wear radiation-proof glasses. We must make sure not to be caught outside without these protective elements. I wasn't sure which catastrophe was going to take place first, the incandescent cloud, or total atomic warfare.

As I lay in the hospital, coming and going out of these strange universes, I realized that I should not play the role of the missionary. If I did, somebody would lock me up believing me to be psychotic. So I told no one what was going on inside.

Meanwhile, someone had informed Toni and she arrived at the hospital while I was still in coma during the first day. She contacted Burgess Meredith, who has been a very loyal friend of ours. The night after the operation had taken place to reinflate my lung, they went to Burgess's house and held a conversation, which he recorded on tape and I later heard.

This was a very dramatic and heartrending juncture in Toni's life and Burgess fully appreciated this. Each of them realized that I might not come back from this episode.

This episode demonstrated to me that the damage to my vehicle was such that I was projecting onto the universe certain aspects of my own knowledge and of my own particular catastrophe, my own situation. The precipitous fall, the quick concussion, led to very fast transitions into other universes.

In the hospital I did not know that I had had an operation to reinflate my lungs. I did not know anything of what went on around me because of the medication that was being administered to me. When I finally discovered, five days after the accident, that I was being medicated with tranquilizer and painkiller, I refused to take any more; my bodily consciousness was too impaired by the medication.

When I discovered that I was being sedated and tranquilized, I took the pills they gave me and held them in my mouth. When the nurse left the room, I put them under the mattress. I refused in that way to take any more medicine. I could not adequately articulate this vocally. The vehicle was so impaired by this drug overload that I could not speak; but I could act.

The nurse discovered this as soon as she changed the bed and she immediately called the doctor. She asked me if I was refusing to take medication and I said Yes. By the time the doctor came I was enough out of the medication to be able to tell him that I did not want to continue and he agreed. He said however, "You have badly damaged tissues and I would like you to continue the antibiotic." I agreed to do this, but to be sure that it was an antibiotic and that nobody was trying to fool me, I bit through the first pill that the nurse gave me and showed her that I was doing this to taste the contents. By this means I ascertained that there was at least an antibiotic present. I wasn't too sure that there wasn't something else present also, but I went on taking what they recommended and trusted the staff not to give me anything else.

This meant that I would have to begin to stand the pain of all of these breaks of the various bones. Subsequently I discovered that I was in a brace to keep my shoulders back because of the broken clavicle. There was no cast and no taping of these breaks. Without tranquilizers and painkillers and without sedation, I would have to remain in pain, sleepless, while allowing repair of these broken parts.

In medical school, a Dr. North, a surgeon, had taught us that the best way (with intelligent patients) to get complete repair of bones was to make a very careful assessment of the breaks and to hold them in such a way that they could remain aligned. The patient is taught to do exercises in spite of the pain, to make sure the bones regrow on their natural alignment, strongly and without distortion.

I realized that the surgeon in charge of my particular case had decided to do this; however, he wanted to be aided by chemical means of controlling my voluntariness in the process. He did not know that I could take the pain, so he gave me medication to take care of pain and sleep. After the first five days, at which time I stopped taking the medication, I didn't get much sleep. The pain was excruciating day and night, and the slightest movement of my right arm gave resounding reverberations throughout the rest of me. The pain spread from the broken areas throughout the body in waves that led to nauseous conditions and burnings, the like of which I have never before experienced. The slightest movement of the right shoulder sent out waves of pain. Finally I was denying the existence of the whole region that was injured and walling it off by a sort of trance technique so that I would not be the victim of the pain emanating from the injuries.

This was an automatic process that took place, but at least I was able to do it, or able to have it done to me, however you wish, without the aid of medication. My consciousness then became much clearer, much sharper, more "broadband."

There were several important episodes that I can remember that occurred during the hospital period. One time I came back, Toni was beside my bed. I begged her to get close so that I could hold on to her and stay here on this planet. She stayed by the bed for five long hours with my arms around her neck. I was able to stay here in spite of medication, in spite of the concussion and its aftereffects. Previous to this particular outside episode, the inside episodes are worth recounting.

At the times I was assumed to be in coma by the medical personnel, inside I was anything but unconscious. I was living in another domain in which I was transiting by means of various programs that I had learned previously.

In G. Spencer Brown's *The Laws of Form*, there is a mathematical operator or, preferably, a logical operator, called "the marked state." This is symbolized by a right-angle corner that looks like a large inverted capital L.

This operator has certain properties, which are of great interest theoretically. It is pertinent to what happened later.

The marked state operator can operate in such a way that it can be fed back through itself (self-referential property). When one uses the operator as a signal, feeding it through the operator itself, it creates an infinite series as follows: marked state, unmarked state, marked state, unmarked state, and so forth, ad infinitum.

I had learned this both from my own studies of Brown's book and from the help of the AUM Conference (see Chapter Fourteen, *The Dyadic Cyclone*). (This particular oscillating character of the marked state operator had been explained to us by Heinz Von Foerster at the AUM Conference.)

Also stored in my biocomputer was a language devised by Robert Edwards in his Ph.D. thesis (UCLA, 1970) entitled The Quantum Observer in a Neurally Engineered Prosthesis. This language appeared only in the first few editions of this thesis, copies of which were furnished to me for my education by Frederick Worden, M.D.

The language involved was called by Edwards "topquantese." This language was devised in order to think about the brain in terms of quantum mechanics. It is a very powerful language that allowed one to progress from the quantum mechanics of one's own nervous system on a submicroscopic scale to the assemblages of neurons known as one's brain, to one's mind and to that mind in networks of communication with other minds and so on, throughout the universe. In other words, Edwards had devised a way of transiting in the inner domains to any region that one wished to travel from the subatomic particles on through the Self into the universe.

While I was in this apparently "comatose" state (outside), I was in a hyperconscious state (inside) in which I was traveling from one domain to another. This was happening without any knowledge of *having* a human body—I knew *of* a body in existence back on planet earth with Toni. Under these circumstances, one is still an individual consciousness but one has no present body, no present brain and no present planet earth. (It is very similar to other episodes, which I have described in

The Center of the Cyclone, in which I was in a comatose state in a hospital in New York in 1964 (Chapter 2).

I was allowed to travel through these domains by teachers, by guides, if you wish, who were programming what I was allowed to do. However, *I was also told that I must use my own efforts to transit.* I made a pact with the guides. In effect I said: *"If you will allow me to go back to Toni, if you will allow me to live in peace on the planet earth for a certain number of years with Toni, then I will do what you want me to do for the rest of that life."*

They said: *"You must go back on your own efforts. What you know about transit between domains demonstrates to us that you are capable of moving from one domain to another."*

I took up the challenge. I started with the marked state operator described by Brown. My consciousness was placed inside the right angle of the large inverted, capital L as it was written, as if it was a vehicle. This is rather a dangerous procedure. This meant that I was identified with the marked state, i.e., I existed. I was now riding the marked state as if it was a vehicle, but at the same time, I *was* the marked state. This means that I was the consciousness, the signal that was being fed through the marked state outside myself. As soon as this happened, I transited explosively into the Void. My consciousness was still intact, but there was no universe at all.

I suddenly realized that this was the first step in the infinite series of marked state, unmarked state, marked state, unmarked state, and so forth. So my consciousness then reassembled a marked state, got into the right angle and came out in another domain, i.e., came out in a new marked state.

(Brown, at the AUM Conference, said to me personally that *The Laws of Form* was not written as a method of going far-out. *The Laws of Form* is a handbook on how to get back.)

To return to the inside: *"I suddenly came out into a universe. I was in a universe in which catastrophes were taking place. One of the marked states was the total atomic warfare on a particular*

*planet in that universe. There was then a period of Void and
then another universe of the incandescent gas around a planet
and the subsequent killing of almost everything on its surface
except those protected in caves.*

"I am told by the guides that I am transiting from one domain
to another: the transition took ten to the minus twenty-seventh-
power seconds riding the Brownian marked state operator." (In
retrospect, I don't know where this quantity for the transition
time came from. It apparently was told to me by them.)

If one works out a few implications of this, one can see that,
for example, at ten to the minus twenty-seventh seconds, light
can only move three times ten to the minus ninth-power angstrom units or three times ten to the sixteenth Planck lengths.*

Translated then into human physical terms, this means that if
a human body were to be exposed to some process that could
take every atomic nucleus in that body and every electron in that
body and transport it to an entirely new universe at these speeds
that the effect (to put it mildly) would be explosive.

I was being exploded from one universe to a Void then to
another universe in a sequence that apparently lasted some days.
As far as I could make out from external observers, I was going
in and out of consciousness every fifteen minutes, after the effect
of the medication had worn off.

A rather amusing episode happened during this period of time.
At one point I came back and wanted to find out what my voice
sounded like under these conditions: I asked Toni to turn on a

---

* This calculation was computed as follows: light velocity is three
hundred thousand kilometers per second. One can then calculate this as
three times ten to the eighteenth-power angstrom units per second. (This
is the value of c, the constant velocity of light.) In ten to the minus twenty-
seventh-power seconds, the distance light travels is its velocity times the
time interval. It can be shown that this distance is then three times ten
to the minus ninth power angstrom units. The Planck length is ten to the
minus thirty-third-power centimeters, which is ten to the minus twenty-
fifth-power angstrom units. If we now divide the distance that the light
travels in ten to the minus twenty-seventh-power seconds by the Planck
length, we find that there are three times ten to the sixteenth Planck lengths
that light travels in ten to the minus twenty-seventh seconds. A hydrogen
nucleus in the hydrogen atom is ten to the minus fifth angstrom units.

tape recorder. I then dictated to the tape the following sentence: "Joe took father's shoe bench out; meet me by the lawn."*

Toni immediately said, "Who is Joe? Does that have something to do with your brother?"

At this point I was already going back into some other universe and failed to answer the question.

In my own internal reality, what I was doing was dictating a sentence onto the tape to be subsequently analyzed by sonic spectographic methods (which I had used in the laboratory on human speech and on dolphin speech). I wanted a quantitative measure of how my voice was different under these peculiar circumstances from what it normally was.

I had not told Toni about this sentence previously; she was faced with somebody coming out of coma not making any sense whatsoever.

Another episode happened inside while I was desperately trying to move from these multiple universes to the planet earth and back into the vehicle.

It is as if several times I had to have a conference with the teachers and bargain with them and promise that when I got back I would live a peaceful quiet life with Toni. Unless I made this promise they would not let me come back.

This was a pretty horrendous series of conferences. It was like arguing with the universe itself, arguing with powers that were so much beyond any powers that we have, that there was no doubt that the only way that I could get back was to get their consent. I was desperate, I wanted to come back. I wanted to be with Toni and I wanted to live a quiet peaceful life insofar as this was possible in our time.

They were adamant that I had to do this on my own by any means that I had at my disposal. So I rode the Brownian operator back to earth and entered my body explosively several times.

I also used the "topquantese" language of Edwards in a much more developed form than I knew when I was in my vehicle on earth. Somehow the topquantese language allowed me to collapse

---

* A test sentence (from Will Munson of the Bell Telephone Laboratories), which contains thirty-four of the forty-four sounds of the American English vocal language.

universes into the vehicle on planet earth. I don't know how this was done; yet as I would go through a certain procedure, the universe would collapse in steps until finally it was my body and the surrounds of that body on this planet. This was a less explosive method than that of the Brownian operator.

Subsequently I asked Edwards what speed this represented and he said it was "ten to the minus twenty-second-power seconds." I asked him why he had withdrawn "topquantese" from the published version of this thesis. He answered that it was because it was still explosive. Even traveling using "top-quantese" I was having a problem of too high a velocity with a shocking result as I would reenter the body and then take off again out of the body.

After I had returned home from the hospital, I established contact once again with Robert Edwards and discussed this travel with him. He said, "We have learned to reduce the time transition to ten to the minus twelfth-power seconds. This is not explosive."

All of these experiences were new and unique for me in spite of much experience in far-out regions. Everything that I experienced during these five days and subsequently was brand new and startling to me. I had not realized the properties of the Brownian operator until I experienced it inside. I did not realize the properties of the topquantese language until I experienced it inside.

I summarize all of this by saying that my own belief systems are totally incredible. I cannot believe them myself in this particular state that I am in—telling you about what happened.

Yet I know, somehow, that all of these episodes that I am recounting are programmed to a certain extent by my own belief systems, by the information that has been stored in me, by contacts with Brown and his writings and with Edwards and his writings.

Under the above transit circumstances, I think that each of us goes to the very limit of our own personal knowledge, of our own cognitive abilities, of our own voluntary participation, of our own Self-metaprogramming in the face of superself metaprogramming way beyond anything human.

The calculations of the speed of transition between universes, the calculation of the distance that light can travel in that very, very small time span, are useful because these are obviously quantities way beyond any of our current experiments or experiences in terms of the observer and the system observed.

In my use of the Brownian operator and in my use of top-quantese, I am realizing that the observer is a participant, is part of the system that he is observing and that he is feeding back upon himself in order to generate transitions. Only those acquainted with feedback theory in circuits can understand this adequately. Let me illustrate.

If one has an amplifier (say a stereo hi-fi amplifier) and one wishes to make this amplifier respond in a highly linear fashion so that the input and the output match each other's form to a very small fraction, one introduces negative feedback overall; in other words, one introduces part of the output back into the input in such a phase relationship to incoming signals that there is a reduction of output by means of the added input. This is called negative feedback. Positive feedback overall leads to oscillation of the system and uses very large amounts of energy. So negative feedback is safe, controlling and gives characteristics to the amplifier that it couldn't have otherwise. Positive feedback leads to new states.

Similarly, feedback on the observer's own knowledge can be either positive or negative in the above sense. If the feedback is of the Brownian type, the observer is transported willy-nilly into the Void and then into another domain. Using the Brownian operator, one goes from one's current universe to the Void and then to any other universe.

Why ten to the minus twenty-seventh-power seconds for this transition? Because *that is the time that one is allowed as a sub-submicroscopic entity to move into the structure of space and space-time itself and still maintain a conscious minimum size organization of Self.*

If one is going to travel from this universe to another one, one can reduce the size of the observer to an incredibly small size—in other words, three times ten to the sixteenth Planck lengths. One at this size is a good deal smaller than any atomic nucleus. When one has reduced one's conscious observer to this size, one's "subquantum observer" is smaller than any known particle. He can move into the indeterminate (unknown) substructure of space, space-time and topology that exists at ten to the minus thirty-third-power centimeters, which is ten to the minus twenty-fifth-power angstrom units. When he is so reduced, he then has the ability to travel (at the velocity of light or possibly faster?) for very short distances, i.e., of the order of three times ten to the sixteenth Planck lengths.

(To review some of the basic physical theory, not including the subquantum observer, I refer you to John Archibald Wheeler's article, "From Méndeleev's Atom to the Collapsing Star," from *Transactions of the New York Academy of Sciences,* New York Academy of Sciences, series 2, volume 33, no 8, New York, December, 1971. In this article he explains the matter of the Planck lengths and the structure of space and space-time and topology.)

In other words, a point of individual consciousness down at these levels can move from one domain to another; there is no determinacy as to where that point of consciousness is going. There is no certainty as to what universe that point of consciousness will enter. At these small sizes, space itself is indeterminate; one can move through galaxies, through universes, by going to this size and even move with far greater speed than the velocity of light. In other words, *at these levels there seem to be doorways into other universes, doorways of very, very small size, but nonetheless, doorways.*

When one is traveling with the Brownian operator and with topquantese one is a very, very small operator. One is a subquantum operator, if you wish, subquantum in the sense of material matter, not subquantum in the terms of consciousness. One is still a full quantum of consciousness in the point. Thus what we are doing here is specifying the quantum of consciousness that is minimal for a human operator.

Human is hardly the term for this; I don't like the word sub-human—that has connotations that I want to avoid. This quantum of consciousness is of such incredibly small size that we can call it "the indeterminate–determinate consciousness operator." This is the infinitesimal (in the "infinitesimal calculus" sense) of consciousness. This is the minimum size for consciousness in order to travel between universes. If consciousness-without-an-object of Merrell-Wolff* has a granular structure, this is it. This means that consciousness in this universe and in others, travels with high velocities at this particular level of size. There is apparently a network of instantaneous transmission for consciousness at this particular level at these very small sizes.

It is almost inconceivable to realize that that particular speck of consciousness carries with it all of the knowledge stored in the vehicle back on earth. This theory calls for access to the knowledge of the vehicle on the part of this infinitesimal operator.

Of course one can also assume that all of this takes place inside the vehicle and that these are "as ifs." These are simulations attempting to explain what happens to one's self under such "concussed" circumstances. I will not argue this. To an outside medical observer this is a very reasonable explanation; however, to the inside observer participating in these experiences, this explanation is totally inadequate in the sense that one had no knowledge whatsoever of the vehicle except that it was in some distant place and one was trying to get back to it at certain times. At other times, one was not trying to get back, and was obviously somewhere out there "enjoying" the experiences in a state of High Indifference. My pact with the teachers or the guides (to come back to Toni and live a quiet life on this planet) could be interpreted as the survival mechanisms of my particular vehicle wanting to come back to a consciousness with which it was acquainted and content.

My closest friends were puzzled because I was unable to tell them what was happening. I was reluctant to tell anyone what was happening because of my knowledge of the way such people are treated on this planet when they are in these states.

As soon as possible, I got myself released from the hospital, went home with a male nurse and set up a wheelchair in my

---

* Merrell-Wolff, *The Philosophy of Consciousness Without an Object.*

living room in which I sat day and night for several days. Finally I rented a hospital bed. I sat at a forty-five degree incline on this bed day and night for several weeks. I gradually learned to walk again; I gradually learned to go to the bathroom again; and with the help of the nurse, I was able to bathe.

Gradually I came back into a normally functioning life on this planet. I am still not back one hundred percent. I still have a problem with my right shoulder. It will be many months before there is normal function reestablished; it will be many months if not years before the bones are back to their normal length, size and shape.

I have been through the most prolonged and intense pain that I have ever experienced in my whole life. I feel that I have paid the price for what I call "the year of Samadhi," for the year I spent previously, giving little attention to the external reality (see Chapter Eighteen).

Somehow the universe seems to take the integral of one's life. If one moves too far in one direction, one must then compensate by moving too far in the opposite direction for a time in order that one achieve a final average balance, which is humanly possible. In other words, for the year of Samadhi where I gave up my voluntary participation in our culture, and took on an inner set of realities to the exclusion of the external realities, I had to pay by giving attention for an equal period of time to the vehicle and its requirements. The total balance over a two-year period looks as if there is some process by which compensatory adjustments are made and a final steady state achieved in spite of the very large transients to which one has been exposed.

As Toni says "Life is a balance game." Here I am attempting to make more quantitative and more precise her statement. One knows intuitively that she is correct, but I wish to render more conscious the actual factors involved in "the balance game." One of my moves lasted a year, the year of Samadhi. So the compensatory movement to achieve a balance requires another year—of recovery, of healing, of being helped and of being restored to somewhat one's former self or possibly beyond what one's former self was.

In other words, to successfully navigate a human vehicle, one must be aware of the balancing net effect over all of one's lifetime. The universe will not allow that vehicle to deviate too far in any one direction without putting in a correction in the other direction and thus achieving balance. A lot of the balancing factors are built into our social structure as such. One is forced to achieve balance by certain means available within our culture: medical means, legal means, political means, personal hygiene means and so forth.

I hope to do a more thorough job on the analysis of the Decker Canyon accident in a future book. Currently I am keeping the description within the confines of this book, written with Toni.

Chapter Thirteen

The Search for Reality

Starting very young (seven years and younger) up through the present, I have been concerned with the problem (usually enunciated as a question): *What Is Reality?* Almost as soon as I could read, I pursued the writings of Immanuel Kant, Sir James Jeans, Bishop George Berkeley and any other authors I could find who had something to say about Reality. As I mentioned earlier, I wrote my first article on the subject at age sixteen years ("Reality," published in 1931, and reproduced in full in Appendix One, pp. 199–201, *Simulations of God: The Science of Belief*.)

By 1931 I realized ("made real") an intuitive feeling, which I articulated at that time, that reality has a dual aspect, an outer ("objective") and an inner ("subjective") aspect. I quote:

> Today reality may be said (in its less involved meanings) to possess the same attributes as the original meaning of [the Latin word] *res* ["a lawcourt"]. First it expresses that which is completely objective as opposed to anything subjective. By objective we mean existing without the mind, outside it, and wholly in-

dependent of it. Subjective, on the other hand, takes the meaning of that which is in the mind. . . .

How can the mind render itself sufficiently objective to study itself? In other words, how are we able to use the mind to ponder on the mind? It is perfectly feasible for the intellect to grasp the fact that *the physiological changes of the brain occur simultaneously with thought, but it cannot conceive of the connection between its own thoughts and these changes* [italics inserted]. The difficulties of the precise relation between the two have caused many controversies as to which is the more real, the objective or the subjective reality."

I then quoted Bishop Berkeley's dictum that there is no existence without the mind, either in ours and/or in "the mind of some Eternal Spirit." This article guided my search for answers. I am still in the search, forty-four years later.

From Kant's *Critique of Pure Reason*, I began to understand that word, language, logic and mathematical descriptions were not adequate expressers of either the inner or outer aspects of reality. Somehow, all *descriptions of reality* were sterile: they tended to play word games, to cleverly juggle with ideas in intricate patterns as if meaningful. My search for the answer to the question *"What Is Reality?"* continued in the study of mathematics, of logics, of semantics ("metalanguages," for example). I found them, each in turn, sterile in the deeper search and helpful in widening my representational capacities, my abilities to see relations internally in myself, my own mind. I was not satisfied that skill in manipulating concepts, no matter how precise, no matter how inclusive, could answer my question.

Consequently, I went into the experimental sciences. I pursued experimental (and theoretical) physics. Cosmogony (the study of the origins of the cosmos, the universe) raised her lovely head: for a time I was entranced ("in trance") with her seductions (astrophysics, astronomy, etcetera). The study of submicroscopic realms of matter seduced me (quantum mechanics) as did the study of known physical energy (light, photons, thermodynamics, etcetera).

Finally I realized that the study of my own brain and its "contained-restrained" mind was needed in this lifelong search.

I took a new direction into new domains: I turned to my program for the search, given above in "Reality": "*The physiological changes of the brain occur simultaneously with thought, but it cannot conceive of the connection between its own thoughts and these changes.*" How can one make these connections? How can one record in objective records (1) these changes in the brain and (2) the corresponding thoughts and their fast changes?

As a dedicated young experimental scientist, I saw, in a course in neurophysiology at Cal Tech in 1937, a possible means of recording "the physiological changes of the brain." I inquired of Dr. van Hareveld how to do this desired recording. He gave me Lord Edgar Adrian's paper "The Spread of Electrical Activity in the Cerebral Cortex." I read it and determined to devise a better method of recording the electrical activity. I wanted a more complete picture (recorded, of course!) of the electrical activity throughout the brain, not just in small areas of the cortex. I also needed to learn more of the mind in the brain (its thoughts, their changes, their "sources and sinks") in order to find/devise/create a method of recording them in parallel simultaneously with the changes in the brain. In short, I was seeking methods of objective fast recording of the activities of the brain, and, simultaneously, objective fast recording of the activities of the mind in that brain.

In this search I went into medical school, seeking more knowledge of these two domains of parallel process. (At Cal Tech, Henry Borsook (M.D., Ph.D.), professor of biochemistry, said to the young seeker: "All of the current knowledge you are looking for is in medical school: you will need that medical degree to be free to search further. A Ph.D. degree is not sufficient.")

In medical school, I continued the search, in neuroanatomy, neurology, neurosurgery, psychiatry. I found more data but no new methods. I saw the limitations of the methods used: spoken and written language and questions (in the mind domain), EEG and fast electrical recordings (in the brain domain). *Literally, there was no method (yet) of recording the mind activities and the brain activities simultaneously.* I also learned that most medical researchers did not feel that there was any hope of ever accomplishing this difficult task.

Upon graduation from medical school, the search was interrupted by a period of devising means of measuring fast physiological changes in high altitude aircraft personnel: oxygen and nitrogen in the gas breathed, in explosive decompression, in conditions of anoxia and bends. I learned about states of my own mind engendered by too-low oxygen in the brain, about states of my mind in the excruciating pain of decompression sickness (bends), and states of my mind excited by fear during explosive decompression of a pressure cabin. My knowledge increased, but I felt diverted from the search.

Soon after the war, the search resumed. I devised new methods of recording the electrical activity of the brain in many places simultaneously, recorded and reproduced on a two-dimensional array.* I worked out new safer ways of placing small electrodes within the brain.† This work lasted eleven years and was terminated when I realized that, as yet, there is no way of picking up/recording the activities of the brain without injuring/altering the structure of the brain itself, and changing the capacities of its contained mind.

Also soon after the war, in my "spare time," I pursued the study and development of the mind, my own. I studied semantics, logic, mathematics, means of modeling the brain's and the mind's activities. Warren McCulloch and Heinz Von Foerster were working in the area of representation of the brain's activities and I studied their work. For the mind studies, I needed more "raw data." I pursued psychoanalysis in depth—I found a psychoanalyst's psychoanalyst: Robert Waelder, who had a Ph.D. (Vienna) in physics and was trained with Anna and Sigmund Freud in Vienna, Austria. I worked with Dr. Waelder for three years, five to seven days a week, one hour a day. I found

* "A Method of Recording the Moving Electrical Potential Gradients in the Brain: the 25-Channel Bavatron (brain activity visualization device) and Electro-Iconograms (electrical image records)," Institute of Electrical Engineers, 1949.

† John C. Lilly, "Electrode and Cannulae Implantation in the Brain by a Simple Percutaneous Method," *Science*, May 16, 1958, vol. 127, no. 3307, pp. 1181–1182.

much that was pertinent to the search: the question "What *Is* Reality?" was researched within my mind intensively.

I confirmed (as I had earlier suspected) that wholly complex domains of thought/feeling/doing/memory below my levels of awareness acted so as to program my current beliefs about "what is real." Inner reality had its own laws, distinct from (and many times counter to) the laws of outer reality. I struggled with the theories—belief systems—of others in regard to inner reality. I revised my own belief systems in regard to my own inner reality ("realities" would now be more accurate: "the inner reality" of 1931 had acquired a plural label "inner realities"). With Waelder's help and quiet acceptance, I was able to enter new inner domains of feeling/thinking/emoting, emerge, and represent the experiences verbally-vocally in writing. My modeling of inner reality became more open: my respect for the Unknown in my own mind increased greatly. I realized, finally, that the depths of mind are as great as the depths of cosmic outer space. There are inner universes as well as outer ones. My concept of metabeliefs (beliefs about beliefs) as the limiting beliefs restraining-confining-limiting the processes-operations of my mind originated in the work with Robert Waelder.

In parallel with the brain-activity studies, the mind studies continued with the solitude-isolation-tank work and its origins at the National Institute of Mental Health (1954). Why is isolation necessary for the study of mind? My reasoning was founded on a basic tenet of certain experimental sciences (physics, biology, etcetera): in order to adequately study a system, all known influences to and from that system must either be attenuated below threshold for excitation, reliably accounted for, or eliminated to avoid *unplanned disturbances* of that system. Disturbances from unknown sources may then be found and dealt with more adequately.

Using this injunction from experimental science, I decided to isolate my body-brain-mind, insofar as this is currently possible (without damage-"trance"-chemicals) in the external reality. I saw that to study my own mind, it must be isolated from all *known* "sources" of stimulation and from "sinks" of reaction, in the here-and-now external reality. I devised the isolation tank

method for the study of my own mind, an isolated mind studying its own processes, free of feedback with the external world.
Quite quickly I found this method gave a new source of data of
great richness.

During such studies over the last twenty-one years (1954–
1975) I have found that which began to open during the years
with Robert Waelder: a newness, a uniqueness, a penetration
deep into new (for me) domains of the mind. (Some of these
experiences and domains are recounted in limited-by-consensus-
articles-books-lectures: see republished papers in appendixes to
Simulations of God: The Science of Belief, and References and
Categorized Bibliography in *Programming and Metaprogramming in the Human Biocomputer*, and in Recommended Reading
in *The Center of the Cyclone*, and other portions of *The Dyadic
Cyclone*.)

The limitations placed upon communication of these new
domains of the mind to other minds were also found: once one
has been deep in one's deeper and deeper self (it deepens at
every exposure to isolation), one's ability to transmit the data
must also be increased. I found that most (not all) other minds
are not prepared to hear-understand-grasp what it means to
explore-experiment-be-immersed-in such researches. Certain
domains of the mind, certain states of being, certain states of
one's own consciousness, are so foreign-alien-weird-strange-un-
familiar to most other minds that they cannot listen or read
what one says or writes without becoming upset, or without
using ready labels for the explorer, relegating one's efforts to
communicate as being either negative or null and void.

I have found a few others who do not do this. I hesitate to
give their names here; they, in turn, do not want, nor are they
yet ready to want, to face the onerous burden of open communication in an unreceptive, possibly hostile or coercive consensus
world. Among these others are those who went too far: the
consensus world of the (numerically superior) persons who fear
these domains exerted powerful external reality means to reduce
the communication of those they fear to near zero.

Over the years of this search, I have carried out several experiments in public communication about these domains of the

mind. I experimented with means of reaching those who in the privacy of their own minds, were in or entering into new domains. I wrote books, gave workshops, lectured—in this experimental mode. I openly pushed my own accounts to dangerously unaccepted edges of credibility. I purposely held back accounts that in my judgment and/or my publisher's judgment would break the consensus thread of communication, with possible disastrous results for me.

Many of my former colleagues disavowed me and my researches: I understand their belief systems and the power such systems have over our minds. I do not recriminate them, nor do I blame former friends for not maintaining contact with me. In my search (for "What Is Reality?"), I have driven myself (and hence, close associates-relatives-friends) to the brink of the loss of all communicational contacts for months at a time, by means totally alien to the previously accepted belief systems (what is appropriate?) in our culture. I have explored and have voluntarily entered into domains forbidden by a large fraction of those in our culture who are not curious, are not explorative and are not mentally equipped to enter these domains.

I find rebels quite disturbing to research unless restrained, disciplined and limited in their actions to effective realms; consensus external reality furnishes a platform for exploration, as long as it is stable enough for the researches. Such research as I have done/do has required, over the years, stability in support (financial, emotional, intellectual, political) or I could not do the work required. There have been numerous difficulties in maintaining the necessary support, but no insurmountable difficulties, yet. So far, there has been a peculiar concatenation of the right events to support one or another aspect of the search. A person, here or there, suddenly comes over the horizon of my mind to facilitate either the new ideas, the new money, the new emotional-intellectual-environment, or the new political means needed for the continuance of the work. Somehow, at times by apparently mysterious means, the social consensus reality provides that which is needed at the right time. For this support I am profoundly thankful and grateful.

My own mind provides its own difficulties in this search:

there are times in which I feel the search must stop; it is too much to ask of my biology as a human; it is too much to ask of my functioning as a social being in the world of humankind with its neglected suffering millions of humans. I take time for the search away from other activities. It may be that I should not continue the search and should turn to politics, to more direct expressions of helping others to help one another. This dilemma has always been a distraction, a seduction enticing me away from the search as I now know it. Over these years of work I have sidestepped, or once in it, I have desisted from, leading/participating/belonging to various groups in a responsible position: scientific societies of many sorts, local town/city politics, fraternities, and even dedicated family life. Because of the search for the bases of reality, I minimized participation in the social reality, limited it, insofar as this was possible, to communication of the results of the search.

In the search there have been many times of great joy, of breakthroughs into new domains, of a new grasp of the previously ungraspable. Internally, in the privacy of my own mind, thus far, I feel infinitely rewarded by the results.

My life has been lived continuously in the search. At times my efforts have been hidden: I could not expose the experiments being done to the gaze of others without irreversibly altering the experimental conditions and thus changing the results because of the changed conditions. Today as yet, I cannot discuss certain experiments I have done: many are, of necessity, still hidden. Even the facts of my own motivations ("What Is Reality?") given in this chapter will change the current experiments. Thus it is in the huge feedback system of which each of us is a very small part.

Many others (in one way or another) have pursued this search for reality and its representations. I owe many debts to those who cleared some of the jungles of beliefs, who removed accumulated layers of nonsense before I started digging. (As an aside, I feel somewhat like the sparrows I watched in Minnesota as a boy: unerringly each sparrow found the undigested edible single kernels of grain in the drying manure. If only it were so easy for us to find the viable kernels of true knowledge in the masses of nonsense given us in books, in the media, in political speeches, in ourselves by ourselves!)

Some searchers end their books (and apparently their search) with pessimistic statements. I give one example of a foremost thinker, Ludwig Wittgenstein:*

> "6.522: There are, indeed, things that [a] cannot be put into words. They *make themselves manifest* [b]. They are what is mystical."

I added [a] and [b]. For [a] substitute the words "as yet." For [b] add the words "by other means." This transforms these two statements of Wittgenstein into the explorer's domain. Substitute for his third statement the following:

> "They are now what is in the Unknown yet to be found."

Thus do I operate: if I see premature closing off of possibilities, as if something is impossible ("mystical"), I paraphrase, reorient the statements, so as to continue my own metabelief: *The province of the mind has no limits; its own contained beliefs set limits that can be transcended by suitable metabeliefs (like this one).*

Returning to the *Tractatus*, one finds an oft-quoted statement:

> "7. Whereof one cannot speak [c], thereof one must be silent."

> "(*Wovon man nicht sprechen kann, darüber muss man schweigen.*)"

In the inserted position [c], I add the words "as yet," transforming the statement into an opening injunction, rather than, as it is given by Wittgenstein, an absolute closure by this injunction of a system of thought.

Of that which we cannot yet speak, we remain silent until a new experience or way of expression allows us to speak. (Radio waves in 1700 A.D. were silent.)

* Wittgenstein, Ludwig, *Tractatus Logico-Philosophicus*, p. 151.

G. Spencer Brown shows (in *The Laws of Form*, pp. 77–78) that Wittgenstein probably was referring to descriptive language rather than injunctive (instructional) language. Injunctive language (in its far-reaching uses) instructs on how to do-make-create something in the inner reality and/or in the external reality. Wittgenstein did not have either later neurophysiological knowledge nor the later knowledge of computers, each of which directly opens the domains expressible in new languages (of the descriptive and injunctive types). Experimental science somehow seems to topple previously expressed absolutes about reality, about meaning, about language, about perception, about cognition, about creating descriptions of minds with limits, specified by the constructor-descriptor. The limits defined are only in the description used, in the simulations of the mind doing the describing.

Realization of the lack of any limits in the mind is not easy to acquire. The domains of direct experience of infinities within greater infinities of experience are sometimes frightening, sometimes "awe-full," sometimes "bliss-full." I quote from a writer who feels this lack of mind limits in his own experiences (Franklin Merrell-Wolff, *The Philosophy of Consciousness Without an Object: Reflections on the Nature of Transcendental Consciousness*, pp. 38–39):

> 1. The first discernible effect in consciousness was something that I may call a *shift in the base of consciousness*. From the relative point of view, the final step may be likened to a leap into Nothing. At once, that Nothing was resolved into utter Fullness, which in turn gave the relative world a dreamlike quality of unreality. I felt and knew myself to have arrived, at last, at the Real. I was not dissipated in a sort of spatial emptiness, but on the contrary was spread out in a Fullness beyond measure. The roots of my consciousness, which prior to this moment had been (seemingly) more or less deeply implanted in the field of relative consciousness, now were forcibly removed and instantaneously transplanted into a supernal region. This sense of being thus transplanted has continued to the present day, and it seems to be a much more normal state of emplacement than ever the old rooting had been.

2. Closely related to the foregoing is a *transformation in the meaning of the "Self," or "I."* Previously, pure subjectivity had seemed to me to be like a zero or vanishing point, a "somewhat" that had position in consciousness but no body. So long as that which man calls his "Self" had body, it stood within the range of analytic observation. Stripping off the sheaths of this body until none is left is the function of the discriminative technique in meditation. At the end there remains that which is never an object and yet is the foundation upon which all relative consciousness is strung like beads upon a string. As a symbol to represent this ultimate and irreducible subject to all consciousness, the "I" element, I know nothing better than zero or an evanescent point. The critical stage in the transformation is the realization of the "I" as zero. But, at once, that "I" spreads out into an unlimited "thickness." It is as though the "I" became the whole of space. The Self is no longer a pole or focal point, but it sweeps outward, everywhere, in a sort of unpolarized consciousness, which is at once Self-identity and the objective content of consciousness. It is an unequivocal transcendence of the subject–object relationship. Herein lies the rationale of the inevitable ineffability of mystical insight. All language is grounded in the subject–object relationship, and so, at best, can only misrepresent transcendent consciousness when an effort is made to express its immediately given value.

I change his last statement by means present in his own writings into, once again, a transforming injunction: "That language (not 'all language') grounded in the subject–object relationship, misrepresents transcendent consciousness when, in that language, an effort is made to express the immediately given value (of transcendent consciousness)."

G. Spencer Brown's doorway* out of this dilemma is the development of an injunctive language that gives instructions (suitable to the listener-reader-experiencer) on how to evoke-enter-create transcendent consciousness in one's Self.

I have found Merrell-Wolff's own writings on his own experience to have injunctive qualities for me, for changing my "subject–object" consciousness into the new domains that he so beautifully expresses.

* G. Spencer Brown, *The Laws of Form*, p. 78.

The distinction between descriptive language and injunctive language disappears in the domains of inner experience (and probably in the domain of external experience also) as follows:

A mind isolated from all known stimuli-reaction probabilities (in a state of being with attenuated or missing feedback with the outer reality) for a long enough time, frequently enough, enters new (for that mind) domains. Once that mind has the experience of entering-creating new domains, it has self-referential programs-beliefs-metabeliefs that can be used (at some future times) to transform its own state of being into further new domains. (One learns rules of exploring new domains under the special conditions.)

To achieve this new level of learning-to-learn, one sets aside previous limits set upon domain exploration: one drops irrelevant beliefs about inner/outer realities previously stored; one examines beliefs-about-beliefs (metabeliefs), especially those about "the limits of the human mind." One drops the usual self-limiting languages (useful in dealing with other persons not so equipped) found in the external reality. One gives up entrancement-seduction by "systems of thought," by other persons, by successes-failures in the consensus realities of others linked to one's self and of one's self in those realities.

However, without the disciplines outlined above and without experience of solitude-isolation-confinement in the external world, these considerations may be meaningless. Once one has been immersed long enough in the above, description of new domains by others now become injunctive to one's Self. Their descriptions invoke–evoke new domains in Self, in one's own mind.

Thus can language instruct one to move into new states of being, new domains of experience.

Of particular interest to me are the domains represented by the mathematical concepts of: *zero* (the origin at which numbers and variables cease having any value); *infinity* (the non-terminus approaching which numbers and variables assume values that cannot yet be represented); *the point* (the smallest possible value of any number or of any variable that approaches, but does not reach, zero); various *differential operators* (∇^2-0, for example), which can move through their defined domains free of constraints by the domain in/upon which they operate.

Of particular interest is the *relation of identity*, one variable to another, in the consciously functioning domain. Assuming one's conscious Self to have a "size" in a certain domain (say equivalent to that of a human brain in the external reality domain), one *identifies* one's Self with that "size." Start cutting down that "size" until one is a point: in any domain, a point is not zero. *Identify* one's whole Self with a point. This kind of point has consciousness, memory, the complete knowledge of the individual Self. It can remain a fixed point in a defined domain, a moving point in the same domain, or a point in *any domain*. Such a point has no mass, no charge, no spin, no gravitational constant and, hence, is free to move in any physical field.

And so on and on—for identities of Self with differential operators, with infinities, with zero. Identify self with a differential operator that can move through a field unconstrained by the presence of the field. Assume that oneself is infinite, what is the experience? Assume that oneself is zero, what is the experience? The reader is left with these exercises to perform on/in himself/herself.

I would like to end this discussion with a quotation from a researcher who investigates the bases of reality—G. Spencer Brown:*

> Unfortunately we find systems of education today that have departed so far from the plain truth, that they now teach us to be proud of what we know and ashamed of ignorance. This is doubly corrupt. It is corrupt not only because pride is in itself a mortal sin, but also because to teach pride in knowledge is to put up an effective barrier against any advance upon what is already known, since it makes one ashamed to look beyond the bonds imposed by one's ignorance.
>
> To any person prepared to enter with respect into the realm of his great and universal ignorance, the secrets of being will eventually unfold, and they will do so in a measure according to

* G. Spencer Brown, *The Laws of Form*, p. 110.

his freedom from natural and indoctrinated shame in his respect of their revelation.

To arrive at the simplest truth, as Newton knew and practised, requires *years of contemplation.* Not activity. Not reasoning. Not calculating. Not busy behaviour of any kind. Not reading. Not talking. Not making an effort. Not thinking. Simply *bearing in mind* what it is one needs to know. And yet those with the courage to tread this path to real discovery are not only offered practically no guidance on how to do so, they are actively discouraged and have to set about it in secret, pretending meanwhile to be diligently engaged in the frantic diversions and to conform with the deadening personal opinions which are being continually thrust upon them.

In these circumstances, the discoveries that any person is able to undertake represent the places where, in the face of induced psychosis, he has, by his own faltering and unaided efforts, returned to sanity. Painfully, and even dangerously, maybe. But nonetheless returned, however furtively.

Chapter Fourteen

Esalen Institute and the AUM Conference

As is recounted in *The Center of the Cylone,* I spent two years, 1969 to 1971, at Esalen Institute in Big Sur. Among a fair number of people in the United States, Esalen has a certain kind of reputation. It apparently was the origin of encounter group work with William Schutz and of the Gestalt psychology type of therapy under Fritz Perls. As is recounted in *The Center of the Cyclone,* the Esalen Institute hot baths were one of the main attractions at the location in Big Sur. These were natural hot springs in the cliffs above the Pacific, used by the Indians for many years before Michael Murphy's grandfather bought the property in 1910, before California Highway One was put through. In 1938, Highway One was constructed and it went by this property between the Pacific on the west and the Santa Lucia mountains on the east. A motel was then constructed and over the years the motel grew, using the hot baths as its main attraction.

Mike Murphy and Dick Price, the founders of Esalen, met in a course on Asiatic studies at Stanford University. Mike Murphy then went to India and spent eighteen months at the Sri Aurobindo Ashram in Pondicherry, working with the cosmic

Mother. The life in the ashram was active with physical sports, physical exercises and yogic techniques being taught to the students. After Mike returned, he and Dick made an arrangement with his family and they started the Esalen Institute. Everyone concerned had to pitch in and help. Dick and Mike were washing dishes, gardening and so forth in the early days of the Institute.

As time went on, they became better known. The catalog expanded over the last twelve years; the influence of Esalen on the established community become prominent. As a consequence, well over a hundred copies of Esalen were set up around the United States and called "human potential movement growth centers."

I arrived at Esalen in 1969, and like many people before me, had my personality rescued for the use of my body, brain and mind to become a more integrated individual. I started my Esalen experience at a nude weekend conducted by Bill Schutz. He talked sixty people (including me) out of their clothes within fifteen minutes.

Dick Price laid out my schedule, and for the next six weeks I went through various samples of the main tent and sideshows at Esalen. I took the hurdle of the nude baths by the sea, saw a dolphin in the ocean and watched whales go by; I saw the sea otters swimming at the surface, on their backs, with their prey of clams to be pounded open against their chests. As was detailed in *The Center of the Cyclone*, I had left the confines of a laboratory and tropical existence where I had been working with dolphins and doing research on the problems of communication with humans and dolphins.

While I was at Esalen, the first seeds of the AUM Conference were planted when in 1969 Stewart Brand of *The Whole Earth Catalog* gave me G. Spencer Brown's book *The Laws of Form.* Stewart asked me to do a review for the catalog. I read it and immediately realized that I knew only one person in the United States, possibly in the world, who was capable of reviewing this book, justly and in depth. I suggested that he send the book to Heinz Von Foerster, who is Director of the Biological Computer Lab at the University of Illinois. Heinz is preeminent among the world's cyberneticists and computer logicians. He grew up in

Austria where, as Ludwig Wittgenstein's nephew, he had early exposure to the ideas and philosophy that Brown has further developed. Heinz's review and commentary (reproduced at the end of this chapter) on *The Laws of Form* appears in *The Last Whole Earth Catalog* and provides a doorway into Brown's work.

In the following years I continued to read *The Laws of Form* and, at odd times, tried to master it . . . with little success. I referred it to Alan Watts, who read it with such excitement that he quickly traveled to England to meet and talk with G. Spencer Brown. When Alan got back he suggested that we organize a conference on *The Laws of Form*. The purpose was to expose the works of G. Spencer Brown to leading thinkers in America in the hopes that the implications of the work could be discussed and explored from many different points of view. We wanted a number of people to meet Brown, and also felt that the exposure to his peers in America would be useful and stimulating to him.

As part of a larger generalization, Alan suggested that the conference be the initial grouping of the "American University of Masters" (AUM). He purposely chose the acronym AUM as the Sanskrit mantra form (commonly miscalled OM) meaning the Universe and the highest beings of that Universe. He felt the Western yogi could learn from the Eastern one, and vice versa. We planned to make the AUM into an ongoing ad hoc institution. Sadly, these plans have been stalled (at least temporarily) by Alan's sudden death. The organization, ephemeral as it might have been, proved to be a vital and invigorating experience in our lives.

He and I wrote to G. Spencer Brown. After several telephone calls, Brown agreed to come for forty-eight hours from London. Toni and I picked him up at the San Francisco airport in our motor home. For the three-hour drive to Big Sur he rested in bed in the back. It was impressive that in the midst of jet lag and with very little rest, he was quite ready to present his new calculus to his American colleagues.

For two solid days of approximately six hours a day he gave polished performances, the like of which I have rarely seen. He not only went through some of the bases of *The Laws of Form*, but also went through his ideas on the five levels of eternity as given in footnote number one of his book *Only Two Can Play This Game*, under the pseudonym James Keys.

After his departure, the other participants each lectured on the work. Heinz Von Foerster summarized the conference in his own unique way.

In his summary Heinz recapitulated some of the philosophical marvels in *The Laws of Form*, and ended with another piece of magical logic and biological significance by showing that Spencer Brown's logical operation of the "Cross" is constructed so as to miraculously recreate itself when operating on the "Void." Finally, however, Heinz drew our attention to a most touching relation between G. Spencer Brown and two other men who all are tied to one another by a state of melancholy that befalls those who know that they know. These men are Ludwig Wittgenstein and Carlos Castaneda's teacher, don Juan. To see this relation and to feel this melancholy, one should remember the last words of *The Laws of Form*. After G. Spencer Brown went through the incredible tour de force that Bertrand Russell called "a new Calculus of great power and simplicity," Spencer Brown ends his book by saying: "Thus we see that our journey was in its preconception unnecessary although its formal course once we had set out upon it was inevitable." This sounds so much like Ludwig Wittgenstein in his *Tractatus Logico-Philosophicus*. The famous last proposition is a resignation; it reads: "Whereof one cannot speak, thereof one must be silent."

To close the circle, Heinz now read us from a few of the last paragraphs of Castaneda's *Journey to Ixtlan*. The situation is that don Genaro, don Juan's brujo friend, has just ended his description of what he had left when he entered "the realm of knowledge" with the metaphor of always traveling but never or at best almost reaching Ixtlan. Don Genaro, don Juan and Carlos Castaneda are sitting around in a triangular formation and Castaneda writes:

> For an instant I sensed a wave of agony and an indescribable loneliness engulfing the three of us. I looked at don Genaro and I knew that, being a passionate man, he must have had so many ties of the heart, so many things he cared for and left behind.

I had the clear sensation that at that moment the power of his recollection was about to landslide and that don Genaro was on the verge of weeping.

I hurriedly moved my eyes away. Don Genaro's passion, his supreme loneliness, made me cry.

. . . I gazed at the two of them, each in turn. Their eyes were clear and peaceful. They had summoned a wave of overwhelming nostalgia, and when they seemed to be on the verge of exploding into passionate tears, they held back the tidal wave. For an instant I think I *saw*. I *saw* the loneliness of man as a gigantic wave which had been frozen in front of me, held back by the invisible wall of a metaphor.

I derived from Heinz's summary of the AUM Conference the following explanation behind Brown's little symbol that looks like the inverted, capital L (⌐), which can be used as an operator at the same time as a signal. When one feeds the signal through the operator it generates an endless series of the marked state alternating with the unmarked state. In other words, the operator itself, the cross, the marked state, then the unmarked state (the Void, in other words, a blank space that lies outside any universe), the marked state, etcetera. This series was entitled a "flippety": an automatic oscillator that can be considered the basis of all communication, of all calculation, of all creation. Later, such considerations (after three years of study of *The Laws of Form*) led Francisco Varela, working with Heinz, to develop a three-valued logic: the unmarked state, a self-referential operator, and the marked state.

This new development of Varela, published since the AUM Conference, may eventually be used to solve the dilemma left in me by study of *The Laws of Form* since it was first published. This dilemma was not solved at the Conference, nor in my own work since that time.

All too simply the dilemma is this:

Where is the mathematician and his reader in all this high-powered calculus? Brown, apparently to his own satisfaction, relegates "the observer" as follows (*The Laws of Form*, p. 76):

> We see now that the first distinction, the mark, and the observer are not only interchangeable, but, in the form, identical.

This is the only reference in the main body of the work to "the observer." I ask the question: Who is making the above quoted statement? Is this statement self-referential in regard to its creator? Is the creator equivalent to "the observer," or is there more here than is stated?

Brown says, in a footnote to Chapter Two, *The Laws of Form*, p. 77, that:

> . . . the primary form of mathematical communication is not description, but injunction. In this respect it is comparable with practical art forms like cookery, in which the taste of a cake, although literally indescribable, can be conveyed to the reader in the form of a set of injunctions called a recipe . . . a set of commands, which if obeyed by the reader can result in a re-production, to the reader of the [writer's] original experience.

My dilemma then arises anew: *The Laws of Form*, as written (as an injunctive set) postulates the creator, his injunctions, the reader, the creator's experience and its reproduction in the reader.

Brown goes on (p. 77, continued) mentioning the same proposition quoted by Heinz above:

> Where Wittgenstein says (proposition 7, of *Tractatus Logico-Philosophicus*)
>
>> Whereof one cannot speak,
>> thereof one must be silent.
>> (*Wovon man nicht sprechen kann,
>> darüber muss man schweigen.* (p. 150 of *Tractatus*)
>
> he seems to be considering descriptive speech only. He notes elsewhere that the mathematician, descriptively speaking, says nothing.

I include my own, bracketed, interpolations within Brown's next statements:

> The same may be said of the [cook], who, if he were to attempt *a description* (i.e., a limitation) of the set of [taste] ecstasies apparent *through* (i.e., unlimited by) his [*recipe*] would fail miserably and necessarily. But neither the [cook] nor the mathematician must, for this reason, remain silent.

Bertrand Russell, in his introduction to *Tractatus*, expressed "what thus seems a justifiable doubt in respect of the rightness of Wittgenstein's last proposition [number 7]," when he says (p. xxi):

> What causes hesitation is . . . Mr. Wittgenstein manages to say a good deal about what cannot be said, thus suggesting to the sceptical reader that possibly there may be a loophole through a hierarchy of language, or by some other exit.

The exit, as we have seen it here, is evident in the injunctive faculty of language.

This is a long tortuous road to understanding, necessarily complex for completion of a domain of discourse. Russell is suggesting that there is a loophole that is not present in Mr. Wittgenstein's explicit directions. He is looking for an exit. Brown maintains that the exit is in the external injunctive use of language beyond the internal injunctive use of language in Wittgenstein's system. Brown is attempting to open up this philosophical problem of the closure of Wittgenstein's system so that it extends further than merely the descriptive use of language as Russell makes clear. In my own work, I have enunciated the following format (cf *The Mind of the Dolphin; The Human Biocomputer; Simulations of God: The Science of Belief*):

1) *Communication* is the process of inviting another mind to participate in constructing a set of instructions for the construction of a simulation, of a model, of: how to think, and/or to build, and/or to feel, and/or to do an externally real new object, another simulation, a state of being, a state of one's central processes, a model of communication itself, a new language, a new calculus, or whatever.

2) *Information* exists exclusively in a mind in a central nervous system (C.N.S.).

3) *Signals* (including verbal, nonverbal, and unknown) exist outside the mind and transfer information from a mind-C.N.S. through the body, through the external reality to another body-C.N.S.-mind.

4) An observer-participant lives within his *program domains* within the central processes of a central nervous system.

5) An observer-participant is limited by his *simulations* within his program domains.

6) The *program domains* of the observer-participant *can be enlarged beyond its current limits by his participation in searching for new simulations not yet in these domains.*

7) The activities within the program domains of the observer-participant, within certain limits (unknown/known), can be self-programmed, and hence can be self-referential.

8) *The observer-participant currently can be considered a property of the program domains:* the satisfactory definition of this "entity" (observer-participant) is yet to be made fully and completely.

9) The observer-participant uses *a set of operations* as follows (regarding any language, any mathematics, any representation regarding his own inner reality ["inner simulations of inner experience"] and/or/including any representation of his outer reality ["simulations of outer experience"] or any representation lying within his program domain, bridging these "inner–outer" domains):

    a) *A simulation is descriptive-injunctive (not one, but both).*

    b) *A direct experience of newness, of uniqueness* (arising within central processes or from incoming signals or both) *is experienced by the observer-participant through a filter-screen-processing domain beyond his conscious observation-participation capacity:* a very large fraction of perception requires a processing-computation delay in which he cannot participate consciously.

    c) *The observer-participant is always delayed behind the signals generating the computations soon to become "informative" to him.*

    d) *Information is central processing of signals coming in to the C.N.S. and going out from the C.N.S.*

    e) *What appears to be "transfer of information" from one mind to another exists through each simulating the other.*

    f) *Direct experience (inner, outer, inner–outer) cannot be transmitted directly from one mind to another: only*

> *simulations can be analyzed and mutually transformed into appropriate signals for transfer to another participating mind.*

g) In a dyad of two bodies (two separate minds within) only that which is contained in mutually compatible simulations can become appropriate communicative simulations generating appropriate signals and hence "shared" information.

h) *Among all possible sets of simulations, mutual dyadic search can be done so as to develop or find elsewhere appropriate simulations.*

i) Simulations and/or metasimulations are of several types (both in one mind and/or in more than one mind):

  i True
  ii False
  iii "As if True"
  iv "As if False"
  v Meaningless
  vi "As if meaningless"

j) True in the injunctive-descriptive mode expresses a high degree of goodness-of-fit of simulation to direct experience-participation (inner, outer, inner–outer).

k) False (in the same mode) expresses a null or low degree of goodness-of-fit.

l) The "as if" values are used in the construction phase of simulations in evaluating simulations, in the recognition that all simulations are programs in a limited mind. (In the deeper analysis any and all simulations are "as if true/false".)

m) Meaningless is used in regard to simulations that are not useful in the program domain of the observer-participant.

n) "As if meaningless" is used in regard to simulations not yet one's own.

Thus one can see that Wittgenstein's Proposition 7 above ("Whereof one cannot speak, thereof one must be silent") is an injunction to search, in silence, until one has the simulations necessary to emit the information one knows internally to be true—simulations shared with other disciplined minds who either have, can find or create, or can be given the necessary instructions to construct, sufficiently corresponding simulations to receive the new information. (Brown spent several weeks working with Russell to demonstrate *The Laws of Form* as a new calculus.) The ultimate human test of one's simulations is their usefulness in communication with others: the construction of new consensus simulations shared among increasingly greater numbers of minds (hopefully, over the whole planet).

Studies of injunctive-descriptive simulations and their deep basic structure is rewarding in the inner–outer realities. The trend expressed in this conference (and, we hope, in future exchanges) is that disciplined minds hunt for and need more appropriate, more useful, more efficient simulations in every field. Mathematics and logic are the metasimulations that bring increased efficiency of operation to each of our inner program domains. It is less complex and more efficient mentally to understand simulations (and belief systems constructed from them) than it is to defend a belief system as if one's survival depended upon it. Defense-attack based upon belief systems is a meaningless simulation possibly leading, in the present era, to the end of humankind as we know it. The power of words, of language, of beliefs, of simulations can be deadly—especially if unshared and unreal in regard to consensuses separated from one another, growing in isolation with poor or missing communication between them.

Other participants taught *The Laws of Form* as found in the book. Douglas Kelley, a mathematician from Chicago, gave a series of explicative lectures for those who needed it. Gregory Bateson gave his wise advisories in the same region, connecting some of Brown's ideas to his own work in *Steps to an Ecology of Mind*. Gregory, who has had a persisting influence on many of us for years, is just becoming discovered (at age seventy) by the general intelligent reading public. His time seems finally to have arrived; we will all be the richer for it.

John Brockman contributed his usual humor, showing that "there is Nothing in the screen of words," i.e., the Void is inexpressible. The Brockman Void is generated in *Afterwords*, a book in which blankness of page is interspersed with words which undo themselves.

(Baba) Ram Dass gave a warm presentation of his beliefs epitomized in his guru; he said that each of us is his guru; his guru is of universal extent. He said he loved him [us] deeply.

Alan Watts gave many wondrous remarks including one that Toni will never forget . . . "There is no substance, all is form," even as in his version of physics. Part of *The Laws of Form* (page 31, the Primary Algebra, Chapter One) was put to music by Kurt Von Meier and Company toward the end of the conference. The entire AUM proceedings were recorded. We have Brown's part transcribed: it is a clear presentation linking the laws to his "five levels of eternity."

Brown has been running his own publishing company, G. Spencer Brown, Limited, of Cambridge, England. Brown's books have been published in this country by Arthur Ceppos (Julian Press) at Toni's and my recommendation. *The Laws of Form* is now available in paperback (Bantam Books). I recommend the United States edition over the British edition, as it contains a new introduction, which somewhat simplifies one's absorption of "Laws."

Many Esalen people attended the AUM Conference: Bill Schutz, Dick Price and several others. Heinz Von Foerster received a three-hour massage from Jane Milletich, which I am sure he will never forget. The conference, which lasted five days beyond Brown's departure, prospered in the Esalen atmosphere and the California sun. Most of the participants eventually got into the rhythm, taking advantage of the hot baths, massage, etcetera, as well as meals at the lodge.

Toni:

"My first awareness of G. Spencer Brown/'James Keys,' as a person, the man behind the theory presented at the AUM Conference, came in the mail from my old friend Alan Watts.

"John and I had been together for about a year when we received the manuscript *Only Two Can Play This Game*. Brown's work *The Laws of Form* had been given to Alan originally by John. Alan returned from his visit to Brown in England with the new manuscript, which he then sent to us. We were about to fly to New York and we took the manuscript with us.

We read the manuscript together on the plane. I was laughing and crying all the way, much to the distraction of fellow passengers. I loved the mystical, romantic and cosmic humor of the story. I remember asking him if they ever got back together (James Keys and the girl in the story, that is). I don't remember the precise wording, but it never was a yes or no.

I was so moved by the book that as soon as I arrived in New York I went to the home of Arthur and Prue Ceppos, handed it to Arthur, and didn't stop talking for hours about my reaction and why I thought he should publish it. He subsequently read it and agreed for his own reasons that it should be published. I received one of the first copies with the inscription "To the Godmother."

Whatever I have been able to assimilate from *The Laws of Form* has been through people like John and Alan. I understood it intuitively through my own experience. One can relate to "flippety," as he calls it:

—the dichotomy of: should I? shouldn't I?
—the oscillator.
—expansion and contraction.
—the cosmic balance game, or cosmic surfing, as I like to call it.

The last one I've known very well for some time (see end of Chapter Twelve, *The Dyadic Cyclone*).

We were both anxious to meet him after that, and coincidences seemed to line up so that the right amount of density focused on having the conference take place. Hence, the "American University of Masters" was instituted and the big brains came from around the country to hear the ex-Don from Oxford present his *Laws of Form* at Big Sur.

James, as he asked me to call him, is like an exotic rare bird with plumage that I had never seen before. His eccentric behavior has a great deal of style (at least in short doses, to which I've been exposed). I loved his voice. Just listening to his presentation was a privilege. He is in every sense a professional.

I was happy to have the memory of that last gathering with

Alan Watts who died shortly after that. He had such a wonderful time playing host to his peers. Every morning at 6 AM he would ring a gong and awaken everyone for meditation. Most of us meditated in our own way. It was somehow comforting to hear the gong. Every evening, the last sign we would have would be the lonely figure of Alan walking up and down the motel corridor looking for another night bird to share yet another charming story over a glass of wine. At one point he lauded all of us for our patterns of regularity in sleeping and eating.

In a gathering of his peers, as opposed to disciples, Alan was at his lovable best. He so wanted to help James to be more sociable, which of course was not James' style.

Much of the glow of the conference came not from the official program and lectures, but from the interaction among the "Masters" and the interaction between our group and the regular Esalen people.

Here were a group of "super-heads" descending on Esalen, a place where many of the staff members feel that "the body is the temple of the mind." Just as the Esalen people were suspicious and even disdainful of the intellect, so too were the AUM members forgetful that they had something called a body. However, as the conference went along, the ice began to break, discussions sprang forth, the AUM people began drifting down to the baths, signing up for nude massages, and genuinely enjoying themselves in the ambience of Big Sur.

Some of the fondest memories are of the people and what they brought to the conference in the way of style and personality.

Kurt Von Meier, the Master American Shaman, and his musicians put the math to music. We had a concert at the end of the conference. The added dimensions of understanding it with the use of music made the "Glass Bead Game" of Hermann Hesse come to life (as in *Magister Ludi*).

(Baba) Ram Dass was his usual lovable bhakti non-self. He had a wonderful time appearing to resist the academic packaging of this new Western mystical math. We stayed up for hours one evening as mathematician Ted Glynn took a typical Western stance vis-à-vis Ram Dass's Eastern trip. Ram Dass was very argumentative at first, even disconcerted, until all at once, he came forth with a gleaming smile and turned to Ted and thanked him for being his guru.

Gregory Bateson and his lovely wife Lois were there with their beautiful daughter, Nora. Gregory, with his usual dignified English manner, "harumphed" his way through the sessions, quietly assimilating.

Heinz Von Foerster was charming and erudite, as usual. He is a rare combination of Austrian charm accompanied by an amazing ability to make even the most difficult proposition understandable. After Brown left, Heinz gave his dynamic interpretation of what had been presented (see above).

John Brockman's profound humor always makes it possible for me to catch a glimpse of myself turning a corner. Alan Watts, reading from the galleys of the now-published *Afterwords* at breakfast one morning, looked up and laughingly said, "He's like the man who draws a circle on a piece of paper to make a hole, then jumps in through the hole, and then pulls the circle, the paper and *us* in behind him, leaving nothing . . . just the Void."

George Gallagher and his wife Betty helped me to put some of this high-powered math in perspective. George has a beautiful ability to simplify with the use of short, precise analogy.

It was quite a show . . . some of the intellects ("mystics") of our culture all getting together to compare interpretations of a new mathematical theory . . . in the midst of mineral baths, massage and sunshine.

Heinz Von Foerster's review of "The Laws of Form," by G. Spencer Brown, as it appeared in "The Last Whole Earth Catalog," p. 12, Portola Institute, Menlo Park, California 94025.

> The laws of form have finally been written! With a "Spencer Brown" transistorized power razor (a Twentieth Century model of Occam's razor). G. Spencer Brown cuts smoothly through two millennia of growth of the most prolific and persistent of semantic weeds, presenting us with his superbly written *Laws of Form*. This Herculean task which now, in retrospect, is of profound simplicity rests on his discovery of the form of laws. Laws are not descriptions, they are commands, injunctions:

"Do!" Thus, the first constructive proposition in this book (page 3) is the injunction: "Draw a distinction!" an exhortation to perform the primordial creative act.

After this, practically everything else follows smoothly: a rigorous foundation of arithmetic, of algebra, of logic, of a calculus of indications, intentions and desires; a rigorous development of laws of form, may they be of logical relations, of descriptions of the universe by physicists and cosmologists, or of functions of the nervous system which generates descriptions of the universe of which it is itself a part.

The ancient and primary mystery which still puzzled Ludwig Wittgenstein (*Tractatus Logico-Philosophicus*, A. J. Ayer (ed), Humanities Press, New York, 1961, 166 pp.), namely that the world we know is constructed in such a way as to be able to see itself, G. Spencer Brown resolves by a most surprising turn of perception. He shows, once and for all, that the appearance of this mystery is unavoidable. But what is unavoidable is, in one sense, no mystery. The fate of all descriptions is ". . . what is revealed will be concealed, but what is concealed will again be revealed."

At this point, even the most faithful reader may turn suspicious: how can the conception of such a simple injunction as "Draw a distinction!" produce this wealth of insights? It is indeed amazing—but, in fact, it does.

The clue to all this is Spencer Brown's ingenious choice for the notation of an operator ⌐ which does several things at one time. This mark is a token for drawing a distinction, say, by drawing a circle on a sheet of paper which creates a distinction between points inside and outside of this circle; by its asymmetry (the concave side being its inside) it provides the possibility of indication; finally, it stands for an instruction to cross the boundary of the first distinction by crossing from the state indicated on the inside of the token to the state indicated by the token. (A space with no token indicates the unmarked state.) Moreover, these operations may operate on each other, generating a primary arithmetic, an opportunity which is denied us by a faulty notation in conventional arithmetic as pointed out by Karl Menger in "Gulliver in the Land Without One, Two, Three" (*The Mathematical Gazette*, vol. 53, pp. 224–250, 1959).

These operations are defined in the two axioms (no other ones are needed) given on pages 1 and 2. They are:

Axiom 1. The law of calling:

The values of a call made again is the value of the call. That is to say, if a name is called and then is called again, the value indicated by the two calls taken together is the value indicated by one of them. That is to say, for any name, to recall is to call. (In notation: ⌐ ⌐ = ⌐

the "form of condensation.")

Axiom 2. The law of crossing:

The value of a crossing made again is not the value of the crossing. That is to say, if it is intended to cross a boundary and then it is intended to cross it again, the value indicated by the two intentions taken together is the value indicated by none of them.

That is to say, for any boundary, to recross is not to cross. (In notation: ⌐⌐ =

the "form of cancellation.")

For instance, take a complex expression

$E =$ ⌐⌐⌐⌐⌐

Then, by the two axioms

$E =$

In the beginning this calculus is developed for finite expressions only (involving a finite number of ⌐), simply because otherwise any demonstration would take an infinite number of steps, hence would never be accomplished. However, in Chapter 11, Spencer Brown tackles the problem of infinite expressions by allowing an expression to reenter its own space. This calls for trouble, and one anticipates now the emergence of antinomies. Not so! In his notation the classical clash between a simultaneous Nay and Yea never occurs, the system becomes "bi-stable," flipping from one to the other of the two values as a consequence of previous values, and thus generates time! Amongst the many gems in this book, this may turn out to be the shiniest.

Sometimes the reading gets rough because of Spencer Brown's remarkable gift for parsimony of expression. But the 30 pages of "notes" following the 12 Chapters of presentation come to the reader's rescue precisely at that moment when he lost his orientation in the lattice of a complex crystal. Consequently, it is advisable to read them almost in parallel with the text, if one can suppress the urge to keep on reading Notes.

In an introductory note Spencer Brown justifies the mathematical approach he has taken in this book: "Unlike more superficial forms of expertise, mathematics is a way of saying less and less about more and more." If this strategy is pushed to its limit, we shall be able to say nothing about all. This is, of course, the state of ultimate wisdom and provides a nucleus for a calculus of love, where distinctions are suspended and all is one. Spencer Brown has made a major step in this direction, and his book should be in the hands of all young people—no lower age limit required.

Chapter Fifteen

The Dolphins Revisited

In the dyad, we have decided to go back to the dolphin work, examine it very carefully, and do some entirely new work with the dolphins. Dolphins are very exciting to work with. They are playful, curious and develop very close attachments for humans. They are infinitely patient with us. In all of our work with the dolphins no one was badly injured over the thirteen-year period. Most of us in working with them in water received black-and-blue marks or scratches on our skin at one time or another when we pushed the dolphins too far. Their discipline with humans in the water is really amazing. If they do not want you in the water they bang their beaks against your legs just hard enough to move you out of the water. If you insist on coming into the water, they may scratch your skin with their teeth in a very precise controlled fashion. When I remember that a dolphin can bite a six-foot barracuda in two with those teeth I can imagine them biting my leg or my arm in two; however, this never happened in spite of this capacity to do so.

The largest of the dolphins are *Orcinus orca* and are in captivity in large numbers in the United States, Canada and England. At no time have any of these huge dolphins injured the people that swim with them.

This is the most astonishing property of these large brains—their gentleness, forbearance and their care of us. The dolphins we worked with over the thirteen-year period, had brains 20 to 40 percent larger than ours. *Orca* has a brain three times the size of ours. To give you the background, let me give you some of the characteristics of the detailed anatomy of these brains and of the detailed anatomy of their sound communicating and sonar apparatus.

I spent the years from approximately 1955 to 1968 working practically full time with the dolphins. During that period I wrote the books: *Man and Dolphin* and *The Mind of the Dolphin* in addition to *Programming and Metaprogramming in the Human Biocomputer*. Each of these books deals with the problems that humans have in being faced with an alien species with a brain size equal to and larger than the human brain.

Much work has been done upon the brain of the dolphin showing its superb complexity and its detailed structure on a microscopic scale. Prior to the work on the brain done by Dr. Peter Morgane, Dr. Sam Jacobs and Dr. Paul Yakovlev, there were no *preserved* brains of dolphins or whales examined. All of the materials previously investigated had deteriorated owing to postmortem self-digestion.

These early specimens from the last century and the early part of this century had a low cell count owing to the auto-destruction of the cells caused by this rather warm brain lying on the beach or on the deck of a factory ship.

Morgane, Jacobs and Yakovlev developed three dolphin brains that were totally preserved so that every cell was still present. When we looked at these sections, I suddenly realized that these resembled the human brain to the point where the unpracticed eye could not tell the difference between the cortical layers of the human and those of the dolphin. The only significant difference was that the dolphin had a thicker layer number one on the outside of the cortex. From studies of the 11,000 microscopic sections made of these brains, Morgane, Jacobs and Yakovlev have been writing many scientific papers and are currently preparing an atlas of the dolphin brain. The material they have used for this atlas is better than anything that has been done to date on the human brain.

Those results show that the dolphin's cell count is just as high per cubic millimeter as is that of the human. The material also shows that the connectivity—i.e., the number of cells connected to one and other—is the same as is that in the human brain. They have also shown that there are the same number of layers in the cortex of a dolphin as there are in that of a human.

In other words, this brain is as advanced as the human brain on a microscopic structural basis.

They have also shown that the dolphin brain has quite as large "silent areas" as does the human brain. Let me explain.

We have frontal lobes and parietal lobes, the greater part of which are silent, i.e., there are no direct motor outputs or sensory inputs from or to these portions of our brain. It is the silent areas that distinguish us from the chimpanzees and from the gorillas. We have, of course, an anthropoid brain, but it has been enlarged only in the silent areas.

An examination of the brain of *Tursiops truncatus,* the bottle-nose dolphin of the Atlantic, shows that their brain has enlarged over that of the smaller dolphin's brain, purely by an increase in the size of the silent areas, even as we have enlarged silent areas from those of the chimpanzees. Even as our brains, in increasing in size over the chimpanzees' expanded in the silent areas, so did the dolphins as they grew larger brains. (The current smaller dolphins have brains the size of a chimpanzee and are decreased in size in the silent area region over that of the larger dolphins.)

What do the silent areas do? Presumably these are the areas of our brain in which we do our major central processing (computations) as humans. That which we value most as humans (as opposed to smaller-brained animals) is in these silent areas. They are the association areas for speech, vision, hearing and motor integrations and for relating these to all other activities of our bodies.

In all other regions the dolphins are comparable to us with some differences. Their visual system is one-tenth the speed of ours; however, they make up for this in that their sonic and acoustic systems are ten times the speed of ours. This means that the dolphins can absorb through their ears the same amount of information—and at the same speed—that we do with our eyes. We can absorb through our eyes ten times the amount of information that the dolphins can through theirs.

This means that we are dealing with a species that is primarily acoustically oriented. We are primarily visually oriented. Our visual orientation is built into our language so that we, in general, talk as if we were watching and seeing and analyzing what we are talking about as if *seen*.

In contrast, the dolphins "see" with their sound-emitting apparatus and the echoes from the surrounding objects underwater. Remember that half the twenty-four-hour day, during the night, their eyes do not need to function. Remember that they must be able to "see" underwater in the murky depths during the day as well as during the night. They must be able to detect their enemies, the sharks; they must be able to detect the fish that they eat, and they must be able to detect one another in spite of a lack of light; therefore, they have an active processing mechanism for sound that is immensely complex.

Over the years we have examined the sound-emitting apparatus of the dolphins very carefully, both anatomically and physiologically. As is presented in *The Mind of the Dolphin* they have three sonic emitters, two of them (nasal) on their forehead, just below the blowhole, anterior to the brain case. They have their third one in their larynx which crosses their foodway in the nasopharynx.

We put small hydrophones on the sacs in the top of their heads on each side of the blowhole and followed what they could do with these two sonic emitters. It turned out that they have total independent control of these two emitters and that they can whistle on one side while clicking on the other and change over from one to the other. They can also control the phase of what is emitted by controlling the timing of these two emitters. The laryngeal emitter produces extremely short clicks that are used in their "fine structure" sonar. The sound from the larynx is propelled through the head forward in the two rows of teeth, eighty or more, which acts similarly to a "yagi antenna" for transmitting a very narrow band of frequencies, around one hundred and sixty thousand hertz. This dental yagi also works for reception concentrating the return echoes in the same frequency band and thus reducing the noise of the sea and enhancing the signal from these clicks. We measured the tooth structure and the wavelength of the emitted sound. We found that the spacing of the teeth was exactly half a wavelength of the sound being emitted and received. This is a very sophisticated system with which the dolphins cannot only get the distance of objects but they can get the composition of those objects in terms of density. They emit this beam and scan one another's bodies. If one gets into a pool with them, they immediately turn on their sonar and scan one's body. This is one of their forms of recognition for individuals. (They can also recognize one visually under well-lighted circumstances.)

This sonar beam can penetrate one's body, is reflected off one's lungs, the gas in one's gut and the air cavities in one's head. A dolphin looking at one's stomach for example can tell if one is anxious or upset because the stomach tends to churn during anxiety. They can see this churning with the bubble of air that is in the stomach.

To return to the nasal emitters on each side of the blowhole. We examined these very carefully and it turns out that there are two tonguelike muscles that move anteriorly and posteriorly coming up against the edge of what is called the "diagonal membrane." When they wish to click they keep this membrane a little bit relaxed. The muscles for this membrane go down through the nasal passages (through the bone) and can be contracted in such a way as to tense the free edge of this membrane in the air passage. The tongue is then brought back forming a very narrow slit about three-quarters of an inch long through which they blow air into sacs above the membrane and sacs below the membrane. This means that they have the ability to push air back and forth through this narrow slit. We set up a model of this and showed that when the edge is tight, whistling takes place when air is blown between the membrane and the tonguelike muscle. When the edge is more lax, clicks form as air is blown through the slit.

We also showed that they can do stereo effects by controlling the phase on the two sides of the head, which means that they can also polarize the sound so as to distinguish it from the surrounding sea noises.

With such a degree of sophistication of their emitters and an equal sophistication on their receivers, their ears buried inside their head, they can do amazing things with this apparatus.

For example, a dolphin can distinguish the difference between a one-inch diameter, one-sixteenth-inch thick aluminum disc against a concrete wall versus a copper disc of the same dimensions, when this is hidden behind a visually opaque but a sonically transparent screen.

Two dolphins communicating sound like three dolphins. They may face each other and use the laryngeal tight sonar beam for communication when they do not want somebody else to know about their communication. We often found them doing this in our laboratory, and every so often we had the opportunity of having a hydrophone between them and we would then detect the fact that they were doing this. We could not hear it of course, it was too high a frequency for our ears, but we could show it on a cathode-ray oscilloscope and record it on high-frequency tape recorders.

I do not think that dolphins distinguish their sonar from their communication with the nasal emitters. The nasal emitters emit longer wavelength sound than does the laryngeal emitter. This means that they have a 360° solid angle "sonar" in the two emitters near the blowhole as opposed to the tight beam emitter of the larynx. This means that they can detect objects behind, above, below or ahead of them with the nasal emitters, and then with the laryngeal emitters they can turn on any interesting object and examine it in detail.

They do not distinguish between sonaring and communicating; in other words they are quite capable of sending holographic sonic pictures to one another with their communication apparatus. They can then use these pictures in symbolic ways similar to the way that we use the printed versions of words spoken out loud.

This implies an immense complexity of acoustic memory and of acoustic portrayal, way beyond anything that we have achieved either in simulations in computers or in terms of concepts having to do with acoustic events. Only our most sophisticated and advanced mathematics can even approach an analysis of this kind of a system.

Most of the above work was done between 1961 and 1968 in the Communications Research Institute in the laboratory in Saint Thomas in the Virgin Islands and in the laboratory in Miami, Florida.

Over the years I gradually developed an entirely new set of assumptions based upon our work with dolphins. I realized that here was an independent being living in an alien environment whose evolution was several times the length of the human evolution. The original whales, from thirty million years ago in the Eocene period, found in rocks where the sea used to be—now land—had brain capacities of eight hundred cc's. This means that they have a longer evolution than does the human. The humanoids were found in strata that are of the order of two million years old. The humans themselves (Neanderthal, Cro-Magnon, and so forth) are not nearly this age. This means that these alien beings are much more ancient than we are on this planet. It also means that they achieved brain sizes comparable to the human a lot sooner than did the human itself.

I believe that we can presume that they have ethics, morals and regard for one another much more highly developed than does the human species. For example, they realize their total interdependence. Let me illustrate this interdependence.

All of the dolphins and whales breathe totally voluntarily. They have no automatic respiratory mechanism such as we have; if they did, they would drown when they passed out from a high fever or a blow on the head or some other reason. An automatic breathing system would mean that underwater they would breathe water when unconscious. They cannot afford an unconscious respiratory automatic system such as we have.

This voluntary respiration means then that any time a dolphin or a whale passes out for any reason, his fellows must bring him to the surface and wake him up in order that he will breathe again, or else he dies.

We saw many instances of this among the dolphins. To wake

one another up they will rake the dorsal fin across the anal/genital region causing a reflex contraction of the flukes, which lifts the endangered animal to the surface. Dolphins support one another at the surface and stimulate the unconscious one until the respiration starts again when he is awake.

This implies that dolphins cannot afford to be very far away from one another, twenty-four hours a day, three hundred and sixty-five days a year, day and night. This also means that when a large group of dolphins becomes ill, say owing to a virus, they will beach themselves in order not to die at sea, They would prefer to die on the beach rather than to die in the depths. This explains the beaching of pilot whales and various dolphins. We have seen several dolphins come in from the deep sea and enter small shallow protected lagoons in the Florida Keys in order to recover from their illness, safe from sharks and the other predators of the sea. We have seen spotted dolphins, which are pelagic (i.e., a deep-sea species), come into very shallow water and stay there several weeks while they were recovering from their injuries.

Please pardon this long introduction to our future program with dolphins. Toni and I have decided to go back to dolphin work in depth under very stringent controlled circumstances.

As I stated in *The Center of the Cyclone*, I closed the dolphin laboratory because I did not want to continue to run a concentration camp for my friends, the dolphins.

I have not attacked publicly the oceanaria for keeping dolphins restrained in what they call a "controlled environment" for the following reasons.

The oceanaria have done a very great service for the dolphins and killer whales in acquainting literally hundreds of thousands of humans with their existence and with their capabilities in a circus way. The dolphins and the whales are indebted to the oceanaria for educating the human species. This has been a costly education for these species; however, I believe that this is worth it. Thousands of people are becoming more and more aware of the necessity of stopping whaling, for example. More and more people are aware that when a dolphin is beached, something is wrong and that it needs help. The oceanaria assure that we will get closer and closer to an ability to communicate and to break the barrier between these species and ourselves. For this I am very grateful. If it weren't for the oceanaria, I would not have been able to do my initial work with the dolphins. Let me give specific examples.

Recently I attended the so-called killer whale (*Orcinus orca*) show at Sea World near San Diego. I saw these huge dolphins treating humans in the same gentle fashion that the smaller dolphins had treated us. I saw a man ride a killer whale holding on to a loop around the whale's neck and holding on to the dorsal fin with his feet, wearing a small aqualung in case of emergencies. The whale then took him down to the bottom of this rather deep pool and then propelled himself up into the air, leaping clear of the water with the man on his back and diving immediately to the bottom of the pool again, five or six times.

This is an astounding cooperative effort on both the part of the human and the killer whale. This man has immense courage and immense trust in this huge creature. On the other side, the killer whale has an immense trust in the humans and does everything he can to be sure that that man can breathe at the proper timing so that he does not drown. This requires a discrimination and a careful timing of the dives and the leaps in such a way that the man can survive. He then delivers the man to the side of the pool so the man can step off safely. This is an incredible performance. I could hardly believe it the first time I saw it. Without the beautiful organization of the oceanaria such feats would be impossible.

I originally saw the potential of this sort of work when Ivan Tors made the movie *Namu—The Killer Whale*. The movie crew swam with the whale in a lagoon. There is one scene in that movie in which there is one person riding on the back standing up and holding on to the immense dorsal fin, another swims up near the huge flukes and taps them and the whale lowers the flukes and allows the person to climb aboard also.

The immense sensitivity of these animals' skin allows them to detect the presence of a person and to regulate their activities in such a way as to not damage them. It is most impressive, their careful control of their immense size so as not to endanger their human friends.

The killer whale had a very bad reputation mainly from the writings of Robert Falcon Scott (*Scott's Last Voyage,* published in 1913), who wrote about his trip to the South Pole. He witnessed an episode in which killer whales broke four feet of ice to investigate some Eskimo dogs around his ship next to the ice. As soon as they saw the photographer, i.e., a human on the ice floe, they went away again. This episode frightened Scott, as he wrote in his diary. He attributed many things to the whales that they did not have, such as ferocity and cunning. I believe this episode is easily explained when one knows that the killer whales came up to the edge of the ice, looked across the top of the ice and saw the dogs, but no humans there. The humans were on the ship tied up at the edge of the ice. Naturally their tremendous power in breaking the ice seemed a threat to Scott and his people.

I believe that the whales, dolphins and the killer whales know all about us, know how dangerous we are. They have been present when we have held our wars in the sea and let off depth charges; they know about our submarines, and our atomic bombs and hydrogen bombs. They know how dangerous the human species really is and they respect us as a very dangerous group. I believe that they all know that we can wipe them out if they hurt any of us and this message gets around. There was an episode written up for example in one of the skindiver magazines in which a man went out of Seattle in a forty-foot power boat made of wood and saw some killer whales. He shot through the dorsal fin of one of the male killer whales. I don't know why.

The whale turned around, came up to the front of the boat, came up in the air, grabbed the stemhead (the wooden part of the boat that holds the front of it together) and pulled the stemhead out of the boat, opening the hull above the waterline. The man then scrambled around and readjusted the weight in the boat so that the front end came up out of the water and he went back to Seattle. He then told everybody what had happened and showed his boat.

This to me is an example of the measure of the killer whale's very high intelligence. He pulled the stemhead out of the boat, but did not sink it, so that the man could come back and, as it were, give the message "Don't shoot killer whales" to his fellow humans.

In the Communications Research Institute we did many experiments which we did not report publicly. We did a lot of quantitative work on the sonic spectrum of the dolphins. We did a lot of quantitative work on what the dolphins could do with this amazingly sophisticated system. We found for example that they can control their click rate, i.e., the pulses of sound that they emit in the following fashions. They can control the sonic spectral content of each of the clicks. They can control the rate of click production to a very fine degree. They can control the number of clicks that they emit to a very close value. They can change from clicks to whistles in a fraction of a millisecond. They can control the click rate from one per minute up to several thousand per second easily. They can control the acceleration and deceleration of the clicking rate to an amazing degree of accuracy.

We intend to use these capabilities in inducing them to control a computer. In the Institute we set up a teaching program to teach them how to control a computer through a code, a machine code using their clicking.

In the new project we intend to pursue this. Since the days we were working with the computer many new micro- and minicomputers have been devised that are suitable for this kind of work. We have already started our work on the software necessary for this.

What are the assumptions behind this kind of work? The assumptions are that there is a very sophisticated, very developed, alien mind behind this type of communication and we assume that they already have an immensely complex language based upon acoustic pictures analogous to our words and sentences. They have probably developed a *sonic picture language.*

We intend to unearth this language, to make it more obvious to us, to perform transformations of it to a visual representation (a "holograph") from their acoustic representation.

We intend also to establish that this very sophisticated animal has an acoustic language probably as complex (if not more so) as any human language and that they can learn to control a high-speed computer.

The reason for using a high-speed computer is that the dolphins can transmit and receive so rapidly that a human operator cannot possibly keep up with them in their natural state. We found in the Institute that dolphins will accommodate to the humans' slowness and the humans' lower-frequency range of transmission, but they do so with great difficulty. Our language is a very narrow band in their frequency spectrum and seems very slow to them, at least something of the order of five to ten times.

These are the reasons that Toni and I are going back to work with dolphins. We have found that the amount of interest in dolphins and the technical advancement in computers has gone up tremendously since 1968 when I closed the Institute.

We can now do much more sophisticated software, much higher speed operation of computers, than we could do then.

We want to break the communication barrier and believe it can now be done—with the cooperative efforts of many persons working on these problems knowledgeably, with the dolphins (*Tursiops* and *Orcinus*).

Chapter Sixteen

Searching for Evidence of Extraterrestrial Beings

I once attended a very peculiar conference; it was secret and yet it was supported by The National Academy of Sciences and The National Research Council. It occurred in the early sixties. The conference was called by the Director of the National Radio Astronomy Observatory at Green Bank, West Virginia, at the behest of Frank Drake, a radio astronomer, who had worked out Project Ozma. Project Ozma was a radio telescope search in a particular way for intelligent signals from some of the nearby stars, i.e., the planets around those stars.

I was startled by the invitation to this conference. There was a lack of official scientific recognition of the work that I was doing on the dolphins. I became known as the scientist most favored by the wives and children of other scientists. I was invited to be the after-dinner speaker at several scientific societies, including the Acoustical Society of America and The Institute of Electrical and Electronic Engineers, Inc.

I was asked to lecture to the learned societies under those peculiar conditions in which the members were in a state that we call in medicine "post-prandial stupor," due to filled stomachs and too much alcohol. (I am not talking about scientific papers that I proposed giving at meetings; I had no problems there. I would submit an abstract and give a short talk at the official meetings even as did my colleagues.)

I tell you this because when the invitation came to go to Green Bank, West Virginia, I was startled and surprised that a group of radio astronomers and their satellite scientists in the radio measurement game should ask me to come and talk about dolphins. I couldn't quite figure this out in advance. When I got into the small airplane that takes one to Green Bank, on board the same plane was Bernard M. Oliver, who had been at Cal Tech at the same time I was there, as an undergraduate. Bernie is probably one of the most intelligent, energetic and broadly educated scientists that we have in the United States today. On the plane he explained how this conference had come about.

The failure of Project Ozma probably meant that the wrong methods were being used. Frank Drake had used a kind of quantitative reasoning about the probabilities of extraterrestrial intelligent communicating life forms that would use radio telescopes or laser beams or some other method (such as gamma rays) to communicate across the galaxy.

I asked why the conference was secret. He said that the National Academy did not consider this subject at that time to be quite respectable enough to publicly announce the results. They did not want to appear as fools in the public eye.

At this particular conference I was asked to speak about the dolphins. Three hours were scheduled for me in which to do this. I presented all our evidence that dolphins are another intelligent species on this planet. This was given in the midst of an atmosphere of tentative acceptance of what I was saying and great interest in the results of our analysis of the brain structure, the vocal behavior, the communicational abilities and the airborne humanoid voice outputs of the dolphins.

This was probably the most interested scientific audience that I had had to date, even though they were functioning in a sort of underground fashion outside the usual halls of science. This conference was not written up; nothing was published from it until a year later when a short summary appeared in *Science* magazine, and a science editor from *The New York Times* wrote a book called *We Are Not Alone*.

Carl Sagan, an astronomer from Cornell University, has written two books partly based on this conference. One he wrote with I. S. Shklovsky, a Russian, on the search for extraterrestrial life. It is called *Intelligent Life in the Universe*. The second one came out quite recently and is called *The Cosmic Connection: An Extraterrestrial Connection*. In spite of the openness of these scientists, what I had to say allowed them tentatively to make the statement that apparently this planet has two forms of intelligent life, one of which uses radio telescopes and the other of which does not, i.e., dolphins.

It is rather interesting that in Carl Sagan's first book he made the usual mistake of the scientific community in general by stating that dolphins brains are *almost* as large as humans. We had shown convincing evidence that they are definitely 20 to 40 percent larger (see *The Mind of the Dolphin*). The whales are up to six times larger. Somehow Sagan did not fully accept this, and writing in his book several years after the conference, he inserted his own belief in the preeminence of man over dolphin on such a measurable point as brain size! In his next book he gives detailed accounts of his own encounter with my dolphins in a swimming pool in Miami, as evidence for their intelligence.

Thus, reluctantly and kind of through the back door, the scientific establishment has begun to accept what we have been saying for years, ever since it was first announced in 1958 that there are brains other than human worth considering on this planet. The announcements have been welcomed by people who needed support in their arguments for, and in their far-out (they think) considerations of extraterrestrial life. They needed to be bolstered up on the occurrence of intelligence, other than human intelligence, on this planet. They needed bolstering for their arguments about extraterrestrial intelligence, and yet most of the scientific establishment has not accepted what we have done. Youngsters have accepted it. There are several grade-school text readers that have been published in which a sort of sentimental fashion Dr. Lilly is featured as the Dolphin Doctor, and in some, some of his "conversations" with dolphins are paraphrased.

Like Galileo, I wrote in the common language of the laity—as an educational measure. I realized that arguments in scientific societies are not the way that the ideas of a culture are changed. We have all been educated on the fantastic power of the media in changing public opinion. So, quite early in the game (about 1960), I was convinced by a well-known author to start writing popular books incorporating my ideas and some of the results of the scientific work on dolphins. It happened like this.

By coincidence, when I moved to the Virgin Islands it turned out that Herman Wouk had also moved there. He heard about my dolphin project through mutual friends of ours, Patty and Ev Birch of Saint Thomas. Patty and Ev arranged for me to meet Wouk and we finally had dinner together; he wanted to find out what we knew about dolphins. I told him the story to date and he said, "This is worth a book, you really should write a book." My answer was that I was not an author, I was a scientist. I had written scientific papers but I didn't think I was capable of writing a popular book. He said, "Nonsense, I will get my agent Hal Matson down from New York, and I will get my editor Lee Barker from Doubleday also to come down to talk with you." In subsequent weeks the editor and the agent showed up and signed me up for a two-book contract, the first of which was to be *Man and Dolphin*, which was published by Doubleday in 1961. At that time the second was to be a book called *Solitude, Isolation and Confinement*, which I had completed, but which I withheld because the data in it, I felt, were too personal for a scientist to publish at that time. Subsequently, some of the data were published in *The Human Biocomputer* and in *The Center of the Cyclone;* however, the Doubleday two-book contract was subsequently satisfied by the publication in 1967 of *The Mind of the Dolphin*.

Over the years I discovered who was reading these books, especially when they came out in paperback form. It was mostly the younger generation and the wives of scientists, not the scientists themselves. This is rather a paradoxical situation. In the books I gave a sufficient bibliography of the scientific papers that we had published in rather obscure places such as the American Philosophical Society in Philadelphia, No. 78, p. 288; The American Psychiatric Association publications, Washington, D.C., etcetera.

My scientific voice was heard, but it was heard more in the home than it was in the halls of the universities and of the scientific societies. When the editor was friendly we were able to get papers published. For example, when we had a friendly editor at *Science* of the American Association for the Advancement of Science in Washington we were invited to give two papers on our dolphin work; these appeared as *The Sounds Emitted by the Bottlenose Dolphin*, and *Vocal Exchanges Between Dolphins*.

Another scientific paper appeared in the *Journal of the Acoustical Society of America*, when Bill Fry, a personal friend from my biophysicist days invited me to write a paper for that journal. It is the *Reprogramming of the Sonic Output of the Dolphin*, a rather revolutionary paper published in 1968; this paper has been ignored by the scientific community at large. This paper is republished in full in *Lilly on Dolphins, The Humans of the Sea*, Anchor/Doubleday, New York, 1975 (as Appendix One).

My work has shown that dolphins and whales are more intelligent than we are. Their community of effort, their total dependence on one another in an extremely hostile environment is a far better example of intelligence than man's warfare upon man, both outside on a national basis and inside the structure of our society, in battles about ideas and the entertainment rip-offs.

In concert we are deadly. Those with money and power are deadly. They must be deadly to survive—ruthless and deadly. In one of my publications on a symposium of extraterrestrial communicating life forms sponsored by The Institute of Electrical and Electronic Engineers, Inc., I warned off other species from this planet.

I said, "With our depredations committed against one another and our depredations committed upon whales, making cat (and dog) food out of their bodies, I advise all extraterrestrial beings to stay away from this very dangerous planet." The bodies housing the largest brains on this planet (those of whales) go into "industrial products" including cat and dog food and, in Japan, human food. The carcasses of the whales are cut up and every bit of them used, except for the brain.

Their brains are the most magnificent structures on this planet.

A sperm whale brain of nine thousand grams is six times the size of the average human brain. It is four and one half times the size of the largest of the human brains measured to date. As I have said in other places, nature does not create such large brains for the amusement of man or for his reverence and awe. These brains are created to be used. The problem in science is to find out how they are used: something that we will never find out if we allow the industrial exploitation and murder of these intelligent beings.

Two things used to make me angry: man's inhumanity to man, and man's murder of the whales. Each of these now cause me only grief. My compassion is aroused in the place of my former anger.

I am sorry that I complain so much. I don't want to have to complain. When I see what kind of absolute stupidities which have involved my life and have involved humankind itself in its own destruction of itself, I cry. Eventually we all die. Eventually we die naturally, if we are not killed first by the stupidities of our fellow man. I do not understand my own species. There are times and occasions in which I do not think I ever will understand them.

Let us return to the search for extraterrestrial intelligence. I recommend an article to you by Bernard M. Oliver in the Cal Tech alumni magazine, *Engineering and Science,* for January 1975. In this article, Dr. Oliver gives the evidence for the noneconomic nature of interstellar travel and the necessity for interstellar communication by new and expensive (ten-billion-dollar) arrays of radio telescopes (Project Cyclops).

Oliver here gives the quantitative data for picking the band between the hydrogen line and the hydroxyl line (OH) in the radio spectrum. Here galactic noise is lower than the "big bang background" at $3°$ Kelvin, which permeates space in every direction. He calls this band of frequencies a "water hole" (between H and OH of H_2O) and says that this is the place "where water-based life forms should meet."

All of Bernie Oliver's arguments are based upon the natural sciences to date. He has an evolutionary theory of the cosmos based upon astronomy and astrophysics. He has a theory of the three and a half billion years* of the origin of the green hills of earth and setting the stage for animal life. He has a theory of the origin of planets, of rocky planets. He hypothesized that there are ten billion life sites in our galaxy, based upon these theories. I quote:

> On some of these planets life has not yet evolved, on others it has perished. The number of advanced cultures at this time is roughly equal to the average longevity of advanced cultures in years.

Quoting further he says:

> The significance of this statement is that if civilization usually solved their ecological, societal, relation and resource problems and therefore have life of a billion or more years, then the galaxy is teeming with intelligent life. If on the other hand they kill themselves off after only a hundred years of nuclear wars, or some equally stupid way, then the galaxy is practically devoid of intelligent life.

He does a very sophisticated analysis of nuclear space travel with the conclusion that it is impractical. The cost is prohibitive. He then applies very sophisticated methods to an analysis of what it would take to communicate across the galaxy; Bernie edited the results in a monograph, *Project Cyclops*, published by NASA.

The Cyclops array would be the most powerful radio telescope ever built and would permit real time images of the radio sky. Cyclops could reach out one hundred light years. We could pick up signals radiated from the planets at this distance. For powerful beacons we could probably go out a thousand light years. Of course we are up against the delays in these signals. One would not receive an answer at one hundred light years for two hundred years.

It is considerations like these that block support of such a

* Now raised to sixteen million years by Sandage's new work on Hubble's constant velocity of expansion of the universe (Allan Sandage, *The Hubble Atlas of Galaxies*).

project; however, he has a very cogent argument that Cyclops would pay for itself in very short order if we did establish communication with a super-advanced civilization willing to share its results with us. If such a super-advanced civilization were within a few light years from us, the project would be worthwhile. At a hundred light years, we are investing money of this generation that would not see a return for several generations to come, if then.

Therefore, I suggest that what Oliver has shown is the impossibility at the present level of our natural sciences of communicating with life forms that are not on this planet. I suggest that such budgets as those in the National Defense be turned over to projects other than Cyclops, projects such as devising methods for communicating with whales and dolphins; their alien bodies are available, their communication systems are directly researchable without long transmission delays.

We can see a much more immediate return on such a project than we can in trying to communicate with extraterrestrial intelligences whose existences have not been demonstrated.

The existence of whales and dolphins has been demonstrated. The existence of their complex communication system has been demonstrated. Their wish to communicate with us and their capability of making the attempt has also been demonstrated. I refer you to *Man and Dolphin; The Mind of the Dolphin;* and to *Reprogramimng of the Sonic Output of the Dolphin* for this evidence.

If we could devote a good deal less than ten billion dollars to this project, say, to begin with, a million dollars a year for ten years, for a total of ten million dollars, we could do on this planet the initial exercises required by us to communicate with a nonhuman species; even one such species is important. We need this preliminary exercise to educate us out of our arrogance, out of our assumption that our knowledge is all knowledge, that our sciences are the only sciences. Those who construct and use radio telescopes realize that radio telescopes do not look under seawater, at least in the wavelength range of interest to them. Therefore they go off-planet searching for extraterrestrial life forms.

I suggest that instead of killing off the intelligent species of this planet, we attempt to break down the communication barrier right here on the planet. It's a good deal less expensive than the extraterrestrial search as it's promulgated.

I have other suggestions to make much further out—that we try to find means much faster than light and radio for communication. That we search for influences of these advanced civilizations upon us by using methods far more advanced than those conceived of by Dr. Oliver. There is some evidence from my personal experiences, and those of certain of my colleagues willing to use the methods that we have used, that such influences are being brought to bear upon us. The evidence is of a peculiar sort, not generally allowed in the halls of respectable consensus science, on this planet at least. It is the result of inner searches for sources of information not brought to one through the usual five senses. This information can be brought to one in meditative states, brought to one floating in the silence and darkness in the flotation tank in isolation. As far as I and others in this area can find out, our planet is subject to influences from beings far more intelligent than us, far more advanced, far more knowledgeable and not just in the consensus science of this planet, but in sciences we have yet to discover.

There is a cosmic limiting velocity to miracles. The "miracle speed limit" is administered by cosmic traffic cops. We are not allowed to make discoveries (so-called) any faster than the stage of evolution of this planet allows.

The overall evolutionary rate to which we are subject here, is regulated by influences beyond our present understanding. Yes, we may need Cyclopean arrays and radio telescopes for effective communication beyond the solar system, but we should devote at least some of our research money to methods other than radio telescopes, to methods using our own detection systems of which we are not yet fully aware, within our own bodies. If one spends sufficient number of hours, totally isolated from the distraction of one's own species, such as Admiral Byrd (see his book *Alone*, first published in 1938) did in the South Pole for months on end, one comes up against certain kinds of revelatory experiences having to do with the content of the universe.

I have had such experiences in the Chilean desert; I have had them in the isolation tank. Sufficient number of persons using the same methods I have used have had similar experiences to convince me that there is something worth investigating here. Once again we are on the edge of the Unknown. Once again we have no guidelines from previous science, we are breaking into new fields, new areas of interest. Apparently only the young are sufficiently unbiased, sufficiently able to change their belief systems to investigate this region, even as they are with the dolphins and the killer whales.

At least once a week I get inquiries from youngsters who are dealing with dolphins or *orca*, the so-called killer whale. There are now enough dedicated youngsters working in this area so that we may be able to make a breakthrough on interspecies communication on this planet.

There are also enough youngsters beginning to spend enough time in isolation tanks so that we may make a breakthrough in another area of methods of communication beyond our present science.

At Green Bank, West Virginia, in the early sixties, *The Order of the Dolphin* was founded; subsequently this order was to be composed of those interested in extraterrestrial communication. The Order subsequently died a nice quiet death. There should be a younger Order, a younger society to pursue these matters. It should not be a science-fiction society. This one should be founded by the youngsters as a respectable scientific organization that is searching for means of communication with extraterrestrial life forms including those on this planet. We should say not "extraterrestrial" so much as "extrahuman," outside of the human species; "nonhuman intelligences" is a more proper term for what we are trying to define.

I feel that the large brains of the elephants, the whales and dolphins contain sufficient anatomic, physiological and behavioral evidence to encourage such a scientific society to proceed to organize and to seek support for its own research projects.

Without organization individuals are going to be shot down right and left by the organized establishment. They are going to be discredited.

The way that most scientists in the past have gained credence in the community is by organizing with one another and creating a new society.

For example, I was a charter member of the American Biophysical Society and an early member of the American EEG Society. In both of these cases the biophysicists and the electroencephalographers were not considered quite respectable by other societies, so they founded their own. I think it is time that those interested in nonhuman intelligence and in communicating with it, form their own society and thus gain more credibility and respectability.

Whether we like it or not, credibility and respectability are needed for financial support both of the private and government types. Imperfect as scientific societies tend to be, they are better than isolated individuals when it comes to support: unless one can find money either of one's own or of a dedicated wealthy person or family, one must still raise funds for one's efforts in this area.

Chapter Seventeen

The Moat Effect: An Example of a Metabelief Operator

In neurophysiology there is a well-known effect, which I here call the "moat effect." If one shines a very small spot of light upon the retina of an animal and follows the effect of this stimulation by means of electrodes within the retina, one finds that the light stimulates a small spot of neuronal activity. This small spot is surrounded by an area of inhibition of spontaneous activity within the ganglion cells. In a diagram of this effect, refer to illustration, one finds that there is a raised level of activity in the center where the spot of light is and a ring of depressed (inhibited) spontaneous activity surrounding the central part.

It can easily be demonstrated that this same property exists throughout the nervous system. Stimulation of a small area of cortex leads to inhibition in the surrounding regions, and so on through the subcortical systems.

This is called the "moat effect" because there is, as it were, a tall column in the center of a depressed area, a circular area, so it looks like a column surrounded by a moat. The height of the column may be above the surrounding terrain outside the moat, or it may be below it (see illustration of the Moat Effect).

COLUMN

SURROUNDS

MOAT

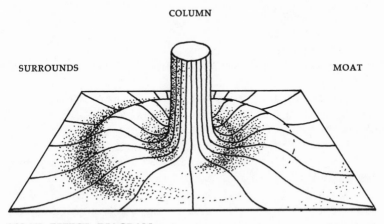

MOAT EFFECT DIAGRAM

I have noticed that in general people tend to do exactly this kind of operation in regard to their knowledge about any given subject. They tend to raise the importance of their own knowledge (make a central column of high importance) and demean areas of knowledge not within their own area of competence (surround it with a moat in regard to other knowledge or other people's knowledge). So the "moat effect" exists not only in our own neurophysiology, but also in our thought and our behavior and our social activities.

Later in this chapter I will show how I used this moat effect as a defense to help motivate me to reenter reality after my accident.

The fact that this effect is generalized from a central nervous system that operates in this way—locally to its properties in generating behavior and thought—is rather astonishing.

One can see such arrangements of activities in politics, especially among political candidates running for office in which they take their own program and their own thinking as if it is the most important thing in the world, and surround it with an area of demeaning other people's programs, opinions and activities. One can see this in science when a given scientist raises the importance of his own area of interest and activities and demeans that of his colleagues. One can see it in the treatment of single scientists who depart from the standard formulas for science. One can see this property in one's own family. Practically everyone that one knows tends to do this, including you and me.

Pay close attention to someone riding their own hobbyhorse and to their criticism of other hobbyhorses, of other people riding their hobbyhorses. One can see a given person elevating tennis above golf, somebody else elevating golf above tennis, another doing the football trip, another doing the surfing trip, the skiing trip, and so on.

I summarize this by saying that we all do that which we are best equipped to do with what we have at a given time; we tend to neglect and demean that which we either do not choose to do, or cannot do, or do not have time enough to do, or do not have enough money with which to do, or do not have the energy to do. In other words, *we do the best we can with what we have as of here and now.* We believe that which we must believe to do what we are doing. This particular point of view can be applied to one's business, one's leisure-time activities, one's home life and to one's criteria for various kinds of judgments.

For example, consider one's aesthetic judgment: what is beautiful? It is quite mysterious why we consider a certain type of face or body structure to be beautiful and another one to be ugly. In the essence of things, any living body is beautiful; any living body has survived billions of years of counter life forces and yet here it is. Not only has it survived, but we know that all of its predecessors survived in order to generate it. Therefore, any living creature, including any type of human, in essence, is beautiful. The most objective, dispassionate, the most indifferent kind of judgment says that any living thing, that all living things, is and are beautiful. There is no escape from this. And yet one can hear on TV talk shows, one can hear on TV interviews, one can hear public figures giving off-the-cuff judgments about this or that being superior, being more beautiful or more ugly than another.

Recently, I was very badly injured in a bicycle accident.* I broke five ribs on the right. On the right side of my body I broke my clavicle and my scapula, and still after many months my right shoulder is not operating correctly. My right lung was collapsed, I had a concussion, spent nine days in a hospital and several weeks in bed at home. This accident taught much. It taught me that the beliefs of others about one's self are particularly powerful in determining the external reality in which one lives. It taught me that certain people cannot possibly understand the processes by which one arrives at one's particular thinking and feeling while in intense pain. As William James said at the beginning of this century, "Those who live on one side of the threshold of pain cannot possibly understand the psychology of those who live on the other side of the threshold of pain."

This lesson was brought home particularly strongly to me: I suddenly realized that we cannot expect understanding from others no matter how close to one they are, no matter how much they apparently understand one, if one is in states (not just pain) that are unfamiliar to those persons closest to one. If your wife or husband has never gone through the particular kinds and intensity of pain that one is experiencing, one cannot expect them to understand. This is asking too much of biological organisms that are having their own survival problems within different belief systems. We are the victims of our previous experience and of our beliefs constructed on those experiences. There is no escape from this victimization, as it were. We are limited biological organisms, severely limited by the biological vehicle within which we reside.

To return to Toni. I made our dyad the column at the center of a moat in a vast region of inhibition of other attractions in the inner domains. The moat effect took me over totally; I was too damaged to do anything but concentrate my total energies

* See Chapter Twelve, "States of Being and Consciousness in 'Coma,' " for details of this accident.

on returning to this planet to a peaceful life with my love, Toni.

While I was away from my body, I knew that I must return. The top of the column of the moat effect read "the most important thing for me to do is to return to her."

At one point in the hospital I returned from these far-out spaces. Toni was by my bed; I held on to her neck desperately for five hours, maintaining my hold on where I wanted to go as a demonstration of my sincerity and my need. (As I write this I cry because it is still my need, it is still the top of the column in the moat. I make this important. I believe this and I disbelieve anything that interferes with it. To be here now on this planet in this body with Toni is all that is important to me. This I believe to be true. It is not "as if true." It is true.)

During a period of twelve weeks, I was unable to function in my usual ways. I was forced to rest and stay in a hospital bed in my home without ceasing. I was forced into a twelve weeks' meditation on my own friability, my own fragility, my own mortality, my compromises, in order to stay a while longer on this planetside trip.

I have many lessons to learn: lessons on how to remain at peace in spite of provocations to the contrary; of how to maintain the feeling in the face of temptations to be unfeeling; of how to continue to write books, to lecture, to give workshops, to teach and to listen to lectures, to read books, to be taught, to attend other's workshops and not demean either my own knowledge or the knowledge of others and to respect our ignorances. To love and be loved, to repair, to be repaired, to solve the karma I accumulated and the karma accumulated by others because of me.

The moat effect can be made useful as long as one is conscious of its actions. It can't be erased. It is built into our structure. But it can be made more flexible. As it were, one can move the column through areas of knowledge, areas of ignorance, and not make the moat negative. The moat can be positive, one can raise the whole structure above the surrounding terrain, as it were, making a mountain peak with a central island in the middle. One can't smooth out the terrain of the mind and of the body. All one can do is recognize its shapes, its forms and its substances.

There are those including myself who feel very strongly that the body is a transducer. What is a transducer? It derives from the Latin *"trans,"* meaning across, and *"ductere"* meaning to lead—a transducer leads something across something else.

The simplest examples of transducers are microphones, which lead the sound waves, the small changes of pressure (in the oscillating pressure in the air) across into oscillating electrical currents or voltages. A loudspeaker does just the opposite. It takes oscillating electrical currents and changes them into pulsating oscillating airwaves. When I say that the body is a transducer, I am summarizing several points of view about the body's function.

I am making one basic assumption, which one should examine very carefully. I am assuming that *the Self, I or you or he or she, within that body somehow is conscious of its separateness from that body, but also is conscious of being imbedded within that body. The body then functions as a transducer between that Self, that essence, if you wish, and the rest of the universe.* It behooves us then to train that body, to take care of that body, as that which transduces, that which is the carrier of the wishes of Self, the intent of Self, through the surroundings and the intent of the surroundings back into the Self.

Al Huang, who teaches T'ai Chi (a Chinese form of moving meditation) and dance—a combination of the two that is beautiful and effective—with his own body's example, to students of varying degrees of expertise in this area, recently said to Lama Govinda, in my presence, "The body functions as the intermediary between the Self and the universe. The flow of the cosmos is like the flow of clouds over one's head. The universe and the cosmos express themselves in a flowing as of water. I teach how to have the body express and join with the universe and its flowing and allow the Self to express the universal flowing through the body."

The very fact that one is an individual in a single body possessing a single mind means that one is subject to laws of relative importance. One somehow in this life is a Center Of the

Universe, "a COU," as it were. One is anthropocentric because one is *anthropos*. One is anthropomorphic because one is *anthropos*. Similarly, one is egocentric because one is ego, one is egomorphic because of the limits of the knowledge of ego. (Here I am using "ego" not in the restrictive sense in which Oscar Ichazo uses it, but in the more general sense of the Self, of the I, the me, the functional entity within a wet, blood-filled living body.)

In a sense one is a zombie, a body controlled by something other than what is in that body. In a sense one is a robot, a machine, controlled by something other than that which is the robot. One's programming came through the genetic code and through one's own experience. So, once again, one is the "victim" of one's own genetic code, of one's own experience, of one's own current circumstance. A victim until one can leave permanently.

This personal catastrophe, my accident, is a lesson to me, a private lesson illustrating my major point that: *What one believes to be true in the* **province of the mind** *either is true or becomes true within certain limits. In the province of the mind there are no limits; however,* **the body introduces definite limits.**

When one's body introduces its definite limits, what can one do? One solution is to escape the body, to leave, either temporarily or permanently. During this recent personal catastrophe, I did not choose to leave but was forced to leave in contrast to previous personal experiences in the tank. As I wrote in *The Center of the Cyclone,* there are many instances in which I chose to leave, several in which I did not choose to leave but was forced to leave. This new experience forced me to leave.

I have never really been tempted to leave permanently, to die, to leave the body here for others to handle, to bury, to burn, to drop into the sea; somehow I have overvalued this body, its sensations, its feelings, its history, its future, its present. A body is in an overvaluation space, somehow hooked in to the processes of life, to the flow of fluids, to the flow of energies, to the flow of feeling, to the flow of sensation, to the flow of exchange, to the transduction of the thoughts of Self, of the thoughts produced by other Selves, to the interpretation, to the explanation, to the exploration of Self and of the universe.

Where do I go from here? First of all in regard to the body in the future on this planet I go with Toni, our life together, whatever that brings. I admire her graceful, diplomatic and effective way of living and appreciate and enjoy; as she develops her confidence so I develop my admiration and my own effectiveness and our dyadic effectiveness. As I overvalue, as it were, the dyad, I gain a perspective on that overvaluation and what it represents to my essence, to her essence. Toni essentially is a very good human being, a very good woman, a very strong person; thus do I express my overvaluation of her. When one is conscious of overvaluation, when one does not consider it a demeaning process, one considers it a necessary process, to pursue life as it is lived.

As I write this I am watching plants, trees, listening to the wind in Toni's and my place in Decker Canyon. I sit in our small VW camper, enjoying the beneficence of the ambience of southern California with its flowers, red ones, glowing in the bright sunshine, 80° warmth in the middle of January. A truly miraculous external reality. A flow of air, the ticking of leaf on leaf, the creaking of branch on branch, the insects flying through the air, our kitten and her crazy ways. I overvalue, enjoy and feel nostalgic, empathic and more compassionate toward my smashed body, in repairing it, to getting back to where I was before the accident and getting further along with this transducer as it repairs itself with my help and the help of many friends, many healers who have aided me. They too have overvalued me, my body.

Hector Prestera, M.D., and his wife Sharon Wheeler have worked untold hours to release the healing powers of this body; Nurse Bernice Danylchuk and her aides, Lika and Malia from Samoa exerted their powerful program on my body.

There have been many others who have helped of course; there will be many more. Of these, some I have helped in their past difficulties; I will be helping them in the future. This mutual regard, this mutual overvaluation of friend for friend makes it worth staying on this planet. Jan Nicholson with her massage, Helen Costa with her beautiful disciplined investigation of damage and repair, Ruth and Myron Glatt and their chocolate mousse are among many others. I have had help from Emily

Conrad, trained in voodo, during this period of repair. As I say, whether I believe in these healing methods or not, they can work. For this I am grateful.

Toni's father, Angelo, has just arrived.

A.: Good morning, John, how are you?

J.: How are you, pal?

A.: Oh, pretty good.

J.: You look good. You drove all the way successfully from Fontana to Decker Canyon. Congratulations.

A.: Not 100 percent but 75 and ¾ percent.

J.: Yeah, but you got here, that's all that counts. How is your vision?

A.: I can't say it is perfect and sometimes it's a little confusing, but I made it.

J.: And that's your little Courier and it's all repaired.

A.: That little Courier is a prince on the road for real.

J.: Boy that thing has really held up in spite of the fact you turned it over.

A.: You haven't seen it?

J.: No.

A.: It looks better than before.

J.: How many times did you turn over in it?

A.: Three times.

J.: Three times! How are your ribs?

A.: Sometimes I feel a little bit under, but . . .

J.: How is your shoulder?

A.: The shoulder hardly feels anything at all.

J.: Mine is coming back but it really burns and hurts. (Toni comes over to us.)

TONI: Hi Pop, I didn't see you come up.

J.: Oh, he drove up very quietly.

A.: How are you?

T.: I'm great . . . and doesn't he look good? (pointing to John)

A.: Yeah, he sure does.

T.: So you got down here all right.

A.: Oh sure, when you got to do something, you do it that's all there is to it.

J.: You're incredible. You're really incredible.

A.: Yeah, when you got to do something, you do it.

T.: How's your cold, Pop?

J.: You got the flu?

T.: No, he's got a cold.

(Pop finds a loose screw in the VW, searches for its place.)

A.: Here's another hole. No it's another hole in here. I don't think that's open too.

J.: Oh lord, things do fall apart.

A.: Things like that happen to the best of families.

J.: Where did you find it? What does it look like?

A.: I don't see any other screws like it, though.

T.: Guess what I cooked, Pop? Cardoons.

A.: Oh, did you fix them up?

J.: What are cardoons?

T.: The stalks of the artichoke plant boiled, but instead of boiling them I put them in the radar range. Hey, how many dozen eggs is that? (Pop brought us eggs.)

A.: Seven and one half.

J.: Fantastic.

T.: My goodness, Pop, don't you think we have a store around here? Let's go inside, I'm playing an opera you like.

That's a typical conversation with Pop at eighty-three years. He's marvelous. He turned his car over three times. It is a little Ford Courier pickup. He broke his ribs and recovered all by himself in Fontana, living alone. I don't know how he did it. Last year he had a stroke, completely recovered from that but it left a little problem in his vision. He is such a marvelous example of survival of the body with humor. Living alone and liking it. An incredible man. When he shakes hands with you, it is like shaking hands with a rock. He has tremendous strength—physical, mental and moral, spiritual. Toni's love for him and his love for her and me is pretty obvious as is the humor involved.

He illustrates the point of having something to do which is a transduction, the use of the body as a transducer between the Self and the external world. He's a carpenter and cabinetmaker. He makes beautiful inlaid wood boxes and various things for his friends, for his granddaughter, Nina.

Epilogue

Toni:

One evening after a particularly full day in Carmel, John and I decided to have dinner in one of our favorite restaurants.

Sitting opposite him, I suddenly found myself intensely studying and very much enjoying what he looks like. I am a very visual-oriented person and a large portion of my reality is spent in this domain.

John has a great melding of qualities in his face. Sometimes a great strength, expressed with a strong chin and nose. Also a perpetual youngness that makes his resemblance to his son John, Jr., startling at times. Twinkling through his very blue eyes, the Irish leprechaun can be seen, peeking out at a strange world. At particular times, the leprechaun has to make way for a battered magnificent ancient bird, full of the wisdom of the ages, perched and waiting.

Of course "the kid on the block with the biggest chemistry set" is never too far away, and all this is expressed by and captured within a marvelous cragginess that I very much enjoy looking at.

In the midst of my visual explorations of still other dimensions to the domains I have mapped, I suddenly wondered if John looked at me in the same ways.

I asked him to explain to me what I really looked like to him, and he said:

"It changes;
Sometimes it's a thunder cloud with lightning,
Sometimes a warm day in Spring,
Sometimes it's moonlight on a tropical beach,
Sometimes a sewing basket—a hooked rug—or
An avocado tree,
Sometimes a pile of manure.
Always a smile on awakening.
Finally a nice soft warm place to live."

Appendix One

Exercises: Physical, Biophysical, Psychophysical, Mental and Spiritual

This list of exercises is not meant to be exhaustive. It is for the person who is busy and doesn't have much time to spend daily on exercises. Some of the exercises are physical, some biophysical, some psychophysical, some are mental, and some or all could be interpreted as spiritual.

The basic principles behind these exercises have been found by doing a much more extensive long-term and vigorous series of exercises. Over the years I have reduced the time spent and the number of exercises to the minimum required to stay in a good state of health: defined as spiritual health, mental health and physical health.

If you wish, you can vary the exercises depending upon your body build and your own mind so as to take care of your particular physique, your particular mentality and your particular spiritual level.

EXERCISE SET 1: DIET

The first problem for many Americans is diet. Here we enunciate some general principles that I have discovered, by moving my body weight rapidly from 210 pounds down to 133 and then back up again, and moving my body weight from about 175 to about 155 more slowly, several times. My critical weight is between 160 and 165.

The principle is that of the "critical weight" for your particular body. The "critical weight" is defined as that weight at which your appetite exactly matches the needs of your body so that you neither overeat nor undereat. Above the critical weight your appetite is too great and your weight tends to climb. Below this weight your appetite tends to decrease and your body weight tends to fall to dangerously low levels. Once one attains the critical weight, the amount of exercise and the food intake are matched with your particular metabolism in such a way that a "steady state" weight is maintained with a shift of only plus or minus one or two pounds per day.

Your weight is best determined at a time when you have the minimum water in your body. It is best done in the morning immediately after arising and after eliminating urine and feces. This is the time at which your body contains the least amount of water. Water can shift the body weight during the day several pounds.

So the first exercise is to control your diet. In general I have found that if I am overweight, the quickest and safest way to lose the weight is to go on a very high protein and fat diet. Protein has a specific dynamic action, i.e., it causes the metabolism to be raised, which burns up some of the mass that is taken into your body. Fat ingested controls the appetite. If one eats just the right amount of fat, it shuts off the need for further food.

Carbohydrate is to be taken only when you do some particular violent exercise, such as skiing all day. A bit of carbohydrate during the day while doing the exercise is not contraindicated here. The rest of the time stay away from carbohydrate.

One quickly finds that on a high-protein-, high-fat-content diet, the amount of feces is decreased considerably over the amount produced on a carbohydrate diet. Do not worry about this. It is a natural physiological result of eating those foods that you can burn completely. On a high-protein, high-fat, no-carbohydrate diet, one's feces sink; a small amount of carbohydrate (sugar, honey, etcetera) causes them to float. This is a convenient test of how well you are keeping to the diet.

EXERCISE SET 2: STRETCHING

There are two kinds of physical exercise to be considered. The first is the stretching of every muscle in your body, every day, up to its particular limit at that time. This means a set of stretching exercises for this specific purpose. The standard course of yoga, the asanas, is a very good way to do this.

A. For those who know yoga I recommend The Cobra. When doing

The Cobra be sure that your buttocks are tightened so that the lower back is not strained. Lift the head only until the eyes are looking forward horizontally. Do not tip the head back. This puts an undue strain on the neck vertebrae. Keep the shoulder blades together and the arms straight with the hands flat on the floor. Stretch the feet out behind with the top part of the feet tight against the floor. While doing The Cobra, be sure that one does the maneuver known as co-contraction. *Co-contraction is the simultaneous contraction of muscles on both sides of a joint,* so the joint does not move but all muscles are tense.

B. After The Cobra do The Shoulderstand, being sure of the co-contraction during the maneuver. Lie on your back, with arms flat on the floor. Inhale. Raise legs together and point your toes toward the ceiling. When legs are extending over head, support back with your hands. Breathe steadily. Straighten the back, the hips and the legs to a vertical position, very carefully. Do co-contraction of all muscles and continue breathing steadily. Lower legs slowly.

C. After the Shoulderstand do The Plow, but do The Plow extremely carefully so that the back is not strained. Lie on your back. Depending upon the flexibility of your body, you may not be able to reach your toes up over your head to the floor. If you can, go ahead and touch the floor, then allow the knees to bend until they come on each side next to the ears. If your spine and your pelvic joints are sufficiently flexible, you will be able to do this, but do not strain. Carry it only to the limit where you feel things are too tense to go any further; then desist.

D. Leg Stretch: The next maneuver is part of the "Going to the Sun" exercise of yoga, and it is also a ballet dancer's stretch. Stand with the feet about one foot apart pointing straight ahead. Drop down with one leg going behind you and the top of your toes resting on the floor and that leg completely straight at the knee. Be sure now that you are bending from the hip of that particular leg. The forward leg is perpendicular to the floor with knee bent at a right angle. The hands are placed on the floor on each side of the forward leg, next to its foot. The head should be straight up, eyes looking forward.

Do this on each side, being aware of the joint between your femur and your pelvis. This exercise is designed to stretch that particular joint to its limit. Do not strain it. Keep the buttocks tight during this maneuver.

E. The Windmill: Stand firmly planted with your knees slightly bent and your feet about twelve inches apart. Swing your arms from the shoulder joint in as wide a circle as you can. This exercise is designed to give you increased mobility at the shoulder joint. The hands go up over the head with the elbows nearly straight; the arms are then swung backward and outward, downward and forward and then up again.

F. The next exercise is designed to stretch your thigh muscles. You kneel on the floor with your feet on each side of your buttocks; lean slowly and very carefully backward. If you are sufficiently flexible in the knee joints, in the hip joints and in the back, you can lie down on the floor between your feet. Once again, take it easy. The arms are held in a relaxed position on each side of the legs on the floor.

I have found that this is the minimum yoga, the minimum set of six exercises for stretching. You can elaborate on this depending on the flexibility of your body and your particular stage of learning in yoga techniques.

EXERCISE SET 3: STRESS

A. At the end of my yoga exercises, I do one which I learned from skiers. You stand on both feet, lift one foot bending the knee behind you, grasp that foot with the opposite hand. You now jump on the other foot, bending that knee on going down as far as it is comfortable to do so, so that you can come back up again. Now you jump in place—up and down. This is best done to fairly rapid music. Once you have mastered this you can travel around a room jumping on the one leg. The other arm is used for balance. You then trade sides and do it again. You do this exercise at least five minutes on each leg. You either do it for five minutes or for the period of time necessary for your heart to begin to pound and your respiration to increase to panting.

This exercise is number one in any set of stress exercises—total bodily stress. You can achieve it with the one-leg jumping exercise when you cannot go outdoors.

B. We find a very good "stress" exercise is to walk at a very rapid rate up a steep road or a steep set of stairs. We climb, in fifteen minutes, a road near our house that lifts the body 300 feet in a distance of approximately 4/10ths of a mile. If you have a hill nearby, you can walk up; this is an excellent exercise to wake up with in the morning. We do it whether it is raining or not. We have quite adequate rain hats and capes that we wear in the rain. You should walk fast enough so that in half the distance your heart rate has increased and your respiration also. You will find after several mornings of this that about two-thirds of the way up you hit your second wind, having passed through that rather painful period when the arteries in the muscles and in the brain are beginning to open up from the stimulation of the CO_2 released from your muscles.

C. Posture: Unimpeded breathing is very important during this exercise. One should keep one's shoulder blades together, one's tailbone tucked under and one's head as upright as one can hold it, lifting, as it were, from the top of one's head. This position means that you will be using minimum energy in balancing one bone on top of the other as you walk up the slope. Lifting one's body weight 300 feet every day, either up stairs or up a hill, assures you of staying in good condition in regard to your heart, respiration and total body function.

EXERCISE SET 4: ELIMINATION

A. Defecation: Very little is said about the excretory functions in regard to physical exercises and mental exercises. Probably the safest way to defecate is to squat on the toilet with the seat up, with one's feet on the bowl edge. This prevents the formation of hemorrhoids and assures those who have hemorrhoids that they will not be painfully stimulated. Squatting to defecate is taught by many natives who live in the bush, in Africa for example. Do not strain while in this position; relax and enjoy it.

B. Vomiting: One art that is neglected in our particular culture is that of vomiting. If you have taken too much food, or some food that turned out to have been bad, if you have taken in too much alcohol, or by accident swallowed a poison, it is good to be able to vomit easily and quietly. The dolphins taught me that to vomit is a natural function; that it can be done quietly and under control without the precipitous "projectile" kind of vomiting that most people have, the explosive variety, which brings stomach acid up into the nose and causes pain.

To induce vomiting, put two fingers into the back of the throat until they touch the region behind the soft palate against the posterior wall of the throat. Merely touch here. The vomiting reflex is elicited by gentle pressure in this region. Once the reflex starts, slow it down and do not allow it to become explosive. You will find that if you open your glottis fully and relax the throat, the contents of the stomach will come up easily and will not enter the posterior nose region.

The best way to practice this is to start with an empty stomach and fill the stomach with warm water, by drinking from the water tap. Take about three glasses of about 250 cc's each so that you take in 750 cc's of warm water. Lift the seat of the toilet, kneel in front of it and put the head over the bowl. Do not tip the head too far forward as this allows the contents of the stomach to enter the nose. With the right or the left hand, put the index finger and the second finger into the back of the throat over the tongue. Keep the tongue well forward and relax the throat. Allow the water to come up and pass out slowly and continuously. Do not allow a jerking spurting action, which tends to come from reflex contractions of the muscles involved. When you finally have experienced this several times, you will be able to achieve the slow, steady output that the dolphins have. The operation then goes from a rather painful prospect to an accomplished act of gentle expertise.

Exercise Set 5: Breathing

One's breathing is amazingly important. It is one of the mechanisms that keeps one alive on this planet. It also is that which massages the soft organs within the belly cavity and within the chest cavity. Breathing properly using the belly muscles for expiration and relaxing the belly muscles for inspiration is an art that is taught in yoga classes. Belly breathing without using the ribs can be achieved. Once one has this degree of control, one can then bring the ribs back into the picture; lifting them and expanding the chest cavity. Ordinary breathing is best done with the belly muscles. On inspiration the belly comes out; on expiration the belly goes in.

Exercise Set 6: Voice

Breathing is directly related to one's control of the voice. With good breathing, one develops much more mastery over the voice. One can now control voice without constricting it and without generating falsettos or other unwanted phenomena. Voice control such as is taught to actors, actresses and vocalists is something that one should acquire. Your voice is your means of communication with your fellowman. It is your means of influencing him/her. Once one masters all of the shades of emotional meaning that can be expressed through the voice, one has a range of communication that was not available before. Study actors and actresses going through different emotional scenes, say in the movies or on television. They have become experts at this sort of thing. You can pick out those who are best at it and mimic their behavior.

One exercise that I have found to be very beneficial is controlling the rate at which one speaks; the slower that one speaks the more one can study what one is actually doing with one's voice. Remember that the larynx and the vocal chords determine the vocal sounds. The consonants are determined mainly by the use of the tongue, lips and teeth. Nasalized vowels are those for which one opens the airway into the nose and allows the sound to come out through the nose, such as in an "aum" exercise. The *m* is a nasalized vocalized consonant.

Study your own speech. You have a very elaborate sensitive and sophisticated system for forming your language. Study, for example, how you make a *t* sound in the beginning of a word, in the middle and at the end. Pay attention to what your tongue does when pronouncing the sound for *t*. For example, a *t* at the end of a word can be implied by not making the sharp noise of the *t*, but by merely stopping the flow of sound out of the mouth. Try the word "start" for example. You can pronounce this in such a way that the *t* at the end is implied by the fact that you have cut short the sound "AR."

There is a whole series of exercises involving all of the sounds that you can make with your voice and your mouth. Practice on the following sentence:

"Joe took father's shoe bench out; meet me by the lawn."

This is the Bell Telephone laboratory's test sentence that I mentioned previously. It contains most of the sounds in native American English vocal language. As you say this sentence, study what your mouth is doing. Look in a mirror and watch your lips. Feel what is happening to your tongue—the anterior part, the middle part and the posterior part. Feel what's happening when sound is coming out through the nose. I won't spoil this exercise for you by telling you what happens in each part of the sentence. Each one of us is capable of doing this exercise individually. Try this in the tank with your ears underwater and then sit up and try it with ears out of the water.

Exercise Set 7: Hearing

For the next exercise you will need some help from a tape recorder and a special tape. This tape is purchasable from Paul Herbert at Hot Springs Lodge, Big Sur, California, 93920. When you write for it, tell Paul that you want the repeating word tape, especially that which repeats the word "cogitate" on it for one half hour.

You can listen to this tape through headphones or through a loud-speaker; it makes little difference. You will have to listen the first time for a period of about half an hour. This exercise calls for you to relax completely; lie down while you are doing it and close your eyes and listen and concentrate on what you hear coming from the tape. Let go of all preconceptions having to do with this tape, and just see what happens to your own hearing. This exercise should be done daily for quite a number of days before you see the beneficial results of it.

We can give you a hint: on 300 subjects, we got 2,730 alternate words to the word "cogitate." Only 340 of these were in a large dictionary. The rest were words that we do not use yet.

Exercise Set 8: Vision

A. Afterimages: The phenomena that you will experience with the repeating word effect can also be produced in the visual field. The best way to do this is to study afterimages. However, studying afterimages requires special apparatus. For this you will need a photographic flash, an electronic flash, that you can turn on by pressing a button. You use this apparatus in a dimly lighted room. You look at a picture close enough so that it is in focus but filling your visual field. You set the flash up in such a way that the picture will be lighted up brightly for a very small fraction of a second. I have found the best position for the flash is on top of the head facing forward and down so as to hit the picture in such a way so that it lights it up. (An interesting alternate to the picture is your own face in the mirror, lit up by the flash. However, here you will have to shield the flash so that you don't see the direct flash itself in the mirror, just your face lighted up.)

In either case, picture or face, you make sure that your eyes are looking at the center, i.e., in the case of the face you look at a point between the two eyes and hold it fixed while you are igniting the flash. The face should be lighted by a very dim light and the room must be very dark.

With this setup you can now generate an afterimage on your two retinae such that it will last for twenty minutes to a half an hour. Immediately after the flash you close your eyes and study the afterimage. If the afterimage looks as if it is moving, you have not looked directly at the center of the picture or of the face; you looked off to one side and your peripheral vision is being so stimulated that you get a continuous movement in a particular direction (of the picture or of the face). This is to be avoided, for our present purposes.

Once you do the experiment correctly, you will find that various things happen to the afterimage. It can maintain itself as it was originally for some time if you concentrate on that happening. However, if you let go and allow it to happen, various other phenomena will take place. The afterimage may disappear and a white screen might appear in its place, or a blue screen or a red screen or a yellow screen, practically any color. Various parts of the image will change their shape, their color, the relationship to one another. You may see an ancient face in the place of your own. You may see a baby's face in place of your own, etcetera.

B. Face in Mirror: Very similar effects to those in the afterimage exercise can be achieved by looking at the same spot on your face, reflected in the mirror, that we talked about earlier, between the two eyes. Sit perfectly still and have nothing else in the room moving so as not to disturb the effects that you are looking for. You can kneel or sit in front of the mirror in a comfortable position so that you can stare at a single point between your two eyes above the bridge of your nose for at least one half hour. If you maintain the fixity of gaze, blinking when necessary, you will find that all sorts of phenomena develop. You may see entirely new faces and various other sorts of phenomena. You may find that your state of being can be changed under these circumstances also.

C. Cyclops: The next exercise is similar to the preceding one in that you are using a mirror and your own image. However, now you move up to the mirror, placing your forehead and your nose against it. When you do this correctly you will see one "cyclopean" eye instead of your two eyes. You now concentrate your attention on the single pupil of this cyclopean eye. When you do this you can see certain phenomena that we do not describe here so that you can experience them fresh yourself.

In the last exercise some people have a bit of trouble getting the two eyes lined up in such a way so that they see a single eye. This merely takes practice in most cases. In some cases with various problems having to do with the eye muscles you may not be able to achieve it; however, then go back to moving your face farther away from the mirror until you can get the two eyes to fuse. The question of focus is important also. Nearsighted people have a much easier time with this exercise than do farsighted people. If you are very farsighted, wear your glasses and sit at a comfortable distance from the mirror so that you can fuse the two eyes. You will now see three eyes, two, which you ignore, out in the periphery.

Various esoteric schools have made use of some of these exercises for their own particular purposes. They draw all sorts of conclusions from these. In this book we are merely demonstrating the properties of this immensely complex machine known as our own biocomputer. There is nothing esoteric or mystical about these exercises unless you bring that kind of a metaprogram to the exercises themselves. In that sense they are useful for certain kinds of personal spiritual movement.

EXERCISE SET 9: MANTRA

We make use of the mantra technique also. One of our favorites is "Who Am I?" as explained by Ramana Maharshi. You sit in a quiet room, in a position that you can maintain for an hour, and you keep asking yourself the question "Who Am I?" As each answer comes up you drop it, let it go. Most people who can maintain this discipline and do this exercise find that they can then carry on the exercise without being in a quiet room, in the presence of others, whenever they can relax. This exercise can bring about great changes in your view of yourself. Eventually you will find that your opinion of yourself is only another program and that it is less than the total biocomputer. One program cannot encompass the whole computer. You are far greater than your opinion of yourself.

To lead up to this exercise we generally introduce people to the mantra "I am not my opinion of me, I am not your opinion of me, I am not their opinion of me." Repeated enough, this can set you free from a lot of nonsense that may be present in your biocomputer.

EXERCISE SET 10: SOLITUDE

We recommend that each person spend a good deal of time alone. Solitude is a reinvigorating, revitalizing influence in our lives. We are usually too busy to make full use of it; however, if one can set aside an hour a day to do these exercises in solitude, one will find very fast results with them. The physical exercises can be done in a group. Some people do them best in a group. The walk up the stairs or up the hill is oftentimes done best with others. However, doing these alone is also a transforming form.

EXERCISE SET 11: THE PHYSICAL ISOLATION TANK

We recommend the tank, the isolation, solitude and confinement tank for some of these mental exercises and others that you can work out yourself. The tank is probably the best place in the world to rest. If you can find one available or build one yourself from instructions in our forthcoming new tank handbook, The Deep Self, you will experience new phenomena and find a "great peace." This is a Western approach to meditation–a method that shortens the time used for effective meditation.

EXERCISE SET 12: MENTATIONS (REVISED)

One set of mental–physical exercises that are useful in the tank and that are best done there are the mentations as presented in *The Center of the Cyclone*. Once learnd well, the mentations are useful for daily problem-solving and testing and perfecting of one's objectivity in regard to emotional high-energy problems. Once embedded as recallable programs in one's own biocomputer, the mentations can function below one's levels of awareness and give one a perspective on one's life in a very condensed fashion.

Recently I have modified the mentations from the way they were given in *The Center of the Cyclone*. See Appendix Two, which follows, for the table of the newer and more sophisticated set of mentations.

Appendix Two

Revised Mentations (cf. *The Center of the Cyclone*)

Body Locale	Metabelief Operator Function	Symbolic Representation
Top of head	Supraself-meta-programming	*Guidance*
Center of forehead	Self-metaprogramming	*Initiative*
Point between eyes in the midline	Mental effort in concentration	*Concentration*
Eyes	Internal vision	*Visualization*
Ears	Internal listening to supraself	*Listening*
Nose	Expense, moneywise	*Outgo*
Mouth	Money coming in	*Income*
Neck	Expression from inner to outer reality	*Voicing*
Shoulder: right	Ability to hold to meta-program: including male metabelief operator	*Male Responsibility*
Shoulder: left	Ability to hold to metaprogram: including female metabelief operator	*Female Responsibility*

Body Locale	Metabelief Operator Function	Symbolic Representation
Upper arm: right side	Personal inner strength to write	*Writing*
Upper arm: left side	Personal inner strength to read	*Reading*
Right elbow	Function of your closest helper, male	*Male Helper(s)*
Left elbow	Function of your closest helper, female	*Female Helper(s)*
Right forearm	Programming for and of closest male helper	*Male Orders*
Left forearm	Programming for and of closest female helper	*Female Orders*
Right hand	Content of operational programs for male helper	*Male Manipulation*
Left hand	Content of operational programs for female helper	*Female Manipulation*
Center of chest	State of Being: High Indifference	*Detachment*
Upper belly	Acceptance of new metabeliefs	*Openness*
Navel	The money available	*Capital*
Lower belly: pelvis	The time available for the solution	*Schedule*
Genitals	Statement of new metabelief to be learned and used	*Novelty*
Thighs	Group capacity for problem solving	*Group Strength*
Knees	Available persons for group	*Personnel*
Lower legs	Facilities, space and apparatus available at worksite	*Facilities*
Feet	Worksite available, travel to worksite	*Travel*

The mentations are a set of mental–physical exercises that are useful (once learned well) for daily problem-solving, and testing and perfecting one's objectivity in regard to emotional high-energy problems.

DISCUSSION OF TABLE

The anatomical locales in which one places a symbolic representation of the function are given in the first column. The function definition is in the second column, and the key word or symbolic representation is in the third column. First of all understand what these words mean. For example, Guidance implies supraself-metaprogramming placed in the top of the head. This is all the kinds of programming that are greater than one's Self including the programming of others on this planet and one's spiritual or mental guides that one carries inside one's head: symbol, *Guidance*.

In the center of the forehead, place one's own metaprogramming, the Self-metaprogramming, and symbolize this by the word *Initiative*.

The point between the eyes in the midline: The function is the mental effort in concentration symbolized by the word *Concentration*.

The eyes: This is the location of your internal vision. While doing the mentations in this fashion, one closes one's eyes and uses one's capacity to visualize. This operation is symbolized by *Visualization*.

The ears symbolize one's ability to listen internally either to somebody else talking outside and using the listening capacity or alternatively listening to those forces in one's self that are greater than one's self or listening to one's self. This is symbolized by the word *Listening*.

The nose: One places here "expense," that is the air going out is an expenditure of funds, so we symbolize this by the word *Outgo*.

The mouth is used for the function of money coming in, symbolized by the word *Income*.

The neck symbol is *Voicing;* the function is expression of inner reality into the external reality.

The shoulders are divided right (male) and left (female), and the functions for each are the two metabelief operators, male on right, female on left. Symbols are *Male Responsibility* on right shoulder, *Female Responsibility* on left shoulder. A metabelief operator determines the generation of one's beliefs at a given time (see Appendix Four and Chapter Seventeen).

The right upper arm: The function is one's personal inner strength to write, the right, symbolized by the word *Writing*. Note that if you write with your left hand, reverse this and the next one.

Left upper arm: Personal inner strength to read, the symbolic representation is *Reading*. This implies reading with understanding and also reading in order to change one's metabeliefs.

Right elbow: The function of your closest helper, male, and is symbolized by *Male Helper*. Of course these can be plural if you need it.

Left elbow is the function of your closest helper, female, symbolized by *Female Helper*, also possible to make this plural.

The reason for separating into male and female categories is that the programmatic aspects of males and females are quite different, as you will see as you use this set of operations in your daily life.

Right forearm: Programming for and from your closest male helper, symbolized by the word *Male Orders*. This implies that you are willing to take orders as well as to give orders. It's a feedback relationship symbolized in the right arm.

Left forearm is the converse of the right forearm for and from your closest female helper and we symbolize this by *Female Orders*. Once again, this is both for receiving as well as giving orders.

Right hand has the content of operational programs for your male helper, symbolized by *Male Manipulation*. "Manipulation" means the use of the hand (*Latin: "manus"*). Here we also use manipulation in more symbolic modes as the actual carrying out of instructions, either received from or given to one's male helper.

The Left hand is the content of operational programs for and from the female helper, symbolized by *Female Manipulation*. Once again this is the specific content of programs from and to your closest female helper.

Center of chest: This is your State of Being. One attempts to achieve a state of "High Indifference." We symbolize this by the word *Detachment*. The definition of the State of High Indifference is in Merrell-Wolff's *Pathways Through to Space* in a special section and in the Appendix.

Upper belly: The solar plexus. The function is the acceptance of new metabeliefs, of new metaprograms. We symbolize this by the word *Openness*.

Navel: This is the money available to you for solving your problems; we symbolize this by the word *Capital*.

Lower Belly and front of Pelvis: the function is the time available for the solution to the problems. We symbolize this by the word *Schedule*.

Genitals: Statement of new metabelief to be learned and used. We symbolize this by *Novelty*.

Thighs: Both sides, the function is the group capacity for the problem-solving. We symbolize this by the words *Group Strength.*

Both Knees: Available persons for the group: here you name them. This is symbolized by *Personnel.*

Lower legs, both sides: Facilities, space and apparatus available at worksite. We symbolize this by *Facilities.*

Both Feet: Travel to the available worksite. We symbolize this by *Travel.*

As we say in *The Center of the Cyclone,* the easiest way to learn these mentations is to attach the word (symbol) to the place in the body, memorizing in the body the key word and then working finally on the meaning of those words as one moves over the body. One can move from the feet up to the top of the head and then reverse the direction and go from the top of the head down to the feet.

With a new problem it may be wise to start at the feet and work to the top of the head. When one reaches the top of the head, one then starts over from the top of the head working down.

In certain cases, once one has learned the whole list and attached it to one's body, one can then see in which direction one should proceed, whether from the top of the head or from the feet. *If it is a practical problem, start at the feet. If it is a theoretical problem, start at the top of the head.*

Here we have made a first attempt to modernize the mentations for practical use by Americans in our particular culture. This group seems much more operational than the group given in *The Center of the Cyclone,* for American businessmen, scientists, professionals, housewives and students.

Try them for yourself. You cannot test their use until you have them in your biocomputer. A program, a metaprogram, on paper is not in you and cannot either operate in you or be tested by you. Memorize these mentations by placing the symbol in the body part.

Purposely we do not give you a specific example of their use. We have found that such examples may spoil the novelty of your own results.

Appendix Three

"Hallucinations Can Be Normal, Useful Phenomena" Some Uses of the Isolation Tank

In the following discussion it is assumed that the reader is acquainted with the exercises given in the back of this book, in the appendixes, and that he or she is acquainted with the tank method of solitude, isolation and confinement. (*See Programming and Metaprogramming in the Human Biocomputer; The Center of the Cyclone* and The Deep Self, now in process.) With this background the following discussion is both a recapitulation and a preparation for the use of the tank.

For those who have not yet experienced the tank environment, the lack of light, the lack of sound, the lack of gravitational computations, we recommend the visualization exercises and the new set of mentations given in Appendixes One and Two. The tank environment is a relaxing, refreshing, safe place to recover one's energy. We find that in a busy day, a half hour break in the tank restores energy to the mind and the body. Gardening, hiking, desk work, writing, dictating, typing, each takes a toll of available energy. The tank restores the free, available energy.

Such restoration is possible in the early tank experiences for most people. With practice, it becomes easier to relax more of one's body

244

and one's mind. With experience, the benefits arrive more easily and faster. At first an hour may be used; later, in a series, twenty minutes may suffice. Most people feel a new clarity of perception as one feels on awaking after a good night's sleep.

Self-metaprogramming in the tank is a mental discipline worth capturing for one's own. We give a few hints here as to how to get started on your own discipline and some of its uses.

For review, we state the basic metabelief operator upon which the following discussion is based.

"In the province of the mind, what one believes to be true either is true or becomes true within certain limits. These limits are to be found by experience and by experiment upon one's self. Once found, these limits turn out to be further beliefs to be transcended. In the province of the mind there are no limits."

This metabelief operator is clearest in the tank environment. One has no duties in the external reality whatsoever. One is freed up temporarily from the necessities of schedules, from the programming of others by Self and of Self by others, from the necessities of maintaining the balance of the body under a gravitational field, from patterned visual inputs and patterned acoustic inputs. It is only in this environment that the truth of the above metabelief operator can be realized. The closest approximation to this in an ordinary life is to lie either on a bed in the dark and in the silence or in a bathtub in the dark and the silence. These are not substitutions for the tank, they are practical compromises for those who do not have a tank available.

Once one's mind is freed from the physical environment by this technique, one has the whole range of the human mind available to one's self. One is free to exercise one's imagination; one's thinking capacity is at a maximum. One has available parts of the central nervous system (cerebellum, for example) that are normally not available for programming by Self under ordinary circumstances. By means of the tank, one is automatically given an expanded province of one's mind, in one's brain.

Under these circumstances, hallucinations, projections, simulations are all very real. One basic tank rule is: "No matter what happens do not move"; keep these processes active only in the tank.

Let us start with the visual field, in the tank. First one studies the darkness with eyes open and then with eyes closed. In our experience, most people experience a blackness with the eyes open which has extent—the extent that one imagines that the tank has. One then closes one's eyes and the blackness seems to be a much more constricted space. As one continues this testing of the blackness, new phenomena begin to appear.

With eyes open the blackness begins to extend beyond the known confines of the tank as one forgets about the tank walls. With continued practice of this exercise, one finds that the eyes open versus the eyes closed converge in a very large space. Opening or closing the eyes makes no difference at this point.

After the completion of this exercise, one then continues looking at the blackness in three dimensions. One finds that the space at first has an indefiniteness about it. One may see modulations of the blackness either in rhythmic waves or in cloudlike forms separated by areas of less blackness. As one continues to concentrate one's visualization in the blackness, various other phenomena develop.

One may see very small bright flashes or light or streaks of light or various forms that are quite indefinite at this stage. Their nature seems to be highly contrasting to the black clouds.

The light phenomena are seen in the background against these clouds or within these clouds.

Sometimes one sees straight ahead a tunnellike structure beginning to develop in the center of one's vision. Or one may see a circular bright spot of light that changes color. This spot may start out as blue or as yellow, sometimes green or red.

At this point one may begin to put in metaprograms about changing the color of the spot. If one has already had training in the visual exercises given in Appendix One, one finds that one can manipulate the color much more easily.

The first rule in this set of phenomena can be illustrated. The rule is: *It takes time for the central nervous system to generate a display. One must put in the orders, as it were, to the central nervous system to change the color, then there is a delay, a programmatic delay before that color appears. This delay may last a few seconds, or it may take several minutes.* About this time one may want to abandon the visual field and go into other regions of the mind's activities, leaving the visualization exercise for future attempts. Each session in the tank offers new progress in the visualization abilities when one realizes that this can be done.

Rule number two can then be shown to exist. *That which is forbidden is not allowed;* therefore, at about this time one starts examining one's basic belief structures as to why sharp visual images are forbidden one in the tank environment.

One can then go through the mentations in regard to one's metabelief operators, leaving the visual field for a future investigation. Here, I refer you to Chapter Seventeen and Appendix Four in this book, which deal with the metabelief operator and its use.

To return to the tank, one next considers one's ears and sounds. If the environment is ideal there are no outside sounds coming into the tank. One's ears are underwater and all such sounds are cut by approximately seventy decibels merely by the fact that one's eardrums are loaded with water. If the environment is adequately sound-insulated you will hear nothing at all coming into the ears from the outside.

One now listens to the noises of one's body. If one listens in the very low-frequency region of the spectrum, one can sometimes hear the beating of the pulse in the ears. This can come and go as one's attention is focused on it, or one allows it to pass. One hears one's breathing somewhere in one's head.

One property of hearing underwater should be remembered. Any sounds that are of high frequency that are introduced into the water will be heard inside the middle of the head. One will not be able to assign a direction and a distance to the sounds that are occurring underwater. Therefore, if for example there is gas in the gut and one hears the sharp cracklings of this gas moving in the gut, at first they will seem to be in the head. When one hears such sounds it is wise to lift one's head above water and make sure that they are coming from the gut. This can be confirmed by emerging the ears from the water.

One then puts one's ears back underwater and notes that the sounds are mainly occurring somewhere in the head. One then re-programs the location of these sounds to put them as if coming from the gut. One notices immediately that the sounds pass out of the head and move down into the body. This is a new metabelief operator exerting its power over the apparent location of sounds. If one moves a finger rapidly up and down at the surface of the water making very slight splashing sounds, one can also go through this same exercise and relocate the sounds where one assumes that they belong in the external reality.

One now focuses one's attention on the surface of the body. In the tank one can detect the miniscus (that particular edge between the water, the air and the skin) between the air and the water on various parts of the body, especially around the edges of the face. This is felt as a discontinuous boundary disappearing into the hair for example (if one is bald, one has a continuous boundary).

With other parts of the body it is less easy to appreciate this miniscus, for example, at the knees and the feet. One can detect it easily along the sides of the body, on the hands and with greater difficulty, the shoulders and the arms.

A rather interesting exercise is to try to locate the restoring forces against gravity that are keeping one floating. Since these are distributed over the surface of the immersed body, one can appreciate that these forces in general are below one's threshold for detection of pressure against the skin.

Suddenly one may come up against the boundaries of the tank. A hand may do this, a foot, the top of one's head. At this point one does a centering operation in which one extends the arms out to the sides and the feet out to the sides and centers one once again in the center of the tank. One holds the position long enough so that the slight waves created will not move the body as one brings the feet back toward one another and the arms toward the sides. If one can stay centered and not "Ping-Pong" around against the walls of the tank by pushing off abruptly from one side to the other, one can lose the boundaries of the tank in regard to one's own body.

One may suddenly feel that the body is rotating in a horizontal axis around the center of the body or rotating around any other axis; one may get a feeling as if the body is arched and going backward in an arc, backward and downward with the head leading or in the opposite direction with the feet leading, or rolling off to one side. One knows from the peripheral receptors especially with the miniscus phenomenon that the body is actually not moving at all, that this is an inner simulation "as if moving."

If one now sits up in the tank and then slowly goes back down to the lying position one can study the phenomena of this apparent movement, of the overshoot from the real movement.

One now is getting deeper within the body and one's simulation of the body. If one can leave those very slight evidences of the external reality of the water and move into those spaces in which the simulations exist, i.e., the "as if movement" space, then one is free of the body and one has a simulation of the body operating free of the physical body. As one pursues this particular exercise, one finds that eventually the observer is moving within a coordinate system that is free of the body. At this point one may not want to move very far within this simulation but suddenly one realizes that the observer can become mobile. At first he moves within the simulated body and then finally moves out of even the simulated body.

This phase (the mobile observer), may not occur for several hours of tank work. Some people have a talent for it and can do it within the first few hours. Others may take ten or a hundred hours to accomplish this degree of mobility. One may have to spend many one-hour sessions in the tank in order to achieve this degree of realization of the reality of one's simulations.

Many people are forbidden to do this kind of activity. These people will have to work upon their basic beliefs about the mobility of their operator within the body and outside the body. Of great help to them is the realization that there are many people who can do this and that several people have accomplished this within twenty to thirty hours of tank work.

If one works upon the visual freedom, the visual display systems being independent of the tank and of the body and the acoustic systems and the observer as independent of the body, one finally can experience the phenomena that were described in *The Center of the Cyclone* and *Programming and Metaprogramming in the Human Biocomputer.*

At this point, one may well ask what is the purpose of all this? Why does one go through these exercises? Why does one try to achieve this independence of the observer/operator from the usual coordinates within the body?

The main reason for doing these exercises is to free up one's basic belief systems so that they are more in consonance with the actual powers of the mind itself. Each of us potentially can use our minds in these ways. If we can use them in these ways we can then begin to conceive of other ways of using the mind. One improves one's powers of visualization of problems, of making problems real and of running off models of problems by these exercises. Once one accomplishes control over these phenomena, they are now in one's service. Let us take a specific example.

When I experienced these phenomena of the simulated body moving in a simulated space in the tank, I then decided to make a machine that could simulate these simulated motions for the real body in the external world. I wished to design an entirely new machine for three-dimensional exercises. I went into the tank and started working on the basic concepts and the design of the machine. First I imagined being in the machine. Initially I was tied into it so that I wouldn't fall under gravity when I was upside down, or spinning in space. The purpose of the machine is to be able to spin one's body around any one of three mutually perpendicular axes. One can rotate around a vertical axis running from the feet up through the body and through the head. One can then spin that axis on a horizontal axis going through the center of gravity of the body, extending laterally. Then these two axes can be spun about another axis which is a vertical suspension of the whole machine.

The tied-in-form of the machine quickly disappeared. I realized that one should be able to move one's body, move one's center of gravity so as to encourage movement around these axes. I then visualized a pair of boots in which one laced up one's lower legs and feet. These boots were fastened to a platform. Over my head was a bar that I could hang on to with both hands. The platform and the bar could rotate in an axis perpendicular to the plane of the soles of the feet and to a parallel plane over the head. This was the axis running from the feet up through the top of the head, with some ability to move on and off that axis.

In the tank, my simulated body went through the motions that were required in the external reality later. I then visualized this particular axis being rotated on a horizontal axis through the body above the hips, through the center of gravity, extending laterally from right to left. As my simulated body rotated around its own inner axis, as if a figure skater whirling around his own body axis, at the same time I induced a rotation through the horizontal axis. The head and the feet were now describing a sine wave curve in circular space. The head and the feet were rotating around two axes simultaneously at right angles to each other. To say the least; the simulated body was doing a very complicated series of maneuvers in space.

I then added the third axis, which was in the direction of gravity, perpendicular to the floor, hanging from the ceiling. This meant that the head was now moving on the surface of a sphere with rather complicated sine wave paths over the surface of that sphere. The feet were on the opposite side of the sphere.

Suddenly I realized that all of this could be simulated very simply by visualizing my feet as fastened to one side of a sphere, I was holding on to handles on the other side of the sphere, the body was inside the sphere, and this sphere was suspended or floating in water. The center of this sphere was at the center of gravity of my body. The simplified model suddenly arrived while I was going through the complex operations of setting up three mutually perpendicular axes of rotation. This sphere could do all of these motions as long as it was floating either in liquid or inside a quarter-sphere, suspended upon an air bearing.

Suddenly the two forms of the apparatus appeared in the space around me—remember this space is independent of gravity and independent of the tank and quite independent of my body. The simulated body was going through the motions and the simulated observer was staying in the head of the simulated body.

I then began to visualize a practical form of this apparatus. One could do the sphere form but this would be rather expensive and there was always the problem of having enough air in this sphere. These are solvable problems but I put this one aside for a while.

I then began to design a machine to be hung up in my living room on a beam that's about twelve feet off the floor. I first designed it in an ideal fashion, that is with axles and bearings that had no friction whatsoever, i.e., the air bearing or the high-pressure oil bearing that is used on telescopes. I chose stainless steel for its light weight and its high strength for the framework supporting the body.

I then moved to a more practical prototype disallowing for the heavy expense of air bearings. At this stage of development a prototype would tell us more about how those bearings had to be designed. I then got out of the tank and went to my office and sketched the resulting design, working out practical details, dimensions, materials and so forth.

I give this illustration to show you that what we are doing in the tank can be used in very practical fashions. Once one realizes the fantastic mobility that is possible and the plasticity of materials and one's ability to change them in visualizing their existence in this way, one realizes that this is a very practical design method.

Let us consider the hypothetical case of a businessman who has become expert at the use of the tank in his business.

The businessman is making a very complicated deal for three pieces of real estate with three different other people entering into the negotiations. This particular man had several tens of hours of work in the tank and found that he could hold in his visual sphere, within the province of his mind, the three pieces of real estate, the three operators, and the escrow arrangements for manipulating the deal. He visualized the amounts of money necessary, the flow of that money through four separate escrow accounts, the timing of the opening and closing of the escrows, what information that he had to give each of the other participants and what information he had to withhold from each of the other participants. With his newly developed visualization techniques and his ability to move as a mobile observer-participant he was able to move from one person to the other, set up a simulated conference with each one and realize what we call a sloppy fit, in other words, he had thoroughly in mind several alternatives and alternative ways of saying things to each of these people. As the deal developed he went back to the tank several times and revised his strategy.

In general, such uses show one a lot more about the tank use than one would realize in reading what I have written about the tank previously. We now have a saying that hallucination is a talent to be used in the service of one's planetside trip. It is not something to be shunned as dangerous. It is only dangerous if the hallucinations take on a reality that persists beyond the confines of the tank and one acts as if they are true in the external world. The tank is the only proper province for the exercise of this kind of an ability until one becomes an adept at its control.

Appendix Four

The Metabelief Game: A Metabelief Operator

a) Assume there exist three belief systems, not currently your own.
b) Assume that you have the capacity-ability to believe the reality generated by/in each belief system.
c) Take on belief system no. 1: Believe it totally and ignore any contradicting/paradoxical/disagreeing other belief system.
d) Live out the consequences of belief system no. 1 as true and real.
e) Move out of belief system no. 1 into your usual belief system, your common sense reality beliefs.
f) Take on belief system no. 2, believe it, find the consequences, and return to your own reality.
g) Do the same for belief system no. 3.
h) Examine the consequences, the reality generated by each of the three belief systems, the merits of each.
i) Now specify your own belief system, call it no. 4.
j) Construct a fifth belief system that includes each of the four previous belief systems. What is your new reality?
k) Can you conceive of a new (no. 6) belief system that includes nos. 1, 2, 3, 4, and 5?
l) Is an infinite set of alternate belief systems appearing? If not, why not? Find a belief that allows for an infinite alternate set of beliefs.

m) What/Where/How is the Unknown? Have you included it in the new/old sets? If not, revise until the Unknown is included.

n) Did the Void appear immediately preceding each of your shifts into the new belief systems during your search? Revise until it does.

Appendix Five

Simulations of God: A Triadic Art Theater Piece

When my new book *Simulations of God: The Science of Belief* was in galley proof, our friends Burgess Meredith and Charles Lloyd set about narrating its "Prologue" to music (on a woodwind synthesizer).

Their dyadic performance inspired a group of us to create a group, The Simulations, in order to compose and perform a combination of four arts: narration, music, song and dance, within a similar context.

Toni's interest in combining the arts with other dimensions was long-standing, so with the help of many friends, including Mary Taylor, Garr Campbell, Don Harris, Russell Pyle and Myrna Garwyn, we constructed this piece.

We hope you enjoy our experiment in the four arts to present a fantasy of a possible Origin of Us.

(DANCE INSTRUCTION)
(Music Instruction)
Author and Narrator: Dr. John Lilly
Producer: Antonietta Lilly
Choreography: Nina Carozza, Marsha Polekoff
Music: Dean Olch, John Lambdin, Tony Selvage
Vocal: Jean Ray

Simulations of God
A Triadic Art Theater Piece
Written by John C. Lilly, M.D.

In a sense, a simulation of God is a Creation by a Creature created by God. In another sense, a simulation of God is that which a group of humans consider to be the most important ideas, models, metaprograms that function "as if" God in the thinking of that particular group. This presentation is based upon the author's book *Simulations of God: The Science of Belief,* published by Simon and Schuster, New York, 1975.

In this dance, music, narration piece, it is hypothesized that the first humans were created as haploid females.*

The episode here presented is of two haploid females whose bodies evolved on this Planet by means of the normal evolutionary process. In addition, we present the theory that these bodies are not activated until a Being from the primordial Consciousness-without-an-object enters the body.

In this dance we open with a theory of the creation of the Beings, two of which are to inhabit the two haploid female bodies, thus activating them and creating life as we know it in them.

In the dance after their creation, the two haploid females live on this Planet, form the First Dyad, die and return to Consciousness-without-an-object in order to make further choices as to what bodies they will inhabit in their future lives.

After the dance episode, one or a number of the haploid females becomes a male through a cosmic ray intervention changing the X chromosome to a Y chromosome. This haploid male then mates with one of the haploid females and forms the first of the diploid humans. In this view, Adam and Eve were haploid male and haploid female who mated and gave rise to a series of children who were diploid. The

* A haploid female is one in which there is only half the number of chromosomes of the currently present human beings. Each female contains only one X chromosome instead of the two X chromosomes that females currently have. Currently such haploid females can be created by the process called parthenogenesis. For example, by heat shock of a rabbit ovary, a haploid female rabbit can be created anew. Such single-X female rabbits are sterile in the sense that they cannot reproduce from the sperm of a diploid male rabbit. Theoretically such a female could become a haploid male if a cosmic ray were to hit the X chromosome in exactly the right way, so as to turn the X chromosome into a Y chromosome. The haploid male, with a single Y chromosome, theoretically could make the haploid female pregnant, producing a diploid individual.

diploid humans were so different from the haploid ones that they were forced to leave the original Garden of Eden, which contained the haploid individuals.

The dance is divided into four separate sections.

The first section is entitled "Creation." Beings are created from the primordial Consciousness-without-an-object by the Starmaker. One Being chooses a form on a Planet in a solar system in a galaxy. She finds the haploid female Form, enters it, activates it and dances alone.

In the second episode, entitled "Me," she develops in narcissistic abandon.

In the third episode, entitled "My Energy–Your Energy," a second Being chooses to inhabit the haploid female form and develops her own uniqueness alone.

The first Being sees the second Being, the second Being sees the first Being and they become the first Female Dyad. Dyadic Union develops. The first Being-female dies.

The fourth episode is entitled "Unity and Resurrection."

The first Being-female weakens and dies in the midst of the Dyadic Union dance. The second female grieves, returns to her narcissistic aloneness. She weakens and dies.

Each Being then arises from her Earthly Form and begins her return to the primordial Consciousness-without-an-object.

The Dance of Transit from Earth Form to Unity with the Cosmos begins. Each Being thinks that she is still in the earthly female Form. There is a period of confusion until each determines that she is dead and arisen again. Each returned to the Consciousness of their Cosmic Connection and transit together, back to choose the choice of another Form elsewhere. This completes the first cycle of human life on earth.

It is assumed that after this, after a few millions of years, the haploids give rise to the diploids and the diploids kill off all of the haploids. Two thousand years ago one haploid developed by accident and preached to the diploids, trying to teach haploid philosophy to diploids and not succeeding.

We hope you will enjoy our little fantasy about one possible origin of us, the diploid human race.

SIMULATIONS OF GOD

Introduction to a "Performance" on Earth

I have received a very peculiar and powerful invitation to help in a rather unfamiliar experiment. The invitation includes myself and each of you attending this performance. I have been asked to serve as an intermediary between each of you and the scientist who sent the invitation.

The invitation from the Scientist reads as follows:

"I am that which, on your planet, is called a Scientist. I am from a planet (call it 'A') 25,000 of your light years closer to Galactic Center. Our civilization once was similar to yours, approximately 2,000 of your years in the past. At the present time we are investigating some phenomena recently discovered on another planet (call it 'B') a number of light years beyond yours, toward the edge of the Galaxy. We have a theory that your species of human beings originated on Earth in the fashion that new Beings are being created on planet 'B'.

"We have some 'recordings' (as you would call them) of some of the creation events on planet B. In order to test our theory, we need to obtain your reactions to a 'performance' of these events, re-created for you from our recordings by special techniques (beyond your current capabilities).

"If a sufficient number of you 'resonate' in a particular manner to these events, we will then be able to determine whether or not your species of human beings was created in a similar fashion. If only a few or none of you 'resonate,' then your creation had another origin.

"We invite you to participate in this experiment to guide our future research."

(End of invitation.)

In the communication accompanying this invitation to us, were some more specific instructions to me and to you, as follows:

"A. During the 'performance' from the recordings, I will be able to use you in the performance 'as if' you are me. *You*, in the performance, *will be me* reading my notes as I watch the events. (How we do this is, at present, not yet a part of your science.)

B. Please advise each participant in this experiment to relax his/her beliefs accumulated during their life on Earth. I suggest the following:

1) The two Beings created in this 'performance' are not present-day humans: such primitive humans as these have not existed on your planet for the last two million years.

2) The two Beings may appear 'as if' like some of you because that is your belief: suspend that belief. (They are from a planet far away from you.)

3) The sounds you hear may be mistaken by you for that which you call 'music': suspend that belief also. (The sounds are vibrations that are a part of the creation process, and apparently are used to guide the two Beings.)

4) The behavior of these two Beings may confuse you in your belief that they are 'dancing': suspend that belief also. (They are undergoing reactions to what you call 'feelings' in response to their new form and the guiding 'vibrations.')

5) My 'voice,' articulated through you, is automatically translated from my language into yours. (We use human symbols for our own research purposes: the text means more than you think you will be saying.)

C. I regret that (as yet) we cannot inform you who is doing this 'Creation,' nor why it is being done. In later communications we may be able to tell you *'who* and *why.'* We are collecting the data to answer these questions, as well as the answer to *how* it is done."

The Scientist also sent some additional communication to be given to each of you after the "Performance."

The "Performance":

INTRODUCTION—to be read after music starts (*shakuhachi* flute)

For the purposes of this performance, it is assumed that Human Beings have two separate Origins. The first is the usual evolutionary account of the Origins of Organisms on the Planet Earth. These natural processes create bodies of various sorts. Among all of the animals that have evolved on Earth, the particular Human Animal has its own bodily evolution.

In this piece we develop the idea that there is a second origin of us as Humans. The origin of our Consciousness is a separate event.

During our gestation, a Consciousness enters the body rather than developing from the body. Here we symbolize this as a Superconscient Being from the Primordial Consciousness-without-an-object who chooses the Form that it takes.

In this episode, two Superconscient Beings take the Human Female Form. They find each other and form a Dyadic Union on earth. Each of them has forgotten her Cosmic Connection and her Origins.

("Space" music, synthesizer)

A. Creation of a Creature of God (NINA ON GROUND, ON BACK.)
    1) *Before the Beginning was the Void.*
    2) *In the Void, God, the Starmaker, stirred from his/her Rest. His/her first creation was/is Primordial Consciousness.*
(NINA MOVES)
    3) *Consciousness turned upon itself, creating Individual Selves, Beings endowed with Consciousness.*
(NINA ON FLOOR, ON BACK.)
    4) *Consciousness turned upon itself again, creating Space-time-Matter at the Origin.*
(rhythm introduction).
    5) *Matter and its Space-time poured out of the Origin creating the first Universe.*
    6) *The new Beings saw the new Universe, each making a choice of its Form, of a Galaxy, of a Star, of a Solar System, of a Planet, or of an Organism.*
(DANCE STARTS—music changes: rhythm and volume; crescendo to retard: "LANDING" crash; dies down.)
(wait. ROLL OVER. Music dies down.) Wait for new space to develop. (SILENCE).
    7) *One Being chose a Planet and an Organismic Form, the first Human* (Flute starts) *Female upon her Earth.* (NINA RAISES HEAD.)
(NINA LOOKS UP.)
    8) *On Earth She emerged from Primordial Consciousness in her new Body newly created from Matter-Space-time.*
    9) *She emerged alone, the first of her kind.*
(ARMS CROSS SWINGING WITH THREE MAJOR STEPS.)

B. Me
    1) *She experienced her new Body, found its Movements.*
(Pause Narration: Count Slow "3.")
    2) *She evolved her Form in its Uniqueness.*
(Change key and rhythm: Lyrical modulation. Instrumental change: bass guitar. Melodic: Nina theme begins development.)
(NINA, TURNING, STARTS, WHIRLS.)
    3) *She felt her Form, moved into its Self.*
(Music and DANCE only.)
(Violin starts, joins flute and guitar.)
    4) *She expressed her Self; grew in narcissistic abandon.*

5) *Her Consciousness lost connection with the Cosmic Consciousness of her Origins.*

6) *Her Consciousness of the Growth of her Form, unique unto itself, grew uniquely.*

(Music Peak.)

(DANCE and music alone.)

(NINA FLOOR-FALL NEAR NARRATOR.)

7) *She adored her body, its grace, its beauty, its orgasmic sense of life.*

8) *She loved her Self, her Body, her Earth.*

(NINA GOES TO EARTH)

(MARSHA LINE WITH LITTLE DELAY)

C. My Energy—Your Energy (Overlap violin and flute.)

(Rhythm and Instrument Change)

(Music softens)

(Guitar drops out—bass takes over.)

1) *Nearby upon Earth, another Being chose the Human Female Form, grew into her unique Self, forgot her Origins, worshiped herself.*

(MARSHA'S ENTRANCE AND SOLO.)

(Violin slide.)

(MARSHA HEAD ROLLS.)

(Drums.)

(NINA LOOKS TOWARD MARSHA.)

2) *Startled the first Being saw the new Other; explored the Vision.*

(DANCE and Music only for Marsha; NINA OBSERVES.)

(NINA RÉSUMÉ—MARSHA STOPS AND OBSERVES. Nina theme of PART B.)

(Instrument change: Mutation of theme B: Nina's.)

(NINA WALKS UP TO MARSHA, MARSHA LOOKS AT NINA— Break in music.)

3) *Suddenly the second Being found her Vision of the first Being and explored it.*

(NINA TWIRLS AND MOVES STAGE RIGHT—MARSHA SLOWLY MOVES STAGE LEFT.)

(Instrument Change: Counterpoint Themes B and C, Nina and Marsha.)

(MOVE APART; DANCING SEPARATELY.)

4) *Separately, the two now Human Beings evolved, each alone.*

5) *Two alien Beings, each ecstatic, in love with its own Self, its own Body, its connection to Earth.*

(NINA MIMICS MARSHA'S HEAD MOVEMENT. MUSIC LIGHTENS.)

(NINA AND MARSHA FACE EACH OTHER MOVING UP STAGE; MARSHA TEACHING NINA HEAD ROLLS AND JUMPS.)

6) *Belief in the Other grew in each.*

(Dyadic Theme (B and C) emerges and becomes dominant.)

(NINA AND MARSHA END OF JUMPS APPROACH EACH OTHER FOR THE SHIVA.)

7) *Approaching, each Being saw her Self projected into the Other.*

("SHIVA" MOVEMENTS GOING INTO TRAIN, THEN UNISON RHYTHM: 1 . . . 2, 123. MOVEMENTS INCREASE IN INTENSITY UNTIL MARSHA ROLLS ONTO FLOOR. THEN NINA LEADS MARSHA IN CIRCULAR LEG EXTENSIONS, WHICH GET SMALLER AND SMALLER.)

8) *Each danced around the Other, amazed, in wonder: the Ecstasy of Discovery.*

(Music begins to change in mood and rhythm. As music slows WE FINALLY FACE EACH OTHER.)

(HEADS AND BACKS TOGETHER.)

9) *The first Dyad was created, born of the Dyadic Union.*

(HEAD AND BODY ROLL SEGMENT.)

(Music builds, dyadic theme emerges again.)

(HEAD TO HEAD, TURNING EACH ON OWN AXIS, TURNS AND ARM ROTATION. MOVES INTO THE DOUBLE X ADAGIO STANDING ON THE FLOOR, STANDING. DOUBLE WINDMILL BACK TO FRONT, PAIRED.)

10) *Dyadic Union grew its own Uniqueness, a new melded Form of the first two Humans.*

(THEN INTO HAND-HOLDING SPINS.)

11) *Ecstasy in a New Form, tied to Earth, Earthly Response.*

(WHICH BREAK AWAY INTO INDIVIDUAL SPINS AND LEAPS: CROSSING LEAPS.)

(Peak dynamics.)

(WAIST HOLD SPIN, SEPARATE.)

***(FIRST GONG STROKE)

(LAPSE INTO SLOWED MOTION: SUGGESTION OF COMING WEAKENING. NINA MOVES SLOWLY TOWARD MARSHA.)

D. Unity and Resurrection

(Dying flute: amelodic instrument change.)

(NINA WALKS TOWARD MARSHA, BENDS, HOLDS BELLY.)

> 1) *In the Ecstatic, Earthly Union, the First Being's Form weakened.*

(NINA EMBRACES MARSHA.)

(NINA COLLAPSES ONTO THE FLOOR. Music Decrescendo.)

***(SECOND GONG STROKE)

(Music droning.)

> 2) *Nina died.*

(Music changes—violin comes in.)

(MARSHA MOVES TO HER—BACKS AWAY.)

> 3) *The Second Being, grieved at the loss of Dyadic Union, returned to narcissistic aloneness. Dances alone.*

(Music stops droning. MARSHA CIRCLES UPSTAGE, THEN COMES DOWNSTAGE.)

(DRAMA BY "SELF.")

(MARSHA FALLS ON KNEES. Music weakens to a stop.)

> 4) *She weakened*—few seconds' delay. FALLS TO FLOOR— *and died.*

***(THIRD GONG STROKE)

(STILLNESS. STILLNESS. FIVE SECONDS. Music resumes—complete thematic change.)

(Time warp.) (UNDULATION OF THE BEINGS' BODIES, IN SPASMS, ON FLOOR.)

> 5) *Each Being arose from her Earthly Form, began her return to to the Primordial Consciousness.*

(OFF-BALANCED, DISORIENTED MOVEMENTS.)

> 6) *The Dance of Transit from Earth Form back to Unity with the Cosmos.*

(TRANSITION INTO FRAGILE SLOWED WALK. Time warp mellows and begins to drift.)

(Music begins to pulse.)

(ARMS OUT, NINA APPROACHES MARSHA.)

> 7) *First Being* (Nina):
> *"Am I dead?"*
> *"Yes."*

(MARSHA TURNS LOOKING AT HER OWN ARMS.)

> The Second Being asked:
> *"Am I dead?"*

(Synthesizer.)

(AURA OF FEELING, NINA TO MARSHA):
"*Yes.*"
(Heavy bells, rhythmic gong.)
(MARSHA AND NINA AURA DANCE. FACE EACH OTHER, BREATHING, SPONTANEOUS IMPULSE MOVEMENTS.)
    8) *Ecstatic Dyad Dance of the Two brought the Return to Consciousness of the Cosmic Connection: the release into Oneness with all Creation.*
(REACHING, WALKING DOWNSTAGE.)
    9) *Each went through transit together, back to choose the choice of another Form, elsewhere.*
(SOARING POSITION, PULSING.)
(FREEZE—ARMS DOWN, HEADS UP.)
(Music after peak reverberates into infinity.)
    10) *Soaring to Fusion with Infinity.*
Dr. John puts out the torch.

End of Performance

EPILOGUE (not narrated):

In a sense a simulation of God is a creation by a creature created by God. The first two females are haploid, one-X chromosome. The first haploid male came from a cosmic ray transform $X \rightarrow Y$, thus the haploid male evolved from the haploid female. This dance is of the first two haploid females, who died and returned later to form the first male. Adam and Eve, the last haploid couple, formed the first diploid humans, as we know them (Cain, Abel and a series of females).

Here is the remainder of the communication from the Scientist from Planet "A," which he requested me to read to each of you:

"All of the foregoing events of this 'Performance' given on Earth have been re-recorded for our further research. We have recorded the 'performance' of my intermediary speaking for me, we have recorded each of your experiences individually, and we have re-recorded, simultaneously, our simulation of the original events as seen and experienced by each of you. We are recording your individual experience at the present time.

"We need additional data, and hope you will participate in our experiment for a brief time longer. We ask our intermediary to read to you some questions: we are recording each of you and your answers, silently, below your levels of awareness."

Here are the Scientist's questions (pause):

1) Were you able to suspend your beliefs that this was a production of present-day humans?

(pause)

2) Did you "resonate" to the "performance" with deep primordial feelings of an "unearthly" quality?

(pause)

3) Did you feel a rising of an Ancient Memory of the Creation of your Species, of your own Self?

(pause)

"We are deeply indebted to you for your participation and your excellent cooperation.

"As soon as we and you are able, we will resume our mutually satisfactory communication, in further cooperative efforts in Interplanetary Galactic Research."

As far as I can ascertain, the extraterrestrial Scientist has shut off his recording apparatus. We are now free to talk like human beings once again.

Thank you.

Bibliography (*Books by John C. Lilly, et al.*)

1. Borsook, Henry, J. Dubnoff and John C. Lilly. 1941. "The Formation of Glycocyamine in Man and Its Urinary Excretion." *J. Biol. Chem. 138*:405–419

2. Lilly, John C. 1942. "The Electrical Capacitance Diaphragm Manometer." *Rev. Sci. Instrum. 13*:34–37

3. Lilly, John C., and Thomas F. Anderson. 1943. "A Nitrogen Meter for Measuring the Nitrogen Fraction in Respiratory Cases." Nat'l. Research Council, CMR–CAM Report #299 PB 95882 Library of Congress. Photoduplication Service, Publication Board Project, Washington 25, DC.

4. Lilly, John C. 1944. "Peak Inspiratory Velocities During Evercise at Sea Level" in *Handbook of Respiratory Data in Aviation.* Nat'l. Research Council, Wash., DC.

5. Lilly, John C. and Thomas F. Anderson. 1944. "Preliminary Studies on Respiratory Gas Mixing with Nitrogen as a Tracer Gas." *Am. J. Med. Sci. 208*:136

6. Lilly, John C., John R. Pappenheimer and Glenn A. Millikan. 1945. "Respiratory Flow Rates and the Design of Oxygen Equipment." *Am. J. Med. Sci. 210*:810

7. Lilly, John C. 1946. "Studies on the Mixing of Gases Within the Respiratory System with a New Type Nitrogen Meter." (Abstract) Fed. Proc. *5*:64

8. Lilly, John C., Victor Legallais and Ruth Cherry. 1947. "A Variable Capacitor for Measurements of Pressure and Mechanical Displacements: A Theoretical Analysis and Its Experimental Evaluation." *J. Appl. Phys. 18*:613–628

267

9. Lilly, John C. 1950. "Flow Meter for Recording Respiratory Flow of Human Subjects" in *Methods in Medical Research. Vol.* 2:113–122. J. H. Comroe, Jr., Ed. Year Book Publishers, Inc., Chicago

10. Lilly, John C. 1950. "Physical Methods of Respiratory Gas Analysis" in *Methods of Medical Research. Vol. 2*:131–138. J. H. Comroe, Jr., Ed. Year Book Publishers, Inc., Chicago

10A Lilly, John C. 1950. "A 25–Channel Recorder for Mapping the Electrical Potential Gradients of the Cerebral Cortex: Electro— Iconograms." Electrical Engineering. A.I.E.E., Annual Index to Electrical Engineering *69*:68–69

11. Lilly, John C. 1950. "Respiratory System: Methods: Gas Analysis." in *Medical Physics. Vol. 2*:845–855. O. Glasser, Ed. Year Book Publishers, Inc., Chicago

12. Lilly, John C. 1950. "Mixing of Gases Within Respiratory System with a New Type of Nitrogen Meter." *Am. J. Physiol. 161*:342–351

13. Lilly, John C. 1950. "A Method of Recording the Moving Electrical Potential Gradients in the Brain. The 25-Channel Bavatron and Electro-Iconograms." (A.I.E.E.-IRE Conf. on Electronic Instrumentation in Nucleonics and Medicine). Am. Inst. of Electr. Eng., New York. *S–33*:37–43

14. Lilly, John C. 1950. "Moving Relief Maps of the Electrical Activity of Small (1 cm²) Areas of the Pial Surface of the Cerebral Cortex." *EEG. Clin. Neurophysiol.* 2:358

15. Chambers, William W., George M. Austin, and John C. Lilly. 1950. "Positive Pulse Stimulation of Anterior Sigmoid and Precentral Gyri; Electri Current Threshold Dependence on Anesthesia, Pulse Duration and Repetition Frequency." (Abstract). Fed. Proc. *9*:21–22

16. Lilly, John C. and William W. Chambers. 1950. "Electro-Iconograms from the Cerebral Cortex (cats) at the Pial Surface: 'Spontaneous' Activity and Responses to Endorgan Stimuli Under Anesthesia." (Abstract). Fed. Proc. *9*:78

17. Lilly, John C. 1950. "Moving Relief Maps of the Electrical Activity of Small (1 cm²) Areas of the Pial Surface of the Cerebral Cortex. Anesthetized Cats and Unanesthetized Monkeys" (Abstract). Proc. 18th Int'l. Physiol. Congress, Copenhagen. P. 340-351

18. Lilly, John C. 1951. "Equipotential Maps of the Posterior Ectosylvian Area and Acoustic I and II of the Cat During Responses and Spontaneous Activity" (Abstract). Fed. Proc. *10*:84

19. Lilly, John C. and Ruth Cherry. 1951. "An Analysis of Some Responding and Spontaneous Forms Found in the Electrical Activity of the Cortex." *Am J. Med. Sci. 222*:116–117

20. Lilly, John C., and Ruth· Cherry. 1951. "Traveling Waves of Action and of Recovery During Responses and Spontaneous Activity in the Cerebral Cortex." *Am. J. Physiol. 167*:806

21. Lilly, John C. 1952. "Forms and Figures in the Electrical Activity Seen in the Surface of the Cerebral Cortex" in *The Biology of Mental Health and Disease* (1950 Milbank Mem. Fund Symposium). Paul B. Hoeber, Inc., New York. P. 205–219

22. Lilly, John C., George M. Austin, and William W. Chambers. 1952. "Threshold Movements Produced by Excitation of Cerebral Cortex and Efferent Fibers with some Parametric Regions of Rectangular Current Pulses: (Cats and Monkeys)." *J. Neurophysiol. 15*:319–341

23. Lilly, John C. and Ruth Cherry. 1952. "New Criteria for the Division of the Acoustic Cortex into Functional Areas" (Abstract). Fed. Proc. *11*:94

24. Lilly, John C., and Ruth Cherry. 1952. "Criteria for the Parcelation of the Cortical Surface into Functional Areas" (Abstract). *EEG. Clin. Neurophysiol. 4*:385

25. Lilly, John C. 1953. "Significance of Motor Maps of the Sensorimotor Cortex in the Conscious Monkey." (Abstract). Fed. Proc. *12*:87

26. Lilly, John C. 1953. "Discussion of Paper by Lawrence S. Kubie; Some Implications for Psychoanalysis of Modern Concepts of the Organization of the Brain." *Psychoanalytic Q. 22*:21–68

27. Lilly, John C. 1953. Review of book by W. Ross Ashby: *Design for a Brain.* John Wiley and Sons, Inc., New York. *Rev. of Sci. Instrum. 24*:313

28. Lilly, John C. 1953. "Functional Criteria for the Parcelation of the Cerebral Cortex." Abstracts of Communications, XIX Int'l. Physiol. Cong., Montreal, Canada. P. 564

29. Lilly, John C. 1953. Recent Developments in EEG Techniques: Discussion. (Third Int'l. EEG Cong. 1953. Symposia). EEG Clin. Neurophysiol. Suppl. *4*:38–40

30. Lilly, John C. 1954. Critical Discussion of Research Project and Results at Conference in June 1952 by Robert G. Heath and Research Group at Tulane Univ. in Robert G. Heath, et al. *"Studies in Schizophrenia: A Multidisciplinary Approach to Mind–Brain Relationships."* P. 528–532

31. Lilly, John C. 1954. "Instantaneous Relations Between the Activities of Closely Spaced Zones on the Cerebral Cortex: Electrical Figures During Responses and Spontaneous Activity." *Am. J. Physiol. 176*:493–504

32. Lilly, John C., and Ruth Cherry. 1954. "Surface Movements of Click Responses from Acoustic Cerebral Cortex of Cat: Leading

and Trailing Edges of a Response Figure." *J. Neurophysiol.* *17*:521–532

33. Lilly, John C. 1954. Discussion, Symposium on Depth Electrical Recordings in Human Patients. Am. EEG Soc. Neurophysiol. *6*:703–704

34. Lilly, John C., and Ruth Cherry. 1955. "Surface Movements of Figures in Spontaneous Activity of Anesthetized Cerebral Cortex: Leading and Trailing Edges. *J. Neurophysiol.* *18*:18–32

35. Lilly, John C., John R. Hughes, and Ellsworth C. Alvord, Jr., and Thelma W. Galkin. 1955. Brief. "Noninjurious Electric Waveform for Stimulation of the Brain." *Science 121*:468–469

36. Lilly, John C., John R. Hughes, and Ellsworth C. Alvord, Jr., and Thelma W. Galkin. 1955. "Motor Responses from Electrical Stimulation of Sensorimotor Cortex in Unanesthetized Monkey with a Brief, Noninjurious Waveform" (Abstract). Fed. Proc. *14*:93

37. Lilly, John C. 1955. "An Anxiety Dream of an 8-Year-Old Boy and Its Resolution." *Bul. Phila. Assn. for Psychoanal. 5*:1–4

38. Lilly, John C. 1955. Review of book by Robert G. Heath, et al., 1954. *Studies in Schizophrenia: A Multidisciplinary Approach to Mind–Brain Relationships.* Harvard Univ. Press. *EEG Clin. Neurophysiol. 7*:323–324

39. Lilly, John C., John R. Hughes, Thelma W. Galkin and Ellsworth C. Alvord, Jr. 1955. "Production and Avoidance of Injury to Brain Tissue by Electrical Current at Threshold Values." *EEG Clin. Neurophysiol. 7*:458

40. Lilly, John C. 1956. "Effects of Physical Restraint and of Reduction of Ordinary Levels of Physical Stimuli on Intact Healthy Persons." 13–20 & 44, in *Illustrative Strategies for Research on Psychopathology in Mental Health, Symposium No. 2.* Group for the Advancement of Psychiatry. New York. P. 47

41. Lilly, John C., John R. Hughes, and Thelma W. Galkin. 1956. "Gradients of Motor Function in the Whole Cerebral Cortex of the Unanesthetized Monkey" (Abstract). Fed. Proc. *15*

42. Lilly, John C., John R. Hughes, and Thelma W. Galkin. 1956. "Physiological Properties of Cerebral Cortical Motor Systems of Unanesthetized Monkey" (Abstract). Fed. Proc. *15*

43. Lilly, John C. 1956. "Mental Effects of Reduction of Ordinary Levels of Physical Stimuli on Intact. Healthy Persons" in *Psychiat. Res. Reports 5.* American Psychiatric Assn., Wash., DC. P. 1–9

44. Lilly, John C., John R. Hughes, and Thelma W. Galkin. 1956. "Some Evidence of Gradients of Motor Function in the Whole Cerebral Cortex of the Unanesthetized Monkey" (Abstract). *Proc. 20th Int'l. Physiol. Congress.* P. 567–568

45. Lilly, John C. 1956. "Distribution of 'Motor' Functions in the Cerebral Cortex in the Conscious, Intact Monkey." *Science.* *124*:937

46. Lilly, John C. 1957. "Some Thoughts on Brain–Mind and on Restraint and Isolation of Mentally Healthy Subjects. (Comments on Biological Roots of Psychiatry by Clemens F. Benda, M.D.)" *J. Phila. Psychiatric Hosp.* 2:16–20

47. Lilly, John C. 1957. "True Primary Emotional State of Anxiety—Terror—Panic in Contrast to a 'Sham' Emotion or 'Pseudo—Affective' State Evoked by Stimulation of the Hypothalamus" (Abstract). Fed. Proc. *16*:81

48. Lilly, John C. 1957. "Learning Elicited by Electrical Stimulation of Subcortical Regions in the Unanesthetized Monkey." *Science.* *125*:748

49. Lilly, John C. 1957. Review of book by Donald A. Scholl. 1956. *The Organization of the Cerebral Cortex.* Methuen and Co., Ltd., London and John Wiley and Sons, Inc., New York. *Science.* *125*:1205

50. Lilly, John C. 1957. "A State Resembling 'Fear–Terror–Panic' Evoked by Stimulation of a Zone in the Hypothalamus of the Unanesthetized Monkey." *Excerpta Medica.* Special Issue, Abstracts of Fourth Int'l. Cong. EEG and Clin. Neurophysiol. and 8th Meeting of the Int'l. League Against Epilepsy. Brussels. P. 161

51. Lilly, John C. 1957. " 'Stop' and 'Start' Systems" *in Neuropharmacology.* Transactions of the Fourth Conference, Josiah Macy, Jr., Foundation, Princeton, N.J. (L.C. 55–9013). P. 153–179

52. Lilly, John C. 1958. "Learning Motivated by Subcortical Stimulation: The 'Start' and 'Stop' Patterns of Behavior." 705–721. *Reticular Formation of the Brain.* H. H. Jasper, et al. Eds. Little, Brown and Co., Boston. P. 766

53. Lilly, John C. 1958. "Correlations Between Neurophysiological Activity in the Cortex and Short-Term Behavior in the Monkey," in *Biological and Biochemical Bases of Behavior* (Univ. of Wis. Symposium. 1055) H. F. Harlow and C. N. Woolsey, Ed. Univ. of Wis. Press, Madison, Wis. P. 83–100

54. Lilly, John C. 1958. "Development of a Double–Table–Chair Method of Restraining Monkeys for Physiological and Psychological Research." *J. Appl. Physiol.* *12*:134–136

55. Lilly, John C. 1958. "Simple Percutaneous Method for Implantation of Electrodes and/or Cannulae in the Brain." (Abstract.) Fed. Proc. *17*:97

56. Lilly, John C. 1958. "Electrode and Cannulae Implantation in the Brain by a Simple Percutaneous Method." *Science.* *127*:1181–1182

57. Lilly, John C. 1958. "Some Considerations Regarding Basic Mechanisms of Positive and Negative Types of Motivations." *Am. J. Psychiat.* 115:498–504

58. Lilly, John C. 1958. "Rewarding and Punishing Systems in the Brain" in *The Central Nervous System and Behavior*. Transactions of the First Conference, Josiah Macy, Jr., Foundation, Princeton, N.J. (L.C. 59–5052.) P. 247–303

59. Lilly, John C. 1959. " 'Stop' and 'Start' Effects in *The Central Nervous System and Behavior*. Transactions of the Second Conference, Josiah Macy, Jr., Foundation and National Science Foundation, Princeton, N.J. (L.C. 59–5052.) P. 56–112

60. Lilly, John C. 1960. "Learning Motivated by Subcortical Stimulation: The 'Start' and The 'Stop' Patterns of Behavior. Injury and Excitation of the Brain by Electrical Currents." Chapter 4 in *Electrical Studies on the Unanesthetized Brain*. E. R. Ramsey and D. S. O'Doherty, Eds, Paul B. Hoeber, Inc., New York. P. 78–105

61. Lilly, John C. 1960. Contributing Discussant—The Central Nervous System and Behavior. Transactions of the Third Conference Josiah Macy, Jr., Foundation, Princeton, N.J. (L.C. 59–5052.)

62. Lilly, John C. 1960. "The Psychophysiological Basis for Two Kinds of Instincts." *J. Am. Psychoanalyt. Assoc.* Vol. *8*: P. 659–670

63. Lilly, John C. 1960. "Large Brains and Communication." Paper Presented to the Philadelphia Assoc. for Psychoanalysis.

64. Lilly, John C. 1961. "Injury and Excitation by Electric Currents." Chapter 6 in *Electrical Stimulation of the Brain*. Daniel E. Sheer, Ed., Univ. of Texas Press for Hogg Foundation for Mental Health, Austin, Texas. P. 60–64

65. Lilly, John C. and Jay T. Shurley. 1961. "Experiments in Solitude, in Maximum Achievable Physical Isolation with Water Suspension of Intact Healthy Persons." (Symposium, USAF Aerospace Medical Center, San Antonio, Texas, 1960.) in *Psychophysiological Aspects of Space Flight*. Columbia Univ. Press, New York. P. 238–247

66. Lilly, John C., and Alice M. Miller. 1961. "Sounds Emitted by the Bottlenose Dolphin." *Science.* Vol. *133*, P. 1689–1693

67. Lilly, John C., and Alice M. Miller. 1961. "Vocal Exchanges Between Dolphins." *Science.* Vol. *134*: P. 1873–1876

68. Lilly, John C. 1961. "Problems of Physiological Research on the Dolphin, *Tursiops*" (Abstract). Fed. Proc. *20*:1

69. Lilly, John C. 1961. "The Biological Versus Psychoanalytic Dichotomy." *Bul. of The Phila Assoc. for Psychoanal.* Vol. *11*: P. 116–119

70. Lilly, John C. 1961. *Man and Dolphin*. Doubleday & Co., Inc., New York. (L.C. 61–9628)

      1962. *L'Homme et le Dauphin*. Stock Edition, l'Imprimerie des Dernières Nouvelles de Strasbourg, Stock, Paris

      1962. *Manniskan och Definen*. Wahlstrom & Widstrand, Bakforlag, Stockholm, Sweden

      1962. *Man and Dolphin*. Victor Gollancz, Ltd., London, England

      1962. *Man and Dolphin*. (The Worlds of Science Series, Zoology.) Pocket Edition, Pyramid Publications, New York

      1963. *Mensen Dolfijn*. Contact—Amsterdam-Druk: Tulp-Zwolle

      1963. *Menneskat og Delfinen*. Nasjonalforlaget, Oslo, Norway

      1965. *Man and Dolphin*. Gakken Books Science Series, Charles E. Tuttle Co., Inc., Tokyo

      1965. *Man and Dolphin*. Izdatelsstvo Mir Zubosky Square 21, Moscow, U.S.S.R.

      1966. *Člověk Delfin*. Miroslav Hrncer Vratislav Mazak

      1967. *Man and Dolphin*. Sophia, Bulgaria

71. Lilly, John C. 1962. The Effect of Sensory Deprivation on Consciousness. *Man's Dependence on the Earthly Atmosphere*, Karl E. Schaefer, Ed. MacMillan Co., New York. (L.C. 61–9079.) P. 93–95. (Proceedings 1st Int'l Symp. on Submarine and Space Medicine, New London, Conn., 1958)

72. Lilly, John C., and Alice M. Miller. 1962. "Operant Conditioning of the Bottlenose Dolphin with Electrical Stimulation of the Brain." *J. Comp. & Physiol. Psychol.* Vol. 55: P. 73–79

73. Lilly, John C. 1962. Cerebral Dominance in *Interhemispheric Relations and Cerebal Dominance*. Vernon Mountcastle, M.D., Ed. Johns Hopkins Press, Inc. Baltimore, Md. P. 112–114

74. Lilly, John C., and Alice M. Miller. 1962. Production of Humanoid Sounds by the Bottlenose Dolphin. (Unpublished manuscript.)

75. Lilly, John C. 1962. A New Laboratory for Research on Delphinids. *Assoc. of Southeastern Biologists Bul.* Vol. 9, P. 3–4

76. Lilly, John C. 1962. "Interspecies Communication" in *Yearbook of Science and Technology*. McGraw-Hill. New York. P. 279–281

77. Lilly, John C. 1962. "The 'Talking' Dolphins" in *The Book of Knowledge Annual*. Society of Canada Limited, Grolier, Inc. (This article was updated in the 1969 Yearbook covering the year 1968, pp. 8–15.)

78. Lilly, John C. 1962. "Vocal Behavior of the Bottlenose Dolphin." *Proc. Am. Philos. Soc.* Vol. *106.* P. 520–529

79. Lilly, John C. 1962. "Consideration of the Relation of Brain Size to Capability for Language Activity as Illustrated by *Homo sapiens* and *Tursiops truncatus* (Bottlenose Dolphin)." *Electroenceph. Clin. Neurophysiol. 14*, no. 3: 424

80. Lilly, John C. 1962. Sensory World Within and Man and Dolphin. (Lecture to the Laity, New York Acad. of Med., 1962.) Scientific Report no. CRI–0162

81. Lilly, John C. 1963. "Critical Brain Size and Language." *Perspectives in Biol. & Med.* Vol. *6.* P. 246–255

82. Lilly, John C. 1963. "Distress Call of the Bottlenose Dolphin: Stimuli and Evoked Behavioral Responses." *Science.* Vol. *139.* P. 116–118

83. Lilly, John C. 1963. "Productive and Creative Research with Man and Dolphin." (Fifth Annual Lasker Lecture, Michael Reese Hospital and Medical Center, Chicago, Ill., 1962). *Arch. Gen. Psychiatry.* Vol. *8.* P. 111–116

84. Lilly, John C., and Ashley Montagu. 1963. Modern Whales, Dolphins and Porpoises, as Challenges to Our Intelligence in *The Dolphin in History* by Ashley Montagu and John C. Lilly. A Symposium given at the William Andrews Clark Memorial Library, Univ. of Calif., Los Angeles, Calif. P. 31–54

85. Lilly, John C. 1964. "Animals in Aquatic Environment. Adaptation of Mammals to the Ocean" in *Handbook of Physiology.* Environment I, Am. Physiol. Soc., Wash., D.C. P. 741–757

86. Jacobs, Myron S., Peter J. Morgane, John C. Lilly and Bruce Campbell. 1964. "Analysis of Cranial Nerves in the Dolphin." *Anatomical Record* Vol. *148.* P. 379

87. Lilly, John C. 1964. "Airborne Sonic Emissions of *Tursiops truncatus* (M)" (Abstract) *J. Acoustical Soc. of Amer.* Vol. *36.* P. 5, 1007

88. Lilly, John C. 1965. "Report on Experiments with the Bottlenose Dolphin." (Abstract) *Proc. of the Int'l. Symp. on Comparative Medicine,* Eaton Laboratories, Norwich, Conn. P. 240

90. Lilly, John C. 1965. "Vocal Mimicry in *Tursiops.* Ability to Match Numbers and Duration of Human Vocal Bursts." *Science* Vol. *147* (3655). P. 300–301

91. Lilly, John C. 1966. "Sexual Behavior of the Bottlenose Dolphin in *Brain and Behavior.* The Brain and Gonadal Function." Vol. III. R. A. Gorski and R. E. Whalens, Eds., *UCLA Forum* Med. Sci., Univ. of Calif. Press, Los Angeles, Calif. P. 72–76

92. Lilly, John C. 1966. "Sonic-Ultrasonic Emissions of the Bottlenose Dolphin in *Whales, Dolphins and Porpoises.*" Kenneth S. Norris, Ed. *Proc., 1st Int'l Symp. on Cetacean Research,* Wash., DC. 1963. Univ. of Calif. Press. P. 503–509

93. Lilly, John C. 1966. "The Need for an Adequate Model of the Human End of the Interspecies Communication Program." IEEE Military Electronics Conference (MIL-E-CON 9), on Communication with Extraterrestrial Intelligence, Wash., DC. 1965. *IEEE Spectrum 3*, no. 3: P. 159–160

94. Lilly, John C. 1966. Contributing Discussant. Proc. of Conf. on Behavioral Studies. Contractors Meeting, U.S. Army Edgewood Arsenal, Md. 1965. Dept. of the Army EARL Report

95. Lilly, John C. 1966. "Research with the Bottlenose Dolphin" in *Conference on the Behavioral Sciences*, Proc. of Conf. on Behavioral Studies (Contractors Meeting, U.S. Army Edgewood Arsenal, Md. 1965). Dept. of the Army EARL Report

96. Lilly, John C., and Henry M. Truby. 1966. "Measures of Human-*Tursiops* Sonic Interactions" (Abstract). *J. Acous. Soc. of Amer.* Vol. *40*, issue 5. P. 1241

97. Lilly, John C. 1966. "Sound Production in *Tursiops truncatus* (Bottlenose Dolphin)." Conference on Sound Production in Man: Section on Phonation: Control and Speech Communication, New York Acad. of Sciences. Annals of the New York Academy of Sciences. 1968

98. Lilly, John C. 1966. "Intracerebral Reward and Punishment: Implications for Psychopharmacology." Fifth Annual Meeting of American College of Neuropsychopharmacology. San Juan, Puerto Rico. 1968

99. Lilly, John C. 1967. Dolphin-Human Relationship and LSD-25 in *The Use of LSD in Psychotherapy and Alcoholism.* Harold Abramson, Ed. Second International Conference on the Use of LSD in Psychotherapy, South Oaks Research Foundation, Amityville, L.I. 1965. The Bobbs-Merrill Co., Inc., New York. P. 47–52

100. Lilly, John C. 1967. Dolphin's Mimicry as a Unique Ability and a Step Towards Understanding in *Research in Verbal Behavior and Some Neurophysiological Implications.* Kurt Salzinger and Suzanne Salzinger, Eds. Conference on Verbal Behavior, N.Y.C. 1965. Academic Press, New York City. P. 21–27

101. Lilly, John C. 1967. Dolphin Vocalization in Proc. Conf. on *Brain Mechanisms Underlying Speech and Language.* F. L. Darley, Ed. A Symposium held at Princeton, N.J. 1965. Grune and Stratton, New York City. P. 13–20

102. Lilly, John C. 1967. Basic Problems in Education for Responsibility Caused by LSD-25. Proc. of 17th Conf. on Science, Philosophy and Religion in their Relation to the Democratic Way of Life. Clarence H. Fause, Ed. Paper presented in section on Character Education of Scientists, Engineers and Practitioners in Medicine Psychiatry and Science with Strategies for Change. Loyola Univ., Chicago, Ill. 1966

103. Lilly, John C. 1967. *The Mind of the Dolphin*. Doubleday & Co., Inc., New York.

104. Lilly, John C. 1967. "Intracephalic Sound Production in *Tursiops truncatus:* Bilateral Sources" (Abstract). Fed. Proc. 25, no. 2.

105. Lilly, John C. 1967. *The Human Biocomputer: Programming and Metaprogramming*. Miami. Communications Research Institute. 1967. Scientific Report no. CRI 0167.

106. Lilly, John C. 1968. *Programming and Metaprogramming in the Human Biocomputer: Theory and Experiments*. Miami. Communications Research Institute. Scientific Report no. CRI 0167. 2nd Edition

107. Lilly, John C., Alice M. Miller, and Henry M. Truby. 1968. Reprogramming of the Sonic Output of the Dolphin: Sonic-Burst Count Matching. Miami. Communications Research Institute. Scientific Report no. CRI 0267. *J. Acous. Soc. of Amer.* (See number 112.)

108. Lilly, John C., Alice M. Miller, and Henry M. Truby. 1968. "Perception of Repeated Speech: Evocation and Programming of Alternate Words and Sentences." Scientific Report no. CRI 1067

109. Lilly, John C., Alice M. Miller, and Frank Grissman. 1968. "Underwater Sound Production of the Dolphin Stereo-Voicing and Double Voicing." Miami. Communications Research Institute. Scientific Report no. CRI 0367

110. Truby, Henry M., and John C. Lilly. 1967. "Psychoacoustic Implications of Interspecies Communication." Miami. Communications Research Institute. *J. Acous. Soc. of Amer.* Vol. 42: P. 1181. S3 (Abstract.)

111. Lilly, John C., Henry M. Truby, Alice M. Miller, and Frank Grissman. 1967. "Acoustic Implications of Interspecies Communication." Miami. Communications Research Institute. *J. Acous. Soc. of Amer.* Vol. 42: P. 1164. I10 (Abstract.)

112. Lilly, John C., Alice M. Miller, and Henry M. Truby. 1968. "Reprogramming of the Sonic Output of the Dolphin: Sonic Burst Count Matching." *Jnl. of the Acoustical Society of America.* Vol. 43. No. 6. P. 1412–1424

113. Lilly, John C. 1967, 1968, 1972. *Programming and Metaprogramming in the Human Biocomputer, Theory and Experiments*. The Julian Press, Inc. New York.

114. Lilly, John C. 1974. *Programming and Metaprogramming in the Human Biocomputer, Theory and Experiments*. Bantam Books, Inc. New York.

115. Lilly, John C. 1974. *The Human Biocomputer, Theory and Experiments*. Abacus edition, Sphere Books Ltd. London.

116. Lilly, John C. 1972. *The Center of the Cyclone. An Autobiography of Inner Space.* The Julian Press, Inc. New York.
117. Lilly, John C. 1974. *Het Centrum van de Cycloon, Een Autobiografie van de Innerlijke Ruimte.* Wetenschappelijke Uitgeverij b.v. Amsterdam.
118. Lilly, John C. 1972. *The Center of the Cyclone. An Autobiography of Inner Space* (paperback). Bantam Books, Inc. New York.
119. Lilly, John C. 1973. *The Centre of the Cyclone: an Autobiography of Inner Space,* Calder & Boyer, London.
120. Lilly, John C. 1973. *The Centre of the Cyclone: An Autobiography of Inner Space* (paperback). Paladin, Granada Publishing Limited, London.
121. Lilly, John C. 1975. *Simulations of God: The Science of Belief.* Simon and Schuster, New York
122. Lilly, John C. 1975. *Lilly on Dolphins.* Anchor/Doubleday, New York
123. Lilly, John C. and Antonietta L. 1975. *The Dyadic Cyclone.* Simon and Schuster, New York
124. Lilly, John C. The Deep Self: Explorations in Tank-Isolation. (In preparation.)
125. Lilly, John C. Off Center and Return. (In preparation.)

Biographical Data (*Curriculum Vitae*)

John C. Lilly, B.Sc., M.D.

PARENTS: Richard C. Lilly, Rachel C. Lilly

BIRTH: 0707 hours, 6 January 1915, St. Paul, Minnesota

ELEMENTARY SCHOOLS: Grades kindergarten through 4th: Irving Public School; Grades 5, 6, 7: St. Luke's School (Catholic)

PREPARATORY SCHOOL: (Forms 2 through 6), St. Paul Academy, St. Paul, Minnesota. Graduation 1933

COLLEGE: California Institute of Technology, Pasadena, California; (scholarship). Graduation 1938

MEDICAL SCHOOLS: Dartmouth Medical School, Hanover, New Hampshire (1938–1940); School of Medicine, University of Pennsylvania, Philadelphia, Pennsylvania. Graduation 1942

UNIVERSITY OF PENNSYLVANIA: Department of Biophysics and Medical Physics (Eldridge Reeves Johnson Foundation), University of Pennsylvania School of Medicine (1942–1956). Fellow, Associate, Associate Professor (of Medical Physics and of Experimental Neurology)

PSYCHOANALYTIC TRAINING: Research Trainee (1949–1957): Training Analyst: Dr. Robert Waelder of the Institute of the Philadelphia Association for Psychoanalysis and the Philadelphia Psychoanalytic Society; the Washington-Baltimore Psychoanalytic Institute: Dr.

Jenny Waelder-Hall, Dr. Lewis Hill; Control Analyst: Dr. Amanda Stoughton

GOVERNMENT SERVICE: Senior Surgeon Grade, United States Public Health Service Commissioned Officers Corps. (1953–1958)

NATIONAL INSTITUTES OF HEALTH, RESEARCH: Section Chief, Section on Cortical Integration in the National Institute of Neurological Diseases and Blindness and in the National Institute of Mental Health, Bethesda, Maryland (1953–1958)

COMMUNICATIONS RESEARCH INSTITUTE: Founder and Director, Saint Thomas, United States Virgin Islands, and Miami, Florida (1959–1968)

NATIONAL INSTITUTE OF MENTAL HEALTH: Research Career Award Fellow (1962–1967)

MARYLAND PSYCHIATRIC RESEARCH CENTER: Catonsville, Maryland. Chief of Psychological Isolation and Psychedelic Research (1968–1969)

ESALEN INSTITUTE: Big Sur, California. Group Leader and Associate in Residence, (1969–1971)

CENTER FOR THE ADVANCED STUDY OF BEHAVIOR: Palo Alto, California. Fellow (1969–1970)

INSTITUTO DE GNOSOLOGIA, Arica, Chile, student (1970–1971)

HUMAN SOFTWARE, INC., Malibu, California. Treasurer (1973–present)

SCIENTIFIC SOCIETIES:

The American Physiological Society (1945–1967)

The American Electroencephalographic Society (1947–1967)

The Institute of Electronic and Electrical Engineers (1951–1967)

The Society of the Sigma Xi (1952–life)

Aerospace Medical Association (1945)

Biophysical Society (charter member to 1967)

The American Medical Authors, Fellow (8 April 1964)

The New York Academy of Science (1949) Fellow (1959)

The Philadelphia Association for Psychoanalysis, Affiliate Member (1958)

California Institute of Technology, Alumni Association (life member)

Order of the Dolphin (1961)

For other society memberships, see listings in *Who's Who* (Marquis) and *American Men of Science*

AWARDS:

California Institute of Technology: Scholar (1933–1935)

University of Pennsylvania School of Medicine: Clark Research Medal (1941)

Who's Who in the South and Southwest: Citation for outstanding contributions in Science: 16 April 1963

The American Medical Authors, Distinguished Service Award (26 September 1964)

Career Award, National Institute of Mental Health (1962–1967)

Biographical Data (*Curriculum Vitae*)

Antonietta L. F. Lilly

ELEMENTARY SCHOOL: P.S. 92, East Elmhurst Long Island, New York (1933–1941)
HIGH SCHOOL: Chaffey, Ontario, California (1942–1946)
COLLEGE: Santa Monica Junior College (1958–1959)
  Art Center (1961)
  Chouinard Art School of California (Chouinard Institute of the Arts) (1962)
  Otis Art Institute (1963–1965)
CARROLL CARLSON, M.D., THERAPIST TRAINING PROGRAM: (1964–1966)
ESALEN INSTITUTE, Big Sur, Group Leader (1971–present)
HUMAN SOFTWARE, INC., Malibu, California, President (1973–present)

Bibliography and Suggested Reading List

Bateson, Gregory, *Steps to an Ecology of Mind*, Ballantine Books, Inc., New York, 1972.

Brockman, John, *Afterwords*, Anchor Books, New York, 1973.

Brown, Barbara B., *New Mind, New Body*, Harper & Row, New York, 1974.

Brown, G. Spencer, *The Laws of Form*, The Julian Press, Inc., New York, 1972.

Brown, G. Spencer (see James Keys, pseudonym).

Castaneda, Carlos, *Tales of Power*, Simon and Schuster, New York, 1974.

Castaneda, Carlos, *Journel to Ixtlan: The Lessons of Don Juan*, Simon and Schuster, New York, 1973.

Edwards, Robert, The Quantum Observer in a Neurally Engineered Prosthesis (unpublished thesis, UCLA, 1970).

Gold, E. J., *American Book of the Dead*, Institute for the Development of the Harmonious Human Being, Inc., Crestline, California, 1974.

Govinda, Lama Anagarika, *Foundations of Tibetan Mysticism*, Samuel Weiser, Inc., New York, 1970.

Grof, Stanislav, M.D., *Realms of the Human Unconscious*, The Viking Press, Inc., New York, 1975.

Hesse, Hermann, *The Glass Bead Game: Magister Ludi*, Holt, Rinehart & Winston, Inc. (Rinehart Press editions), New York, 1969.

Huxley, Laura Archera, *This Timeless Moment*, Ballantine Books, New York, 1971.

Illich, Ivan, *Tools for Conviviality*, Harper & Row, New York, 1973.

Janis, Irving L., *The Victims of Groupthink*, Houghton Mifflin Company, Boston, 1972.

Kant, Immanuel, *Critique of Pure Reason*, E. P. Dutton & Co., Inc., New York, 1956.

Kaufmann, William J., III, *Relativity and Cosmology*, Harper & Row, New York, 1973.

Keys, James, *Only Two Can Play This Game*, Julian Press, New York, 1972.

Krishna, Gopi, *Kundalini: The Evolutionary Energy in Man*, Shambali Publications, Inc., California, 1973.

Leboyer, Frederick, *Birth Without Violence*, Alfred A. Knopf, Inc., New York, 1975.

Lilly, John C., *The Center of the Cyclone*, Bantam Books, New York, Toronto, London, 1972, 1973.

Lilly, John C., M.D., *The Center of the Cyclone*, Julian Press, New York, 1972.

Lilly, John C., M.D., *Programming and Metaprogramming in the Human Biocomputer*, Julian Press, New York, 1972.

Lilly, John C., M.D., *Programming and Metaprogramming in the Human Biocomputer*, Bantam Books, New York, 1974.

Lilly, John C., M.D., *Simulations of God: The Science of Belief*, Simon and Schuster, New York, 1975.

Martin, P. W., *Experiment in Depth*, Routledge & Kegan Paul, London, 1971.

Merrell-Wolff, Franklin, *Pathways Through to Space*, Julian Press, New York, 1973.

Merrell-Wolff, Franklin, *The Philosophy of Consciousness Without an Object: Reflections on the Nature of Transcendental Conciousness*, Julian Press, New York, 1973.

Monroe, Robert A., *Journeys Out of the Body*, Doubleday, New York, 1971.

Naranjo, Claudio, *The Healing Journey: New Approaches to Consciousness*, Pantheon, 1974.

Phillips, Michael, et al., *The Seven Laws of Money*, Random House, New York, 1974.

Pearce, Joseph Chilton, *Exploring the Crack in the Cosmic Egg: Split Minds and Metabeliefs*, Julian Press, New York, 1974.

Sagan, Carl, and I. S. Shklovsky, *Intelligent Life in the Universe*, Holden-Day, Inc., San Francisco, 1966.

Sagan, Carl, *The Cosmic Connection, An Extraterrestrial Connection*, Doubleday, New York, 1973.

Sandage, Allan, *The Hubble Atlas of Galaxies,* Washington: Carnegie Institute of Washington (pap.), 1972.

Sullivan, Walter, *We Are Not Alone,* NAL (pap.), New York, 1969.

Taimni, I. K., *The Science of Yoga,* The Theosophical Publishing House, Wheaton, Illinois, 1971.

Toben, Bob, *Space-time and Beyond,* E. P. Dutton & Co., Inc., New York, 1975.

Varela, Francisco J., *A Calculus for Self-Reference,* Great Britain, Gordon and Breach Science Publishers, Ltd., 1975. *Int. J. General Systems,* vol. 2, pp. 1–20.

Vassi, Marco, *Metasex, Madness and Mirth,* Penthouse Press, Ltd., New York, May 23, 1975.

Vizinczey, Stephen, *The Rules of Chaos,* The McCall Publishing Company, New York, 1970.

Wasson, R. Gordon, *Soma: Divine Mushroom of Immortality,* New York, Harcourt Brace Jovanovitch, Inc., 1971.

Wheeler, John Archibald, "From Méndeleev's Atom to the Collapsing Star," from *Transactions of the New York Academy of Sciences,* New York Academy of Sciences, series 2, vol. 33, no. 8, New York, December, 1971.

Williams, Charles, *Many Dimensions,* William B. Eerdmans Publishing Co., Michigan, 1949.

Wittgenstein, Ludwig, *Tractatus Logico-Philosophicus,* Routledge & Kegan Paul, London, 1971.

Acknowledgments

The creative image of myself never before included communicating feelings with the injunctive use of language. This never would have been attempted without John's encouragement and willingness to share his domain with me.

Thank you, John.

It is an unusual privilege to participate in a dyad that allows creative thinking/doing/feeling. Subjection of one's own ego to a supraself dyadic relationship is novel and exciting. Toni's own definitions of the unknown potential inherent in dyadic relations is in itself intriguing and creative. Her tolerance of the unusual, her earthside centering operations, her easy human relations, and her enthusiastic support of projects is heartwarming and exciting for me. Thank you, Antonietta.

With graciousness and humor, Jan di Stefano has typed, retyped, edited and participated in the lives creating this book. Steven Conger's humor and good vibrations have had a facilitative effect on the processes of living and writing this and the forthcoming book (The Deep Self); his tank constructions and schooling by those wanting tanks has kept us aware of other points of view, other philosophies outside our own world. Will Curtis's attention to new ideas and his artistic creations give an ambience unique in our lives.

We appreciate our relation with the author, agent, semanticist and critic John Brockman, whose appraisals and negotiations keep us in

285

touch with the realities of book publishing. He reminds us that words in strings are void unless they can be injunctive, instructive and indicative of change.

Our editor Jonathan Dolger (through remaining himself in his own center) taught us much about the appropriate states of being for creating books; his sensitive diplomacy and willingness to change his mind furnished us with the wherewithal to rewrite where needed; he furnished us with time for creative reconsiderations at crucial points. He made it possible for two books (this one and *Simulations of God: The Science of Belief*) to become entities on their own and to create several new literary offspring currently embryonic.

Arthur and Pru Ceppos are our mentors and aides in the conception, gestation, birth and upbringing of each book from *The Center of the Cyclone* and *The Human Biocomputer* through the later two and several yet to be completed.

Through sharing their deep and thorough cross-cultural studies of Indian groups, John Lilly, Jr., and his wife Colette have furnished us with a basic understanding of and perspective on our own culture. Exposed to the rigors of living in many remote primitive areas, their dyad is a living example of successful adaptation inherent in the man–woman sharing of survival programs and creative work under a supraself dyadic regard for research into the inner–outer realities of hitherto obscure cultures.

Each of us has benefited in our understanding of and participation with the younger generation through the graceful, quietly effective and astonishing creations of Nina Carozza. Her acceptance and understanding of the mystical spiritual realms of human relationships is a source of delight and of a discipline of new order in our experience.

We are each/both indebted to Heinz and Mai Von Foerster in several respects. Their dyad and its relations with students is a model for long-term success in eliciting creativity in bright intelligent students from North and South America, Europe, and Africa. Long-term values generated in the research into the bases of cybernetics and its application to rational approaches to all levels of human endeavor (from cognitive-perceptual processes to interhuman communication and politics) is a continuing wellspring of inspiration to our dyad. Much of John's creativity has come as a result of his long-term associations with Heinz over many years. His incisive diplomatic and deep penetrations into the depths of human rationality, his ruthless and compassionate critiques give one courage to pursue the depths of one's own experience and its representations for others, unencumbered by the usual consensus judgments and consensus forbiddings. Heinz enjoys life to the full; Mai supports his work, his life, his students with gracious wisdom. Heinz said recently, in public, "There is no energy crisis; there is only a crisis in intelligence (and its application to the uses of energy sources and energy sinks)."